The Foggy Bottom Gang

The Foggy Bottom Gang

The Story of the Warring Brothers of Washington, DC

Leo Warring

Parafine Press
Cleveland, OH

The photographs appearing on the cover and in the interior of this book come from either the Warring family collection or the Evening Star archives, used with permission from the DC Public Library.

First Parafine Press Edition 2020
ISBN: 978-1-950843-32-9

Parafine Press
5322 Fleet Avenue, Cleveland, OH 44105
www.parafinepress.com

Book and cover design by David Wilson

Table of Contents

Preface

For my son, the moment came in law school.

On a snowy afternoon in 2013, while doing research in an online database of legal cases, he grew curious and searched for his own name, one he shared with my father: Charles Warring. The search produced one result. My son read about a case that had been unsuccessfully appealed to the United States Supreme Court in 1954 and learned that my father, Charles, and his brothers Emmitt and Leo had operated an illegal numbers operation in Washington, DC. This had brought them wealth, negative publicity, and a string of legal difficulties. In the decision, *United States v. Emmitt R. Warring*, the government's critical evidence to prove income tax evasion had been an examination by Treasury Department agents of a bank safety deposit box that held 240 $1,000 dollar bills and a single $10,000 dollar bill—which equates to almost $2.5 million today. The box belonged to the Warring brothers.

With this happenstance discovery, my son realized that his family had a past that was different from the one he had previously come to know through the handful of colorful stories and anecdotes told by family members, including me, over the years.

The moment had come much earlier for me. I was in my early teens, looking for something under my parents' bed, when I found a large envelope of old, folded newspaper clippings of front-page stories. The articles recounted shootings, arrests, indictments, and trials, as well as the imprisonment of my dad, his two brothers and many associates. The clippings covered events that had occurred before my birth and awakened me to the reality that my family had once engaged in criminal activities—including bootlegging and the numbers racket that had captivated the Washington newspaper-reading public.

But I knew all those clippings drew only a partial picture of the man whom I called Dad and my Uncle Emmitt, both of whom were alive at the time. Now, through technology, hundreds of newspaper articles on the "Foggy Bottom Gang" are available online. A search of the *Washington Post* archives for Emmitt, Charles, and Leo Warring yields almost 300 articles. All are available to my children, and soon to my children's children.

After my son shared his discovery with me, I felt compelled to write a companion to those stories in the Post and the other three dailies that once circulated in Washington. This book addresses the events chronicled in the newspapers but also tells the stories nowhere to be found—the full story of the men I knew as father and uncle.

I hope that this book will give everyone who reads it, including my family, an insight into a time long past and into the characters who graced the Washington scene during one of its most interesting periods.

CHAPTER ONE

From Barrels to Booze

In September of 1951, if anyone in the Washington, DC area was not familiar with the name of Emmitt Warring, they soon would be. Starting Sunday, September 16, the *Washington Post* published a weeklong, front-page series, detailing the life of Emmitt Warring and the gambling empire that he had built with his two brothers. The editor's note to the 1951 story, labeled the "Charmed life of Emmitt Warring," read:

> This is a story of a man of importance and influence in Washington. He is a financial success in a multi-million dollar local business; a contributor to many worthy causes; the employer of hundreds of workers; the first-name intimate of policemen, lawyers and leading citizens. His illegal numbers game is patronized daily by tens of thousands. The purpose of these articles is not to smear with ignominy nor gild with glamour, but to flood with publicity. He has been a hidden power and a secret force in this city. Citizens need to know those who, for good or evil, influence their daily lives. [1]

His brothers Leo and Charles completed the "triumvirate who ruled the Washington gambling world."[2] They were more a presence on the streets than Emmitt. But Emmitt, nicknamed "The Little Man" behind his back, was regarded as the brains or kingpin of the organization dubbed by newspapers as the "Foggy Bottom Gang" or "Georgetown Mob." He usually drew the attention of newspapermen and, more to his detriment, the criminal justice system. A well-known Hollywood actor once called for his criminal prosecution on national radio.[3] The *Washington Post* labeled the Warring brothers' attempted subversion of law enforcement and the courts a "National Disgrace."[4]

If the brothers did not have respect for all aspects of the law, they did have morals. A priest once defended their mixed record by comparing it against those who make "no errors, but no hits and no runs either."[5]

A sampling of the headlines from the September 1951 *Post* exposé read: "Gunfire Punctuated Early Career of Mob," and "Gambler Meets Policemen; Touches off Probe on [Capitol] Hill." Later, in the 1980s and '90s, and even into this century, the Warring name found its way into print any time a story appeared about gambling, corruption, or organized crime in Washington.

The three brothers will forever be associated with two of the oldest and neighboring sections of the city, Foggy Bottom and Georgetown, and their story begins at a much earlier time when Washington, DC, was a much different city than it is today.

ꟹ

Washington, DC, was not always the cosmopolitan town it is in present day. Some observers would say that it remained a sleepy, southern town into the early 1960s. Before that time, there was no Kennedy Center for the Performing Arts, no Watergate complex or Metro subway system. The town didn't even have an elected mayor. Instead, it was governed jointly by three commissioners appointed by the president of the United States. Segregation was, if not the law, the rule. Except for ambassadors and their staffs, the presence of multiculturalism was almost nonexistent. Pat Buchanan, the conservative columnist who grew up in DC, has noted that Washington was a "deeply rooted city" before an influx of newcomers came to the city during the great expansion of the federal government in the late '60s and '70s.[6]

Before the establishment of the new District of Columbia, Georgetown had been a separate municipality. It remained an independent municipal government until 1871 when the District subsumed it entirely. Situated on the fall line of the Potomac River, Georgetown was the farthest point upstream where large vessels could navigate the river. Tobacco growers and farmers in Maryland and Virginia brought their produce for shipment to the port of Georgetown and its neighboring port downstream in Alexandria, Virginia. The presence of these ports influenced the selection of this site on the Potomac for the capital.[7]

Foggy Bottom, which bordered Georgetown on the Potomac, soon became the center of industry in the District. Located to the immediate southeast of Georgetown, Foggy Bottom apparently got its name from the mingling of river fog and industrial smoke in the neighborhood. A large gasworks for the production and storage of flammable gas at 26th and G Street emitted a foul smell that permeated "the Bottom," as the area was called by locals. [8] Although horse-drawn vehicles and later early autos moved on cobblestone streets in both sections, the Bottom lacked the charm that one found in some sections of Georgetown. Two breweries, a glass factory, a lumber mill, and other industry in Foggy Bottom employed most of the male workers in the neighborhood.[9] By the late nineteenth century, many of the European immigrants and African American migrants from the South who settled in Washington lived in Foggy Bottom.

The first of my relatives to call the nation's capital home was my grandfather, Bruce Thomas Warring. Born July 1869 in Prince William County, Virginia, just a few miles from the site of the Manassas [Bull Run] battlefield, Bruce T. Warring was a middle child in a family of at least nine children. His dad John and uncles were coopers, barrel makers, and distributers by trade. There is no surviving family member with knowledge of Bruce's early existence in the Virginia countryside, of the circumstances behind his move to DC, or of how he met his future wife, Julia Galvin. She was an Irish immigrant from County Kerry, Ireland, and one of several sisters who immigrated to the United States and settled in Washington. What is known is that Bruce and Julia married in Georgetown in early 1888. Although his occupation on the marriage license lists him as a cooper, the *Boyd's City Directory* of 1892 shows him as a "conductor," most likely on the city's new streetcar line. But the family trade was in his blood, and later the Warring name would be associated with barrels in Washington, DC—before it became known for something less respectable.

Bruce and Julia's first child, James Thomas, was born in the fall of 1888. Over the next nineteen years, Julia would give birth to a child almost like clockwork every two years (six boys and four girls). The tenth and last child was Charles, my dad.

Early in the new century, Bruce made two major decisions. First, he decided to open his own cooperage (barrel) business, drawing from the experience gained by working for his father. He primarily dealt in wooden barrels mostly used for commodities sold in bulk, such as meats, fish, and dry goods. His shop was located on the Georgetown waterfront at 3256 K Street, just west of the intersection with Wisconsin Avenue (formerly High Street), which was, and remains, the main north/south thoroughfare in Georgetown.

Business was good. A few years later, Bruce moved his growing family from a row house in Georgetown to one of the largest homes in neighboring Foggy Bottom, a white three-story brick house on a hill at the corner of L and 26th Streets. It sat exactly ten blocks due west of the White House and was the jewel of the neighborhood. The Warring boys roomed on the second floor and the girls' bedrooms were on the third floor. The front door faced L Street with a small triangular park separating L Street from Pennsylvania Avenue, which angled away and westward over Rock Creek, the dividing line between Foggy Bottom and Georgetown. The long 26th Street side of the white house faced west and took on a pale orange tone as the sun set in the evening. The house was razed in the 1980s and the location is now home to the Embassy of Egypt's Defense Office.

Bruce T. clearly saw his barrel business as a family business. Coming from a rural culture that viewed children as family workers, he expected that the boys would work in the shop as soon as possible. The girls would help out at home, including caring for the younger children. Only schooling took priority over doing their part in the family business and in the home.

Bruce T. Warring was a serious man. From all accounts, he was the epitome of "old school." He demanded respect and obedience from his children. A wiry man of modest height, he nonetheless towered over the family. Evening supper had a ritual quality. No children sat at the table until their father was seated. Once, some of the boys decided to start scarfing down some food in order to make an evening engagement. Bruce walked in and, in a fit, overturned the dining room table. In addition to the normal place settings, the afternoon paper was placed next to his plate, as he demanded. If anyone was bold enough to read it before Bruce had seen it, they would have to make sure it was perfectly re-folded to remove any suspicion.

He was also lord and master over the family dogs that guarded the homestead. When they were puppies, he started to hone them to do his bidding. He kept them in the basement for weeks and forbade anyone beside him to feed or come in contact with them. To instill a desired meanness and aggressiveness, he laced their food with gunpowder, following an old belief of the times.

Many times, when my brother Richard or I misbehaved, my father would admonish us and add that we were lucky not to have his dad for a father. He said that his father had not hesitated to use his leather belt when his sons stepped out of line.

But his children must have continued to respect "Papa" in later life since at least four grandsons bore the name Bruce as their first name or middle name. In fact, in later years, one of his youngest grandsons fondly remembered his gifts of candy and recalled addressing the old man by the nickname "Bang."

My dad always spoke of his mother Julia with warmth. She was a traditional Irish wife and mother. She spent practically the entire first twenty years of her marriage to Bruce pregnant and caring for babies. She always wore full-length dresses—an image of a woman from the "old country." With a thick Irish brogue and conversation peppered with Irish expressions, no one could miss her heritage. A devout Catholic, she attended first St. Patrick's of Georgetown and later St. Stephen's-Martyr Church in Foggy Bottom, one block east of their home. Saturday afternoons in the fall would find her in front of the family radio with a rosary in hand praying for a Notre Dame victory.

She spoke of her husband in an almost reverent tone. When one of the children did something that would not meet his approval, she would warn, "Bruce T. Warring will not be pleased."

Bruce's main dream in life was to grow his barrel business to lift him and his family up the economic and social ladder. His boys would help him raise his business, and his business would help him raise his boys. But his oldest son James would be the first to leave the father by marrying and starting a barrel shop of his own near a port on the nearby the Anacostia River.

The 1900s saw the birth of the three boys who would make the name "Warring" known to anyone who read the local papers from the 1930s to the 1950s: Leo (born 1903), Emmitt (born 1905) and finally

Charles (born 1907). The three were constant companions. Like the Warring boys before them, when their father wasn't putting them to work, they spent their days fishing in Rock Creek and sledding on the slopes of Georgetown and in Rock Creek Park.

As adolescents they had demonstrated their rebellious spirit by making their father the victim of their mischief on more than one occasion.

Bruce slept at night with his slippers and shotgun near his bed, ready to respond to any intruders. If awakened by the excited barking of his dogs, he would leap out of bed, grab his shotgun, and insert his feet into his perfectly placed slippers before heading for the door. One day, the boys came up with the idea of nailing his slippers to the floor before nightfall and then rousing the dogs after midnight. They were outside the house having just excited the dogs when they heard a shotgun blast. The old man had heard the dogs, bolted out of bed, grabbed his shotgun and slid his feet into his slippers before proceeding to the door. When his slippers failed to budge, he fell forward and squeezed the trigger of the gun. Fortunately, the pellets just blasted into the ceiling.

On another occasion, when Bruce learned that a Georgetown merchant whom he didn't like had died suddenly, he proclaimed that he was glad that he "did not have to look at that son of a bitch's face any more." Hearing their father's statement, the young men hatched a scheme. They knew one of the workers at the Georgetown funeral home where the deceased was kept—and making whatever enticement to the friend that was necessary—they removed the deceased from the premises and drove him to the Warring home. Somehow, they propped up the "stiff" in the vestibule at the front door of the house and knocked, knowing Bruce would answer the door that time of night. The brothers hid across the street suppressing their laughter when Bruce opened the door and was confronted by his nemesis' corpse. His exclamation of surprise quickly turned into screams of profanity when he realized that he had been the victim of a joke.[10]

The oldest of the three, Leo, was only sixteen when Congress passed an act that would eventually give the brothers financial opportunities beyond their wildest dreams: Prohibition.

CHAPTER TWO

Prohibition Comes to Town

Prohibition came early and stayed late in the nation's capital. National Prohibition became the law of the land on January 17, 1920, but Prohibition in the District had begun over two years earlier, on November 1, 1917. Temperance backers had successfully lobbied the Congress to make Washington, DC a model for the nation. Prohibition stayed on the books in Washington until March 1, 1934, months after the passage of the 21st Amendment that repealed it nationally.[1]

In Washington and throughout the nation, Prohibition made criminals out of ordinary citizens. The government had sent young men into the hell of trench warfare in World War I, and many found someone else occupying their jobs upon returning home. Many felt the system did not seem to have their best interests in mind. The economic depression that began in 1929 created the perfect environment for lawlessness, especially among the young adults of the period. Probably no class of criminals has ever found a more sympathetic public than the bootleggers during Prohibition.

Before Prohibition, there were four breweries in the District—two in Foggy Bottom and two in Capital Hill. It was the second largest business in the city after the federal government.[2]

Although Bruce's three youngest boys would gain the most from breaking the Prohibition laws, daughter Esther (Estee) and her husband, Bill Cady, first took advantage of the opportunity that the bootlegging of illegal alcohol offered. Bill's younger brother, Frank, along with his wife—Estee's younger sister, Julie—were recruited to join in the effort.

The Cady's were huskier than the Warring boys, with barrel chests and bulging arms. Both started working as steamfitters. But light-haired Bill was a street savvy operator always looking for opportunities to make an additional buck. In their younger days, Frank generally followed his older brother's lead. Frank was especially good with his hands. As a young man, his reputation for being able to use his fists earned him a challenge from some ruffians on Capital Hill to fight their "king of the hill." The story goes that Frank got the best of his cross-town rival, "Rat" Thomas.[3] But Frank's grandchildren would remember his soft hands and the kind demeanor he showed them.

Soon Estee and Julie's older brother John, aka Jonesy, who was anxious to free himself of his father's strict oversight at the barrel shop, was brought into the endeavor. Jonesy could handle and maneuver barrels around the shop perhaps better than any of the boys. But the lure of lots of easy money was too much to keep him laboring fulltime in the family trade.

Sometimes in a pinch, the three youngest Warring brothers were used to make a run to a customer. They also found it was easier money than laboring in their father's business.

Despite Estee's diminutive stature, she was a strong-willed woman and did not have to take a back seat to Bill in running things. They often clashed in making decisions. Their home, a row house at 2512 K Street just west of Washington Circle and present-day George Washington University Hospital, was the base of operations. Through their labors, the Cady brothers and Jonesy had greatly modified the house by creating underground compartments to conceal their ready supplies of illegal booze.

Initially things went well for the new enterprise. Bootleg whiskey had both plenty of supply—provided from numerous homemade stills making cheap booze in and about Foggy Bottom—and lots of demand.

But the new enterprise soon ran into problems with the law. The stills were often difficult to hide and were susceptible to raids by the cops. As an alternative, Bill Cady arranged to operate a still outside of DC on a country estate in Virginia not far from Chain Bridge, which spanned the Potomac at DC's most northwestern corner. Bill Cady had gained the confidence of the estate's caretaker, who was probably paid well to look the other way.

Through the caretaker, they learned that the owner of the estate, Joseph Leiter, had $300,000 (the equivalent of $3 million today) of "choice wines and whiskies" stored in his cellar. Mere possession of alcohol acquired before Prohibition was not illegal. Leiter's cellar presented an opportunity to make some big-time money by selling "the real McCoy" to a new client base of the well-to-do, who preferred—and could pay for—quality liquor. According to the *Washington Post*, "the bootleggers gave the caretaker a quantity of corn whiskey they had made on the estate, which knocked him out." On the night of October 11, 1921, the men allegedly "bore down on the steel-barred cellar at the millionaire's residence in Virginia and removed the choicest collection of liquors in the Old Dominion [Virginia]."[4]

Three weeks later, on the night of November 1 (probably based on a tip from the caretaker), detectives observed the suspects making a delivery to the home of Colonel Hurly Spencer at 2012 Massachusetts Avenue, just west of Dupont Circle in what was then one of the ritziest areas of DC. When the detectives entered the house, they found twenty-five cases of champagne and identified them as part of the Virginia heist.

Later that evening, the DC detectives and agents of the Morgan Bradford detective services hired by Mr. Leiter surprised Bill, Frank, and Jonesy at the Cady home. The three young men were in the kitchen drinking champagne when the agents rushed through the back door. The men tried to escape through the front door, but the house was surrounded, and the trapped men rushed back in. A "rough and tumble battle followed, lasting 20 minutes before the men were subdued."[5]

The *Post* goes on to detail that "a search of the house revealed 15 cases of champagne, bearing the initials of Joseph Leiter, Washington millionaire clubman and sportsman. All the thrills of an adventure tale are contained in the police description of the search of the Cady residence. Secret passageways, panels and circuitous routes were installed in the house, so that the place took on the tone of absolute mystery."

The article continues: "The police believe they have unearthed the greatest find since bootlegging as an industry joined the six largest revenue producers known in America." Later it detailed the labyrinths built for hiding goods in their house: "By the mere lifting of a step on the staircase leading to the second floor, a cable was brought into play and an entire flooring jerked ceiling-ward, so that those who knew the trick had access to a catacomb where more than 500 one-gallon containers of alcohol were hidden, the police charge. In that same rendezvous, so the police say, were found out branching trenches, little gulleys that led hither and yon like tunnels for cars that carry ore in mines."

Virginia authorities attempted to extradite the Cady brothers and Jonesy. For over 18 months, they were frustrated by the trio's attorney, T. Morris Wampler, who successfully convinced District officials to not cooperate with the Commonwealth of Virginia. In May of 1923, Chief Justice McCoy of the circuit court finally dismissed Virginia's request for extradition that had been signed by Governor Elmer Trinkle. [6]

By this time, Jonesy and his wife Frances (known as Fannie) had two children and another on the way. Frank Cady and Julie had two children, and Bill Cady and Ester had one. The prospect of future arrest and jail time conflicted with parenthood, and they eventually got out of the bootlegging business. Frank decided to concentrate on his day job as a steamfitter, which he held for 40 years until his death. Jonesy continued to put in time at the barrel shop and avoided any big-time bootlegging arrests.

But while doors were closing for Jonesy and the Cadys, the three youngest Warring boys saw a door opening.

Leo and Emmitt decided that, along with their younger brother Charlie, they could take over much of Bill and Estee's customer base in Foggy Bottom and Georgetown. Emmitt had a special relationship with Bill and worked on selling him on the idea. In the meantime, Leo worked to get Estee's blessing. Leo was probably Estee's favorite brother and he seemed to eventually always get what he wanted from her. It was no different with taking over the bootlegging business.

By the mid-1920s, the three younger brothers had reached their twenties and were ready to cut ties with their father's barrel shop. They clearly yearned to find an easier way to make money, and more of it. Although the younger brothers had come to the attention of the law for other issues, they had no bootlegging or other serious charges on their records. The boys would do the work, assume the risk, and make sure that Estee and Bill were financially taken care of.

Working at the barrel shop as a youngster had taken a lasting physical toll on Emmitt, the shortest (barely over 5' 4") and the frailest of the brothers. He had suffered a severe attack of appendicitis and ruptured appendix in his teens, and only emergency surgery saved his life. The operation was invasive in those days, and extensive tissue and muscle had to be cut to remove the appendix. While his job at the barrel shop was driving a mule team to transport barrels, there still was a degree of physical labor involved. The family story was that Bruce forced Emmitt back to work in the barrel shop before he was physically up to it and caused him to permanently position his right shoulder higher than his left.[7] Consequently, he seemed to frequently hold his left hand and forearm up around his left hip when standing instead of letting it dangle beside him in an attempt to draw less attention to his physical peculiarity. Although it's true he likely returned to work too early, his physical appearance was probably caused more by scoliosis, a lateral curvature of the spine, since the condition became more pronounced in later years. In any case, when the opportunity to engage in bootlegging arose, he was ready to leave the barrel shop behind.

> Decades later, the *Washington Post* would print the following apocryphal story:
> "Lift that barrel, boy!"
> A booming voice pitched this injunction—half taunt, half jest—into the fog of soot, smoke and flour dust that lay along Georgetown's K Street.
> Emmitt Warring, a slight young man busily wrestling barrels onto a truck in his father's warehouse, stopped his work. He muttered an oath and stepped off the truck. Swiping his denim shirtsleeve across his forehead, he fumbled for a cigarette and lighted up.
> "All work and no play don't make jack," a visitor joked. Warring, dripping with sweat, sticky with grime, grinned wryly and looked out across the Potomac.
> "You're right. I've just about had it" Emmitt replied.[8]

Such episodes must have occurred often enough in the mid-twenties, when Emmitt Warring was making up his mind whether to quit hustling barrels and start hustling booze.

The three youngest Warring brothers now had an arrangement through which they could leave the barrel business behind. They knew that without a high school education, a life of hard, manual labor was their destiny. Selling banned alcohol to willing customers was, if not legal, at least morally reconcilable.

How did they escape the demanding work of their father's barrel shop to amass power and money that belied their humble beginnings? Basically, it was the complement of their three distinct personalities consolidating at the right moment during a tumultuous time in Washington.

CHAPTER THREE

Leo, Emmitt, and Charlie

Like his brother John, Leo had a little heftier frame than his other brothers—and along with Charlie, was taller than the average Warring brother, standing at 5' 10". He had rugged good looks and could appear quite refined when he dressed well and sported his wire-rim glasses.

His sister Estee could hold her own against any man and would not back down from a confrontation—but Leo was her favorite brother, and had the skill to disarm her. He was the best salesman of the brothers and could be manipulative. When Estee would read him the riot act about his drinking—or anything else—he would softly say to her, "You don't mean that." She would settle down and back off.

Leo was not as controlling as Emmitt and not as gregarious as Charlie. While Emmitt could be coldly direct and Charlie too quick to argue, Leo preferred a softer approach with people.

Leo was probably the least publicly known of the three brothers. Perhaps one reason was that in 1925 Leo had married twenty-two-year-old Audrey Cox and they soon had a family. In contrast, his brother Charles would not marry until he was forty and Emmitt would never marry. The duties of a young family may have helped keep Leo out of trouble at times.

Dubbed by the newspapers as the "hard worker" of the outfit, he oversaw the processing of each day's bets over sheets of notepaper and adding machine tapes. Usually, Emmitt and Charlie would drop by the "office" during the day but Leo opened and closed it daily. However, Leo allowed his younger brother Emmitt to have the last word on any decisions.

Leo did have a fascination with horses—well, at least the kind you bet on. He purchased three or four racehorses, registering them in his sister Esther's name. Leo and Esther even went a step further to hide the Warring name by using the name "Esther Warren" as the horses' owner. Racing under such names as Big Sneeze, Prison Ship, and Leo's Lorraine (the latter named after Leo's daughter, who went by her middle name), the horses were relatively successful racing at nearby racetracks in Hagerstown, Maryland; Cumberland, Maryland; and Charlestown, West Virginia. There is a family photo of Leo with one of his racehorses taken when he brought his wife and two kids to a stable to see one of the colts.

He also took bets on horse racing outside of the numbers business and Emmitt's purview. This was his own operation that his younger brother had no involvement. Besides taking the bets, he also financially backed the operation. Emmitt shunned taking sports bets where certain human elements might try to secretly prearrange the outcome. But the fact that Emmitt was not involved had to give him a sense of personal satisfaction.

It's almost too easy to suggest that Emmitt Warring had a Napoleon complex, but there is no denying that he was short. He was affectionately called "Pudge" (with the "u" pronounced as it is in "pudding") by close family members his entire life. Apparently, Emmitt was so sickly days after he was born that he had been given an "emergency" baptism at home "by an aunt," according to the baptismal records of Holy Trinity Church in Georgetown. The shortest of the Warring boys, he shared his brothers' "iceberg blue eyes" but had slightly sharper facial features.

> In 1951, the *Washington Post* noted Emmitt's small physical presence: His stature has given rise to the third-person nickname of "the little man" or "the little fellow," terms spoken with a degree of respect if not reverence by lesser lights in the community. Some call him "Chief," others "Mr. Emmitt."[1]

Throughout his life, he wanted to be in charge of whatever he was involved in. Following others was not in his makeup. It wasn't a stretch when people, including the newspaper writers, dubbed Emmitt the "brains" of the Warring gang.

From all accounts, Leo and Charlie deferred to Emmitt when it came to calling the shots. Emmitt conducted himself with an air of authority that did not invite opinions or suggestions from others, including his two brothers.

Emmitt understood that information was power before it became a 1980s cliché. As once described by the *Washington Post*: "Warring 'gets the word' through an invisible but intricate network of communication."[2] He maintained an informal web of informants—including bartenders and waitresses, shop owners, household maids, and cooks—to keep abreast of local comings and goings. Sometimes people just volunteered information to get on his good side. Emmitt didn't need to hang out in bars and on street corners; the people who did were his eyes and ears.

More than the actual knowledge or wisdom he may have possessed, the manner that Emmitt approached issues with gave him an aura of intelligence. He dealt only with the facts, and rarely let feelings get in the way. He appeared to stay on one emotional frequency. All his decisions were backed with an assuredness that he knew best. Others, including family, were usually too intimidated to question him. Although Emmitt made some bad choices, he didn't let anyone think that his decisions should be questioned. He felt his dispassionate judgment best served him and his brothers.

Emmitt spoke precisely, with confidence and authority. The *Post* described him as "a man of few words."[3] It seems everything he did and said was with a purpose. He was not into small talk. Although soft-spoken, he commanded people's attention whenever he spoke.

Emmitt appeared to look right through people with a glint of suspicion. When meeting someone, he quickly sized them up and estimated how much they could be trusted. As Emmitt grew older, he concluded that few really could—including the federal government.

Earlier in his life, Emmitt's teachers noticed he was smarter than the average youngster and said he could get straight As if he applied himself to his studies. Whatever interested him at the moment, he would pursue arduously, but if a subject or activity did not catch his fancy, he would ignore it. For example, perhaps because of his physical limitations, Emmitt showed little interest in sports or local sport teams. In midlife when he was besieged by legal troubles, the law consumed his attention. In later life when he was plagued by health problems, medical matters absorbed his interest.

That's not to say that he was much different from other young men his age when it came to having a good time. As a young man, Emmitt had had some brushes with the law for drunk and disorderly conduct—but he later swore off drinking and claimed the smell of alcohol made him sick.

Emmitt never let his diminutive stature stop him from pursuing the ladies, especially redheads. Family photos show him as a young man with one or more girls by his side. Once when Frank Cady Jr. was competing in a Golden Gloves boxing match in DC, he looked down from the ring and saw Emmitt, his uncle, sitting next to a girl that Frank had invited to the fight. After the fight, Frank went looking for Emmitt and the girl but found out they had left together. Though Emmitt would never marry, he rarely seemed to be without a lady friend his entire life.

Newspaper accounts cast Charlie, Emmitt's younger brother and my father, as a "second fiddle." But Charlie's outgoing personality contrasted with Emmitt's natural introversion and resonated more with ordinary people.

Although almost six inches taller than Emmitt, Charlie, who was known by many as "Rags," was clearly the "little" brother to his "big" brother. Emmitt did not hesitate to give advice to his younger brother, and Charlie usually took it, if for no other reason than to avoid Emmitt's disapproval. Charlie's temper as a young man and his fierce sense of protection toward his older-but-smaller brother helped dissuade anyone from taking advantage of Emmitt's size. Later, my father would impress upon my brother Richard and me the need for brothers to stick together.

While Emmitt was deliberate, Charlie was impulsive. The same person could be the object of both Charlie's temper and his good nature in a matter of minutes. My brother and I found out that our dad could give us almighty hell one minute and then ask us to go for a ride to get a treat the next.

While Emmitt desired to exert control over everyone who could affect his operation—the men who worked for him, the police, and the legal system—Charlie was the one wildcard who could frustrate his efforts. Charlie was quick to protect his brothers and their interests, but Emmitt tried to steer him away from any potential violent encounters. Even so, Charlie's emotions sometimes caused him to disregard the threat of a tongue-lashing from Emmitt.

Typically, it was hard to get the best of Charlie. This might have started when he was playing for the neighborhood football team, St.

Stephen's. When I was young, I always heard from my dad that St. Stephen's never lost a game. Later my older cousin qualified my dad's claim by explaining that St. Stephen's never lost a game that was played to completion. If they were behind near the end of a game, Charlie and the rest of the St. Stephen's team would start a brawl that halted the game before it was over.

However, Charlie greatly enjoyed people and relished friendships. Where Emmitt grew increasingly guarded around people throughout his life, Charlie was always inviting. He constantly wanted company. He frequently asked someone to accompany him on an errand, even illegal ones like making a booze delivery or picking up the day's gambling receipts. He enjoyed lending a hand to strangers. During snowstorms, he deliberately drove around looking for people who needed help with their cars.

Charlie delighted in giving gifts. He wanted to share in the goodwill. More than any of the three brothers, he spent the most time on the streets and wanted to be able to give to whomever he met, including relatives. But he had to give from his share of the profits instead of from the general pot. Emmitt, who thought Charlie was an easy touch, giving money to bums and questionable characters who were always ready with an open hand, was in charge of that.

Emmitt once arranged for a new washing machine to be delivered to their Aunt Delia. Charlie was at Aunt Delia's house when the machine was delivered and took credit for the gift. I know from experience that my father really enjoyed buying things for those he liked and he probably rationalized that he had contributed to whatever pot the money had come from. When Emmitt later came over to Delia's house to see if the gift had been delivered, he asked her how she liked it. She responded in her Irish brogue that "it was a great thing that my nephew, Charles, did." Emmitt just shook his head in resignation.[4]

Charlie only finished the sixth grade. There were too many fun things to do during the day rather than sit in a classroom. He probably felt stuck in school while all his older brothers were out making a living, even if it was in their father's barrel shop. One too many truancies in the seventh grade sent him back to his father's barrel shop, where Emmitt was already working after finishing the eighth grade. His abortive attempt at getting an education and the subsequent consequences of his failure caused him to stress the importance of schooling to me and my brother while we were growing up. For the remainder of his life, he had an abiding respect for higher education and for those who held degrees.

His sister Esther had initially introduced her three younger brothers to fine clothes and the latest fashions when the money started rolling in to the Cady bootlegging operation. Emmitt was always well-groomed and neatly dressed in public, reflecting a sense of control. He could put on his best suit and, hours later, his clothes would appear neat and pressed as if he were a mannequin in a store window. But an hour or two after getting dressed, Charlie's clothes started to come undone, with his tie loosened and his shirttail out. The moniker "Rags," which was usually given ironically to a very smart dresser, was given even more ironically to Charlie. Rags was sometimes lengthened to "Ragman" by some acquaintances, but family and close friends stuck with Charlie.

Whether it was Charlie's ragtag appearance, welcoming manner or overall accessibility, he was arguably the most popular Warring brother. And because of his street presence, he captured most of the early headlines.

CHAPTER FOUR

Bringing the Product to Market

From the start, many Americans refused to respect Prohibition and ignored the law. This included those who wanted to drink "intoxicating liquor" and those willing to supply it. The Volstead Act prohibited the manufacture, sale, or transport of intoxicating liquor, but ironically did not make it illegal to possess it for personal use. By the end of Prohibition, three-quarters of all Americans supported its repeal. Many were more than just accepting of the bootleggers' activities; they actually cheered them on as if they were sports heroes. Bootleggers were the daredevils of the day, risking their lives and freedom while standing up to law enforcement and competing bootleggers. One such person was Rags Warring.[1*]

Although all three brothers were actively involved in bootlegging, Rags was the primary point person who delivered the product from manufacturer to consumer. Along with hired moonshine runners, Rags would often make the trip himself from southern Maryland, where the brothers found new supplies in Charles and St. Mary's Counties, carrying the newly-distilled alcohol into the District. Emmitt and Leo managed the business side, primarily through making contacts and gathering information. This included locating potential customers and seeking out policemen whom the brothers could work with.

But Rags took care of most of the street action. He could cajole customers, scare away competitors, and outrun the law in a car chase with the best of them. His devil-may-care attitude was perfect for a bootlegger. It took guts, skill, and a fast car to maneuver the country

1*Note: From this point, I will use Charlie's public moniker Rags in the retelling of public events and stories that were covered by the newspapers. When writing of family matters, I will use "my dad" or Charlie.

roads of southern Maryland and make deliveries to the District roughly 30 to 40 miles away.

Rags saw his attempts to elude police as a game of cat and mouse. Once, he intentionally positioned himself so he would be spotted by the police while carrying a paper bag that looked like it might contain a bottle of alcohol. When approached by the cops, he ran several blocks before being cornered by a team of patrolmen. He took the bag, blew a few breaths into it, and then popped it, revealing it was empty. The cops were not amused, but he was.[1]

When it came to holding on to the Warring territory of Foggy Bottom and Georgetown, intruders quickly learned, Rags was anything but light-hearted. Mary Brown, who lived in Foggy Bottom during Prohibition, gave an example of the Warrings at work during this time. When she was about twelve years old, she walked down I Street in Foggy Bottom and observed a man delivering booze to a house. The man suddenly set his goods down and began to run down the street. The sound of gunshots filled the air, and Mary quickly ducked behind a tree. Mary claims she heard the bullets whizz past the tree towards the running target. She recognized the "Warring boys" doing the shooting as they pursued the intruding bootlegger up the street. She felt that they were only trying to give him a good scare.[2]

But the bootleggers depended on more than being swift of foot. They used fast cars modified to carry a load of alcohol and elude the local cops and "revenuers," a name given to federal agents assigned to enforce Prohibition. While the police usually drove four-cylinder vehicles, most bootleggers had faster, eight-cylinder models. The springs in these roadsters were adjusted to carry a heavy load of alcohol without attracting suspicion. (These factors led the chief justice of the Supreme Court and former President William Howard Taft to write to his brother Horace that "the automobile is the greatest instrument for promoting immunity of crimes … in the history of civilization."[3])

The bootleggers sought more than speed. Often roadsters were modified so the bootleggers could trigger the car to emit either a smoke screen or an oil slick to slow down the pursuing police. Joe Osterman, a former Washington, DC policeman, chased bootleggers during Prohibition. He worked with Lieutenant George Little, head of the local liquor squad, who was described by the *Washington Post* as the "scourge of bootleggers" and whose name was "anathema to such formidable figures as … the Warring brothers."[4] Osterman, who lived to be over one hundred years old, held the philosophy that he had his job to do and the bootleggers had theirs. But he felt the bootleggers went too far when they resorted to smoke screens and oil slicks that placed a pursuing policeman's life in jeopardy. According to Osterman, the cops took their revenge on bootleggers who used such tactics by putting steel shavings in their gas tanks.[5]

In addition to modifying their cars, bootleggers usually had at least one extra car to run interference against the police by driving considerably slower than the fleeing booze-laden roadster and blocking the police's path. (Police cars had yet to be equipped with two-way radio.)

☙

As author and DC historian Garrett Peck notes in his book *Prohibition in Washington, DC: How Dry We Weren't*, the District was already a densely populated area before the housing expansion occurred in upper northwest Washington and into the suburbs of Maryland and Virginia. This density made the bootlegger's job easier.[6] This was especially true in places like Foggy Bottom, Georgetown and southwest Washington. One of the housing realities that led to this density was the presence of alley dwellings.

The influx of European immigrants and freed blacks to the area during and after the Civil War created a need for cheap housing. Because the original design of the city lots provided for space behind most houses, homeowners soon constructed substandard housing in the open space between the primary residence and the intervening alley throughout the city. These dwellings—really shacks—usually lacked electricity and running water. Heat was provided by coal burning stoves. Later, alley houses tended to be small, two-story brick buildings. These homes contrasted sharply with the primary residence in front of the property. Most dwellings were occupied by extended families and sometimes by two families. By 1930, most District alley dwellers were African American.[7]

Crime and disease thrived in these clustered communities. Thousands of under-privileged workers stayed in these crowded dwellings to be near the industrial jobs in Foggy Bottom and Georgetown until the federal government began dismantling them in the 1940s. Foggy

Bottom had a number of alley communities, but one of the oldest and the most populated was known as Snow's Court. (Alleys with only one entrance/exit were frequently called a "blind alley" or a "court.") With roots going back to shortly before the Civil War, Snow's Court was bounded by 24th and 25th Streets (east and west) and K and I Streets (north and south).

Like all alley dwellings, Snow's Court was a close-knit community. People watched each other's children and observed who came in and out of the alley. Outsiders generally were not welcome, especially the police.[8] A former resident of Snow's Court recalled that the police would frequently stop at the entrance of the alley and ask one of the residents to tell another to come out and talk to them. When the police did enter the alley, they went in pairs with their hands usually on their night-sticks. Especially after dusk, poorly-lit alleys could be very dangerous. Joe Goffney, an elderly African American who lived near Snow's Court as a young man, recalled that "he couldn't remember a Saturday night when the ambulance didn't have to go into Snow's Court for someone."

The closed environment of an alley made it a perfect place to distill and sell illegal booze. A percentage of the Warring brothers' bootlegging activity took place in and around Snow's Court and other populated alleys in Foggy Bottom.

Although whites generally headed bootleg operations, they often recruited young black men to make the deliveries. These runners were able to earn much more than they might as common laborers but they faced risks beyond the threat of arrest.

They were on the front lines of an illegal and lucrative activity, which put them at risk when disputes over territories or customers arose. Shooting or killing a black man did not arouse the same interest among law enforcement and civic officials as the killing of a white person. A review of the newspapers of that era clearly reflects an almost indifferent attitude when reporting the killing of a "colored" male. Whether the assailant was white or black, as long as the victim was black, the police apparently did not pursue the case with the same intensity. Thus, a gang could send a message to a competing gang by shooting one of their black "rum runners" with near impunity. Casualties of territorial disputes or "deals that went down wrong" were often found in the Potomac.[9]

Early on, a young black man named Walter "Chick" Edmonds aligned himself with the Warrings and would continue to work for them for decades. Of light complexion and average height, Chick lived at 915 25th Street, just outside the entrance of Snow's Court. The Warrings could count on him, and he could count on the Warrings. Once, when Chick was injured while trying to elude the police, he was brought to the Emergency Hospital and put in a room with a police guard outside his door. As was common in the days prior to photo identification, Chick gave an alias upon arrest. The Warrings were able to find out the floor and room number where Chick was being treated and, at an appointed time, an open truck containing a bed of straw appeared in the alley behind the hospital below his window. Chick opened his window and jumped into the back of the truck and made his escape.[10]

Today, Snow's Court is one of the higher-priced areas in Foggy Bottom, full of expensive townhouses and adjacent to George Washington University.

ᔓ

Not far from the Warrings' residence was another Foggy Bottom landmark, Washington Circle. This was where Pennsylvania Avenue, New Hampshire Avenue, K Street and 23rd Street all converged. During the nineteenth century, the area was called "Round Top." It is unclear if it took that name because it was the high elevation point of The Bottom or because it was also dominated by a criminal gang called the Round Tops. But it is clear that at some point, Rags Warring realized that he did not have to go around the circle when he was in a hurry: he could go through it.

A retired motorcycle cop once recounted how he once chased Rags down Pennsylvania Avenue. When Rags approached Washington Circle in his car, instead of going the regular counter-clockwise route around the circle, he jumped the curb and drove straight through the park in the circle. As Rags was driving right by the George Washington statue, the policemen hit the curb and immediately became airborne, flying off his motorcycle. As the ex-motorman described how he "almost broke his neck," he and Rags had a good laugh, like two former football rivals recalling a game. That wasn't the only time Rags had tried that trick.

Another story regarding Rags navigation of Washington Circle comes from Ralph Hawkins, a leading jazz drummer of the 1930s who married Esther and Bill's daughter, Tibby Cady. Shortly before Ralph passed away, he recalled an event that happened when he was dating Tibby.

During one of Ralph's visits to the Cady home, Rags received a call that a rival gang was selling booze in the Warrings' territory. As Rags broke for the door, something overcame Ralph, and for some reason he blurted out, "Can I go with you?" Rags, always ready for company whatever the circumstances, barked, "Well, come on." Riding in Rags's new Ford with a V-8 engine, they caught up with the car of the offending party around 21st and Pennsylvania Avenue. As both cars sped toward Washington Circle, Rags fired shots in the direction of the fleeing car, and Ralph wondered why in the world he had asked to go along. Rags took his shortcut through the middle of the park. As the lead car made it around the circle and approached the K Street turn, Rags closed in on it. The lead car went even faster as Rags and Ralph drew closer. Both cars raced down K Street to the point where it became Water Street on the edge of the Potomac. The lead car suddenly veered to the left on to an empty lot bordering the river. Two men in the car jumped out and ran east toward Rock Creek Park. Rags and Ralph jumped out, and Rags fired a shot in the air. The offenders had abandoned their car just a few feet from the edge of the Potomac. Rags told Ralph that "we'll just push this thing in the river." Ralph began to lean a shoulder against the trunk of the car when Rags hollered "To hell with that, get in my car," waving Ralph into his Ford. He then placed his car in first gear and slammed into the back of the abandoned vehicle, pushing it into the waters of the Potomac.

CHAPTER FIVE
The Killeen Gang

Before the Warring brothers ruled Foggy Bottom and Georgetown, there was Eddie Killeen and his gang. Killeen was one of the biggest operators in Washington, DC in the early '30s. Although the Warring brothers were growing their operations in areas where Killeen was the dominant force, they were not interested in directly challenging Killeen. In fact, brothers-in-law Bill and Frank Cady had a close relationship with Killeen that went back for years.

Killeen was the black sheep of a respected Georgetown family of devout Catholics. His father was a Democratic leader in Washington and a friend of William Jennings Bryan, who was a major force in the populist wing of the Democratic Party.

Killeen beat a murder rap in 1921. During a party at the Cabin John Hotel just over the District line in Maryland, Killeen drew a gun on man during a quarrel. The man was escorting a woman named Bessie Harris, who jumped between the two just as the gun discharged. When police arrived, they found Killeen and some others singing "Auld Lang Syne" as the woman lay dead.[1]

Although he was tried for murder, Killeen was found not guilty by a jury. Killeen's attorney argued that Killeen had initially pulled the revolver in self-defense, and it had accidentally discharged, killing Miss Harris.[2]

Killeen and his henchmen used strong-arm tactics during Prohibition. A common refrain of his men was "You will buy our beer, or we'll dump any [other] beer you do buy into the street."

On May 12, 1931, gunmen relieved the El Salvador Legation (2601 Connecticut Avenue) of most of their cache of liquor. (Diplomats were legally allowed to maintain a supply since the grounds of the legation were considered foreign soil.) Before the thieves entered the legation, a night manager at the nearby Shoreham Hotel delicatessen observed several men entering and exiting a car to make telephone calls from a phone booth. He became suspicious and took down the license number of the auto. One of the gunmen roughed up the counselor and charge d' affaires, Dr. Don Carlos Leiva, before they made off with the loot. But Leiva bit one of the gunmen in the hand. He was then struck repeatedly with the butt of a gun, subsequently requiring twenty-seven stitches.[3] During the altercation, the same gunman also fired at least one shot into the ceiling to show he meant business.

The tags were traced to Bryant McMahon. Talley Day was later identified as the driver of the car.[4] Both were members of the Killeen gang.

The robbery wasn't the first time that thieves had helped themselves to the ready storehouse of booze at the legation. Another had occurred earlier in the year around Easter, but with no violence. After the second incident, United States Secretary of State Henry Stimson ordered an investigation to determine whether the DC police were providing diplomats the "protection to which they were entitled."[5] Some congressmen complained about the custom that gave diplomats immunity from local liquor laws. But the heat was on the police to solve this crime.

Jack Cunningham, another Killeen man, was a small-time hood whom the police knew well. The word on the street was that the police believed he had knowledge of or participated in the legation heist and were using him for their own purposes. One evening, about a week after the robbery, Cunningham visited the First Precinct station to surrender a gun that had been used earlier in May in a shooting of a man in a 12th Street speakeasy, a shooting which was said to be accidental.[6]

Cunningham was not held, and it took him about an hour to walk home that night. Approaching his residence, Cunningham ducked into a back alley around 14th and I Streets NW. As he ascended the outside stairs to his home, a car sped into the alley. Cunningham turned, and shots rang out in the springtime night air. His wife ran to his aid and found him lying supine on the stairs with a .45-caliber bullet in his stomach. Cunningham died the next day without revealing who had shot him.[7]

The police conducted ballistic tests on the slug taken from Cunningham's body and a bullet found in the ceiling of the El Salvador Legation. The results proved that both bullets were fired from the same weapon.[8] This apparently confirmed police speculation that Cunningham had been killed because he knew too much about the legation robbery. Whoever pulled the legation job must have thought that Cunningham was acting as a stool pigeon when he went to the police station. Ultimately no one was convicted for Cunningham's murder.

One man who was not a suspect in Cunningham's shooting was 24-year-old Talley Day. On the evening before Cunningham was killed, Day had been killed at a reputed speakeasy at 1523 M Street NW. Talley Day's family, like Eddie Killeen's, was respected in Georgetown. His father, Nicholas Day, owned a Georgetown delicatessen. At some point, Talley Day had fallen under Killeen's influence, building an impressive criminal record during his short life.

According to detectives, Day became enraged at the speakeasy when others "razzed" him for complaining because he was losing heavily during a blackjack card game. He threw a drink at one of the men agitating him. Others intervened to stop the matter from escalating.

Throughout the night, Day continued to gripe over his losses and bore the brunt of the others' kidding.

At some point, the main agitator scolded him, "If you can't lose, don't play." He threw his drink of gin on Day. "Now we're even," he said.[9]

Day drew a .38-caliber pistol and began firing wildly. Most of the speakeasy patrons ducked for cover as the gin thrower headed for a nearby door with a companion, John Elmer "Bull Dog" Sweeney, who had a criminal record to match Talley Day's.

As Day aimed his pistol at the men, Sweeney warned him, "Don't do that." Sweeney fired before Day was able to get another shot off. One of his bullets struck Day over his eye and buried into his head. [10]

At Day's funeral services, held at St. George's Syrian Greek Orthodox church on 8th Street, NW, the priest offered a brief sermon, admonishing Day's young friends to "remember thy Creator in the days of thy youth." However, his words fell on deaf ears. At the graveyard, Day's friends assaulted a *Washington Post* photographer and destroyed the picture he had taken during the burial service. [11]

While serving a sentence at the Lorton Reformatory, Sweeney was transferred to Alcatraz for inciting a prison riot at Lorton. In a show of unbelievable hubris, he later sent a note to a DC court while in Alcatraz contending that he had a better right to custody of his four-year-old son than his estranged wife.[12]

Talley Day's companion in crime, Bryant McMahon, would soon find that his life wouldn't be the kind that life insurance agents would want to write a policy on.

McMahon seemed to have a knack for being around when somebody was shot or killed. He and Day together were charged with a series of crimes in the late '20s and early '30s. In a *Washington Post* photo, McMahon sports a nose that evidently had been broken more than once, reflecting a rough-and-tumble life.

But it was evident that McMahon's life was losing value when he was shot and hospitalized a few months after Talley Day was killed. He refused to identify his shooter, claiming a "sniper" shot him.[13] He eventually recovered, but he was fatally wounded in a gunfight at the Houston Hotel near 9th and E Street NW (across the street from the present-day FBI headquarters). A dozen or so racketeers had met in the hotel to discuss control of the area's horse racing wire that provided instantaneous racing results when the fight broke out. Another Killeen man, Sam Melincov, died at the scene. McMahon was brought to Emergency Hospital with bullet wounds in his stomach and hip. Before he died, he adamantly refused to answer police questions about the shooting. "I won't talk," said McMahon. "But if you let me out of here, I'll take care of those mugs myself."[14] His words suggest the real reason why dying men often refused to divulge their killers. It was not so much adherence to a code of silence as it was a denial of their imminent death, and most of all, their plans to even the score. They didn't want to give the police an immediate lead when they carried out their retribution. McMahon's revenge plan was aborted by his own unscheduled death.

Four men were questioned in his death but claimed they could not remember what happened that night to McMahon and Melincov.[15] The police conveniently concluded that the two must have shot each other.

ꟹ

Joseph "Gyp" Nalley might have been the most dangerous member of the Killeen gang. Reputed to be Killeen's primary strong-arm man, he had been arrested over fifty times by his mid-thirties.[16]

In 1921, he was held for assaulting a police officer in Colonial Beach, Virginia.[17] The next year he shot up the small town of Benedict

Beach, Maryland. Jailed in La Plata, Maryland, he arranged for a short vacation when he and two other prisoners beat a guard and made a temporary escape.[18]

In 1924, Nalley was part of a gang that held up two cashiers carrying a Piggly-Wiggly grocery store's cash receipts. Nalley and three other men forced the cashiers to the curb and compelled them to turn over the money at gunpoint. They made off with over $20,000 ($200,000 in today's money).

Later that year, Nalley demonstrated why he was one of the most feared men in the streets of Washington. In December, awaiting trial for the grocery store robbery, Nalley and a man named George King entered a near-beer saloon at 807 North Capitol Street around noon on a Sunday.[19] A "colored" porter known as "Good Old Tom" Brady was busy cleaning up the saloon and told Nalley the place was not open. Nalley and King left after some protest. However, they returned in a few minutes and asked for some glasses to share a drink from a bottle that they had in the car. Brady attempted to sell the men some glasses, and a dispute arose over the price. After they exchanged words and threats, Nalley struck Brady over the head with a whiskey bottle, and King shot and killed him.[20]Nalley and King were arrested but never indicted.

In February of 1925, Nalley was sentenced to serve ten years in prison for the grocery store robbery.[21] However, by 1933 he had been paroled and assumed his role as Eddie Killeen's strong-arm man. Nalley's aggressiveness would soon cause him to cross paths with one the Warring brothers and ruin Emmitt's desire to keep the Warring name out of the headlines.

CHAPTER SIX

Shooting on U Street

If Joe Nalley had not cemented his reputation as a bad actor before he went to jail, he certainly earned it after he was paroled in 1931. In the underworld, he had gained the reputation of being deadly with a knife or gun.[1] Police described him as "a man who under the influence of liquor would attempt anything."[2]

Eddie Killeen knew his liquor profits would seriously dwindle with the imminent repeal of Prohibition. He decided to increase his foothold in the city's gambling houses. In the fall of 1933, Nalley played out his strong man role for Killeen by invading selected locations of speakeasies and smaller gambling houses not under Killeen's control. Nalley and his men terrorized the customers and broke up the gambling equipment including slot machines, dice tables, and roulette wheels. Nalley also reportedly slashed two of "Warring's men" with a knife during a rampage in a speakeasy in the 800 block of 13th Street NW. One of his victims was believed to be one of the Warring brothers. [3]

In the early morning hours of November 7, 1933, Rags Warring drove out to U Street NW from Foggy Bottom with two associates, Victor "Toots" Juliano and Don "Whitey" Wallace. The day before, newspapers had carried the story that the 21st Amendment (repealing Prohibition) had been ratified and signed into law by President Franklin Roosevelt. The three men likely spoke of the consequences of the repeal.

Round-faced, and somewhat plump, Toots was primarily a numbers writer who later financially backed racehorses and boxers. In fact, it was a bet made at a boxing match that caused Juliano and his companion to follow a man they accused of welching on the bet to the man's apartment. Toots' companion at the man's apartment was killed, and Toots took a bullet to the shoulder. [4]

Don Wallace grew up with Rags in Foggy Bottom. He often wore a straw, narrow-rimmed fedora covering his sandy hair. Don insisted on being well dressed. One day he showed up sporting a new suit exclaiming, "Ain't credit wonderful."[5] Don also prided himself on being a good dancer and was kiddingly called "Jitterbug." Don was really not a tough guy. He tended to stutter when excited, and he was easily unnerved for someone in the rackets.

The U Street corridor in Washington was the heart of the largest urban African American community in the country until it lost the claim to Harlem. African Americans could not shop, dine, or be entertained in the white downtown area, so U Street showcased successful black-owned-and-operated businesses and nightclubs. Famous entertainer Pearl Bailey labeled the U Street corridor the "Black Broadway."[6] The nightspots featured first-class African American bands and were patronized by all races.

The Wunder Bar Club (later renamed the Cotton Club after the famous New York nightclub) was such a place, located on U Street near 10th Street. Around 3:00 a.m. on November 7, there were about 200 patrons in the Wunder Bar Club, "both white and colored." During the night, the band likely belted out some of Washington-born Duke Ellington's recent tunes like "It Don't Mean a Thing (If It Ain't Got That Swing)," "Mood Indigo" and "Sophisticated Lady." Perhaps they played Louis Armstrong's big hit of the day "When You're Smiling (The Whole World Smiles with You)."

Although the newspaper accounts differed slightly, the following is a synopsis of the events of that evening:

The drama at the Wunder Bar began when the rival parties were seated close to each other. At one table sat Rags Warring, Toots Juliano and Don Wallace. At the other table sat Joe Nalley, out on the town with two of his men, James Noonan and Charles Kessecker, and two lady companions, Millicent Gooch and Lucille Hughes.

At some point in the evening, Nalley went over to the Warring table and tapped Rags on the shoulder. He said, "Well, let's go outside and settle this thing right now." Nalley and Rags proceeded to the door, but they were trailed by a nightclub bouncer who warned them against any trouble. They assured the man that they were only going to talk, and they did just that for about twenty minutes just outside of the doorway. There was no indication to surrounding patrons that imminent trouble was brewing as they started to walk back to their respective tables. Rags stopped momentarily at his table. He was not satisfied with how the conversation with Nalley had ended. According to newspaper reports, Rags did not sit down, but instead turned and moved towards Nalley's table. Nalley was about to sit down when he saw Rags coming his way. Both men were standing at the table motionless when four shots suddenly erupted in the blare of the jazz sounds emanating from the band. Almost before the fourth shot was fired, the club was virtually deserted. "Excited patrons dashed through the front door, scurried through the rear, sped hands on knees under tables and clambered out windows."[7]

In the end, thirty-four-year-old Joe Nalley lay on the floor dying with three bullets in his chest. Nalley had not fired a shot. A .32-caliber bullet found under Nalley's table matched the three found in his chest. Nalley died at Freedmen's Hospital shortly after his arrival. However, when questioned by police before he died, he reportedly "uttered Warring's name before lapsing into a coma."[8]

As a youth, I got to know Don Wallace pretty well. It is not hard for me to imagine excitable Don exclaiming over and over as the three made their getaway from the Wunder Bar, "Charlie, I didn't know you were going to shoot him."

Given the dearth of witnesses that came forward after the shooting, it is somewhat amazing that the newspapers captured that amount of detail surrounding the shooting. However, there is at least one differing account of the last moments before the actual shots were fired. This comes from someone who was actually at the Wunder Bar Club that night: Rags Warring.

Years later, Rags would provide this slightly different version of events. After walking over from his table, Rags took a seat at Nalley's table. Expecting trouble, he had slipped out a gun from his trousers and held it just under the table, aimed at Nalley. He was sitting close to the table so the gun wouldn't be detected by the others when Nalley suddenly lunged at him with a knife. He quickly rose up and began firing at Nalley. Given Nalley's proclivity for using a knife, and the bullet found under the table, the story may have more credibility than the version the Washington newspapers carried.

After the shooting, the district attorney only needed only one believable witness. There were approximately 200 patrons and workers in the club that night. It would take a minor miracle for Rags to avoid being indicted for Nalley's death.

The police must have received sufficient information from initial witnesses to narrow the focus of their search. Detectives quickly began looking for Rags and his companions. Only after Rags and his companions consulted attorney Myron Ehrlich that same day did they turn themselves in at the Third Precinct station. This was their neighborhood precinct, where there were familiar (and perhaps friendly) police acquaintances.

Although Myron Ehrlich was still in his twenties, he had established himself as one of the leading defense attorneys in the District. A graduate of George Washington University Law School, Ehrlich once said that lawyers who turn up their nose at criminal cases because they are "unstylish" should be "ashamed of themselves." As for judges, he commented that "they have forgotten that they are nothing but lawyers with robes on." [9]

The local newspapers were generous in their treatment of Rags in their follow-up stories. They chronicled Nalley's extensive arrest record and his underworld reputation as a "bad actor" and "strong-arm man" who, according to those in local speakeasies, "got what he tried to give others." [10] The *Washington Times Herald* noted the irony that Nalley, a product of Prohibition, had died as Prohibition was being repealed.[11]

In contrast, the paper reported that "Charles Warring, 26, looks like a college boy, whom police regard as a member of the 'half-world.'" There was little mention of any past trouble with the law, but the paper did state that the police had witnesses who said, "Warring did the killing." The *Washington Post* reported that Nalley purportedly to have recently "hit Warring with an ice pick in a dispute over a woman."[12]

Rags was transferred to the District Jail and charged with murder. Juliano and Wallace were initially "booked" as material witnesses and released on bond. The most incriminating witness, club hostess Courtney Thomas, initially identified Rags from a police lineup of seven men. She later declared that Warring "might have been" Nalley's assailant. The twenty-two-year-old Miss Thomas was "colored" and of light complexion, like many of the employees of the clubs that served a good percentage of white customers. The *Washington Herald* described her as a "vivid night club hostess, with Mae Westian curves and bobbed hair."

At the coroner's inquest, Thomas sat "impassively as an artist's model on a pedestal."[13] In the hearing's most dramatic moment, she was asked to examine the face of every man in the District Morgue Court and say whether he was at the club when the shooting occurred.

She then walked down row after row, apparently not very interested, until she came to the bench where Rags Warring was sitting. Then she stopped, and said so that all could hear: "I don't know whether he was there or not."[14]

In fact, not a single witness at the inquest said they saw the shots fired. No one at Nalley's table that night would identify the shooter. Additionally, detective Floyd Truscott, who questioned Nalley before he died, testified that Nalley kept whispering an almost incoherent answer to their questions: "See Louie, see Louie." Truscott also stated he thought that Nalley once muttered the name of Rags Warring, but he was not sure.

In the end, no one was indicted for Nalley's killing. Emmitt Warring, and perhaps Leo Warring, had probably induced potential witnesses to question their memory of that night's events.

But the public's frustration with the authorities' failure to indict and convict anyone for the series of killings that plagued the city would soon reach the breaking point. In the fall of 1934, the public would be shocked by a murder that would raise its cry for justice to a crescendo.

CHAPTER SEVEN

Reckless Retribution

Edward G. "Mickey" McDonald was one of Washington's better-known "sportsmen" going well back to the 1920s. Tall and thin, McDonald was a colorful big-shot gambler and numbers racket operator who spent his money on the high life. He had a winning personality that endeared him to those on the street.

In 1934, McDonald broke his association with Eddie Killeen, taking some of his old betting customers with him. For this ambitious act, his life became endangered.[1]

Success had allowed Mickey to buy a 12-room country home in Takoma Park, Maryland, just outside Washington, where the area was still rural. When he wasn't spending the profits from gambling operations, he played the role of husband and father with a young child.

In the early fall of 1934, Killeen henchman Albert "Bumps" Sutton hosted a number of out-of-state gunmen in the swanky Alban Towers at Massachusetts and Wisconsin Avenues NW. It was a sign that Killeen had come under the influence of outside forces—namely, Philadelphia mobster Harry Stromberg, alias "Nig Rosen."

Months before, Killeen had complained that he was not receiving any assistance from District authorities in warding off pressure from "Philadelphia interests" for a piece of his business.[2] Out-of-town gamblers had been seen in Georgetown, watching the places that Killeen controlled.

One October morning, McDonald's car exploded when he stepped on the starter. The explosives in the engine ignited, but the stick of dynamite under the driver's seat did not. He miraculously survived without being seriously injured.[3] McDonald took a number of steps to thwart future attempts on his life, including installing a network of floodlights in his front yard.

McDonald now was looking over his shoulder everywhere he went. Someone was definitely out to get him. One day, realizing he was being followed, he walked over to the man tailing him at the corner of 14th and P Streets NW and asked him for a match. McDonald took a good look at the man and discreetly let the man know that he was wise to him.

McDonald had not recognized Philadelphia gunman William H. Cleary. Bringing in killers from out of town to eliminate local competition was common in the gangster world. It made it more difficult to get a lead on the assassin and who had hired him. (One of the best-known examples of such a killing occurred when Al Capone brought New York gangster Frankie Yale to Chicago to kill "Big Jim" Colosimo.)

In addition to Cleary, two others were brought into town to eliminate McDonald. Tony "The Stinger" Cugino was an experienced hired killer from South Philadelphia. Cugino, who was thin and wiry and typically wore a mustache to cover an identifying scar over his upper lip, was the man who had kidnapped "Nucky" Johnson of Atlantic City fame and extracted a $100,000 ransom paid by Harry Stromberg. The authorities believed Stromberg hired Cugino so he could negotiate with the kidnappers and eventually pay a phony ransom to gain Nucky's good graces.[4] The police also believed that Cugino was the individual who had smuggled two pistols in a baked turkey to a couple of buddies of the Tri-State Gang awaiting execution in Richmond, Virginia. The men successfully escaped prison using the weapons, critically wounding a policeman in the process.[5]

John "Slim" Dunn, a third out-of-state gangster, joined Cugino and Cleary on the job. Dunn was out on parole and was already being sought by police for the robbery and critical shooting of a postal guard at Washington's Union Station.

In the early hours of October 23, 1934, Cugino, Dunn, and Cleary hid in the trees and bushes opposite McDonald's home. They were waiting for McDonald to return home late at night after the gambling joints closed up. By 3:00 a.m. McDonald had not shown. There were still no signs of him at 4:00 a.m. The men grew anxious, smoking one cigarette after another. Finally, at 4:15 a.m. car headlights appeared. The driver began to slow down as he approached the McDonald home. Despite a full moon and the floodlights pointed toward McDonald's yard, the gunmen could not get a good look at the driver.

The car stopped close to McDonald's newspaper boxes beside the road. The gunmen presumed they had been spotted and that McDonald had ducked down and was instructing his driver to drive off. Cugino fired two shotgun blasts at the passenger door of the automobile with the intent of hitting the crouching McDonald. The car took the brunt of the blasts, but one pellet went through the passenger window and entered the driver's right arm. Pushing down further on the accelerator, the driver tried to move the gearshift under the right side of the steering wheel into first gear with his wounded arm. As the car lumbered away, Cugino sprung from the bushes and chased it, firing his .32-caliber weapon. One bullet crashed through the rear window and struck the driver in the back of the head. The car veered off the road to the right and came to rest on a mound of dirt. One of the gunmen ran to the car, opened the door, and saw that the driver was not McDonald. He then pumped another shotgun round into the back seat in case Mickey was back there hiding. But no one was there. [6]

It turned out that "Mickey" McDonald had come home uncharacteristically early that night around 11:00 p.m. and had parked his car where the gunmen could not see it from the road. He was asleep in his bed when the shooting took place. The driver was a *Washington Times Herald* newspaper carrier, Allen D. Wilson, of Silver Spring, Maryland.

Mrs. McDonald awoke in time to see two men chasing the newspaper carrier's car down the road. As the gunmen realized their mistake, all escaped into the woods except Slim Dunn, who wandered bewilderedly for a moment along the road. Suddenly another car appeared and unintentionally shined his headlights onto Dunn. The illumination gave Mrs. McDonald a good look at him.[7] Mickey McDonald phoned the police and reported that someone had "pumped some shot" into a man in front of his house. But it was too late for Allen Wilson. His family had lost their husband and father.

Cugino fled back to Philadelphia, throwing the murder weapons into the Susquehanna River as he went.

When the police arrived at the murder scene, all they found were charred cigarettes and burned matches left by the gunmen at their lookout post across from the McDonald home. There were no good leads to find out who had perpetrated this disturbing crime.

The public outcry was immediate. Many had looked the other way when the victims were hoodlums, but this was strikingly different. Wilson was a completely innocent husband and father of three young children: Patricia, age eight; Allen, age four; and Richard, age one.[8] The public grieved for the family left behind.

Although the murder was committed just over the DC line in Maryland, the public felt it was the latest in an embarrassing series of murders committed in the nation's capital. They wanted action and scorned those who were behind local gambling operations.

The gamblers heard the uproar and knew what was coming. Most closed their joints for days after the Wilson killing. The doors stayed shut to escape the eventual "heat" destined to come down on the underworld.[9]

Major Ernest W. Brown, the chief of the DC police, immediately began a concerted drive against crime in Washington and a general roundup of all known "gamblers, gangsters, and criminals." Brown ordered his captains and inspectors to furnish headquarters with information regarding crime and vice conditions in their respective precincts.

Major Brown also was summoned to a conference with the three District commissioners. Afterwards, one of the commissioners announced legislation for increasing the power of police and prosecuting authorities against gangsters. The next day, without the need for any new legislation, the commissioners enforced building code restrictions against gambling houses who rented their premises for illegal activities. Daytime raids were planned to determine if any building, zoning, or fire escape regulations were being broken by the suspected gamblers. Building inspectors were directed to see if barricades, which would violate fire regulations, had been erected by the gamblers to impede any surprise police raid.[10]

To address the public outcry, the Washington, DC Bar Association agreed to host a mass meeting of law enforcement, public officials, church leaders, and ordinary citizens to determine what could be done to reduce crime in the nation's capital. Held in the cavernous ballroom of the Mayflower Hotel, the meeting drew an estimated crowd of 1,200 people. Major Brown, accompanied by Lieutenant George M. Little, chief of the vice squad, outlined the progress his department had made fighting crime over the recent years. Brown assured everyone present that every effort was being made to apprehend the slayers of Allen Wilson. He acknowledged that though the crime had been committed in Maryland, signs already pointed towards District gangsters.

The next day the public saw action. The vice squad raided a gambling establishment in the 1500 block of H Street NW (two blocks from the White House), using crowbars to break through a barricade. Over the entrance was a sign reading "Lawyer's School, Bar Examination Courses," but inside, the police found boards carrying the results of nearby horse racing tracks and other gambling paraphernalia.[11]

Slim Dunn was arrested within a few days for the Union Station robbery. While in jail, he was questioned about the Wilson murder but denied any knowledge of the crime.

Approximately one month later, Albert Sutton was picked up for a possible parole violation. Police wanted to question him about his style of living, source of income, and his place of employment.[12] Sutton had been paroled in 1933 after serving 12 years of a 20-year sentence for robbery and assault with intent to kill in connection with a theft of wine from the home of Rabbi Silverstone at 11th and K Streets NW (Wine could be legally purchased and possessed for religious purposes during Prohibition.)

Based on information received from a counterfeiter at the District Jail, the police focused on the Tri-State Gang, which Cugino had been a member of.[13]

Acting on a tip, New York City police nabbed Tony Cugino at 47th and Broadway on September 8, 1935. He was walking down the street around midnight with his dark-eyed, 23-year-old wife, Frances.[14] After fifteen hours of questioning, he confessed to a number of murders, but he did not mention the Wilson killing.

Despite the fact that the New York police took some precautions to ensure that Cugino did not harm himself—they took his belt and shoelaces—he avoided the electric chair by hanging himself in his jail cell with his necktie and shreds torn from his shirt.

On November 20, 1935, Cugino's young widow Frances was brought to Washington to testify to a grand jury.[15] The authorities hoped she could shed light on who hired the gunmen who carried out the "bungled" killing. The police always suspected Eddie Killeen was behind the killing but could not find any hard evidence to link him to the murder. However, in three days it wouldn't matter.

∽

Those who best knew Eddie Killeen said he was never the same after the bungled shooting of newspaper carrier Allen Wilson.

The walls seemed to be closing in. Perhaps the police were, too. Even though his loyal lieutenant Bumps Sutton had remained silent while in jail, Killeen was in a dark and depressed mood in November of 1935. He particularly feared that other Washington gamblers were out to get him in order to take the police heat off of themselves.[16]

It had not been a good year for "Big Eddie." Even his foray into legitimate business had gone awry. Eddie's beer distributorship had been taken away by District officials because of the strong-arm tactics that his salesmen employed in their sales pitches. It seemed the old habits learned in Prohibition were hard to break.

A number of his men had been killed in various shootouts over the recent years. Others had been incarcerated. Those in prison had kept quiet about Eddie's crimes, but he wondered how long that would last. Now a young girl, Mrs. Frances Cugino, had been brought to town to determine what, if anything, she knew about the Wilson killing. She could now speak of what she knew regarding Killeen's connection to the Wilson murder without fear of implicating her dead husband.

Killeen was estranged from his own wife, Florence, and had taken up with Mrs. Lillian Maddock for over a year. Killeen and Maddock had been teenage lovers in Georgetown but each had married someone else. Recently, their romance had started anew while both were estranged from their spouses. The thirty-five-year-old Maddock, who had a history of narcotics charges against her, was living with Killeen in one of his empty gambling houses on Conduit Road (now MacArthur Boulevard) in Cabin John, Maryland, not far from the DC line. The yellow, two-story stucco structure was barren of furniture but replete with roulette wheels, dice tables, and "bird cages," devices that flipped over to produce a fair roll of the dice.[17]

Killeen and Maddox spent November 21 drinking heavily most of the day and occasionally arguing.[18] The next day, Killeen threatened to leave her and sail to Miami in his expensive cabin cruiser anchored off of Colonial Beach, Virginia. Maddock countered by saying something about Eddie's estranged wife, Florence. Killeen took offense and began beating her, finally threatening to shoot her in her "good leg." (She was already partially crippled in the other.) She then boldly shoved a bed at Killeen causing him to drop the gun out of his hand. In the ensuing struggle, she managed to retrieve the gun and aimed it at him. As he started for a window to escape, she fired twice. The first bullet entered his back. When he turned around, she shot him in the stomach. Maddock then put a blanket over his partially clothed body, threw down a shot of whiskey, and called the police.

When the cops arrived, Lillian Maddock met them at the front door. The policemen inquired as to what was the trouble. She said, "Come on upstairs and see for yourself." Maddock told the police that she "had to do it. He was going to kill me." She later uttered incomprehensibly to police: "I killed him, because I loved him." Police found Killeen's body, still adorned with his two huge diamond rings. There were multiple bruises on Mrs. Maddock's face and body to support at least part of her story.

The Evening Star saw the irony of Killeen's death: "He had been hiding out from gunmen and was killed by a friend." Killeen's gang had literally been dying for months. His death now unquestionably marked the gang's end.

At her trial, Maddock was represented by surprisingly high-priced attorneys, fueling speculation that the faded brunette had been a tool of one of Eddie's enemies. In the end, she would be cleared of all charges in the name of "self-defense."[19]

"Big Eddie" Killeen was buried in a tuxedo and a $1,000 copper coffin (around $10,000 in today's currency). Services were held at the Chambers Funeral Home at 517 11th Street SE. The *Washington Post* described the scene: "Men—big men, hard men, men who looked out of place in the flowery-scented room—wept openly and unashamed. Various floral wreaths were signed: 'The Boys' and 'From a Pal.'"[20] One man showed up with a wreath just before the services were to begin and said, "I never liked Eddie Killeen, but I'm sorry he had to die this way."

Killeen might have gone too far in his last years. The presence of out-of-town gunmen in the Wilson killing brought up questions about out-of-town influence over Killeen. But he was still one of Georgetown's own. *The Evening Star* pointed out that the "Warring boys" were in attendance at the funeral and the two Cady brothers, William and Frank, acted as pallbearers.

The police never produced any hard evidence that Killeen had been behind the bungled Wilson killing, perhaps because Eddie died before they could build any case against him. But with Killeen dead, police and the newspapers were free to implicate him in Wilson's death. In the end, only Cugino's accomplices were left to pay for Wilson's murder.

The break for the police came when William Cleary was arrested in Havre de Grace, Maryland, not far from where Cugino had tossed the murder weapons. Cleary agreed to testify against the others. The accused were tried separately. Mickey McDonald and his wife testified against the men at all their trials. All except Cleary received life sentences.

Tony Cugino's young widow, Frances, was unable to provide any information to police about the Wilson killing or Eddie Killeen's possible connection. They had only been married for three months. She claimed that she knew nothing about her husband's criminal activities and the police believed her. She returned to quiet life in Philadelphia where she lived with her parents and worked at a factory. She refused the advances of a man at the factory and he retaliated by referring to her as "the murder's wife." Tony Cugino had claimed that Frances was the only woman he had loved. Before he took his life in a New York jail, he had written her: "Try to be happy, kid. I'll see you in the next world." Less than a year after Cugino's death, his young, comely widow Frances after returning home after work one day took one of his guns and shot herself in the heart.[21] Apparently, she couldn't wait any longer to see Tony in the next world.

ɞ

With Eddie Killeen dead and "Mickey" McDonald on the sidelines, the Warring brothers expanded their territory, especially in Georgetown.

By reviewing the various newspaper reports of that time, it appears that the fiasco of the Wilson killing stopped a major intrusion by Philadelphia mobster Harry Stromberg into Washington's gambling underworld.

The presence of Stromberg's strongman, Tony Cugino, in the failed attempt to rub out Killeen's competitor, Mickey McDonald, may have been a result of Stromberg's new influence with Killeen. Perhaps Stromberg wanted to show Killeen how the big boys ran things. However, the resultant "heat" that came down after the Wilson murder caused Stromberg to re-think his plans for expanding into the DC gambling world. The Warring brothers benefitted from that change of plans by taking most of Killeen's territory.

Even a congressman offered his observations on outside influence in Washington's rackets. During a hearing of the Special Crime Investigating Committee, William Schulte of Indiana, revealed he had made a survey of crime conditions in Washington and "had discovered that until gangsters from other cities 'muscled in,' Washington apparently was free of murderers among the gambling fraternity."[22] The statement was not exactly accurate, but it highlighted the recent spike in mayhem and murder that seemed to have been the work of outsiders. Schulte put in a good word for the local gamblers by stating that "it was 'unfair' to the Washington gamblers to permit gangsters from Philadelphia, Chicago or any other outside place to come here and control the gambling situation."

National crime syndicates had been leery of entering the Washington scene because of the immediate presence of the federal government. Stromberg's failed attempt to do so apparently reinforced that apprehension.

There were other changes taking place, as well. Eddie Killeen had been willing to use individuals that the public would regard as simple "hoodlums," men who made sensational headlines with their raw tactics to do his work. Emmitt Warring was doing things differently. He sought to keep himself and his operations as low-key as possible.

Emmitt had great respect for those who operated businesses in Foggy Bottom and Georgetown. He wanted to be accepted by them as just another businessman. Early in the formation of the gang, the owner of a drug store at 19th and Pennsylvania Avenue NW gave permission for Emmitt's men to meet and mill about in the pharmacy. Emmitt was grateful to the proprietor and issued strict orders for there to be no misconduct, including drinking. One night a large, imposing member of the gang ducked inside the store's phone booth to take a swig from a whiskey bottle. "Emmitt grabbed him by his shirtfront, jerked him out of the booth and shook him vigorously. 'Once more and that'll be all for you,' Emmitt said to the man, about twice his size."[23] He was known as a "tough little guy"; however, he deplored unnecessary violence. Whenever anyone got on his wrong side, they usually would be treated as if they no longer existed.

Emmitt was very selective when choosing men to hire. He studied the attitude of judges trying cases and discovered that an accused with no prior gambling record would get off with probation or a small fine.

He also eschewed those with records of violence or robbery.

In addition, Emmitt valued honesty in those he hired, making exceptions for only minor thefts carried out as a youth. Honesty and dependability would be important for workers in this new racket that was born before Prohibition died—the numbers game.

CHAPTER EIGHT

The Numbers Game

Critics called it a racket, but those who made a living from it called it a business.

In New York's Harlem and Little Italy, a new betting game emerged during the middle 1920s, the "numbers game." In those days, players could bet as little as a penny on a three-digit number. Bets could be made at work, on the street corner, at the barber shop or beauty parlor. Runners or pickup men would bring the money and betting slips to the bookmakers' headquarters (or "the office") every day. Those who worked in this gambling network made a living by getting a percentage of the take for the day.[1]

The newspapers, and those who played the game on the street, gave it many names, e.g., numbers game, numbers racket, or the name now used by states, the lottery. One amusing euphemism was the "brokerage commission business," a term used by operators to blur the line between those in the numbers business, and legitimate businessmen who worked on "percentages." The terms bookie, bookmaker and numbers writer come from the practice of writing individual bets down on paper or in a book to record who bet how much on what and at what odds.

Gambling equipment—such as roulette wheels found in speakeasies—was considered "gambling paraphernalia" under established case law, but possession of mere names and numbers on paper initially was considered insufficient evidence to charge someone with illegal gambling.

When it came to finances, the only investment a bookmaker needed to run a numbers game was a "bank" to pay off the few winners every day. Earnings made during Prohibition gave many operators the stake they needed to get a foothold in the numbers business.

Besides providing the bank that was needed to get started, the illegal liquor business became the perfect training ground for the numbers business. Many of the same middlemen or runners employed during Prohibition were used to connect gambling customers to the financial backers who would pay the winnings of those who hit the daily number. The same protection system to payoff law enforcement could be used. And when an arrest was made, the same team of lawyers and bail bondsmen could be called on to provide the services they had provided during Prohibition.

Today almost every state has a daily lottery game, and there are at least two national games, Powerball and Mega Millions. The illegal numbers game offered only one game daily, but today states offer multiple games throughout the day, tempting players to part with more of their money. These state and national games are supported by a network of specialized ticket-selling machines and computers generally located in gas stations and liquor stores, all out in the open and under the blessing of the participating states. But before the lotteries were legal, a hidden network provided the same services to countless small-time bettors in most of American cities.

The pyramid-like network consisted of a daily flow of bets starting with individual bettors at the bottom. This money flowed to bookmakers who turned their bets and proceeds over to pick-up men and runners. These eventually passed their collections of the day's wagers and cash over to the game's backers or bankers. Later that night or the next day, the winning proceeds would flow back down the pyramid to the winning bettors.

The headquarters for this operation was simply referred to as the "office" by those who worked there. The office was usually on the second floor of someone's home or a separate apartment rented for the purpose of centralizing and recording the daily action (bets) received over multiple phone lines. The office usually consisted of nothing more than a few card tables and some folding chairs. Arrangements were usually made with someone working for the phone company to set up telephone hook ups that would not reflect multiple phones for one address which could direct police as to where to raid. The "staff" would arrive in the latter part of the morning and stay to late afternoon.

Betting was concentrated naturally where people congregated in large numbers. In Washington, some of the busiest bookies operated in government buildings. A bookie was usually a messenger or someone who ran a snack stand in the building—anyone who came into contact with many people under the cover of another job. The United States Bureau of Engraving and Printing, which produces paper currency, housed one of the largest number books.[2] A congressman from Indiana claimed that almost half of the 8,000 employees in the Washington Navy Yard played the numbers game or bet on horses. "Why, they even have runners in the yard who turn the bets over to agents at the gate at noon," he claimed.[3]

Before the individual states took over the daily lottery, a single three-digit number was drawn each day (except Sunday) for each area. How was the three-digit number fairly and independently determined every day? Initially, a number of sources were used, sometimes differing from city to city. Some bookies used the last three digits of the daily balance of the United States Treasury (as published in the financial pages) or the daily balances of various stock or produce exchanges. Gradually, most operators began using the last digit of the total winning payoffs of three race results at a specified horse race track. The three digits would be determined in sequential order over the course of the day's racing.

Anyone who had bet on a winning three-digit number would receive most often a 600 to one payout for their bet; a dime bet would pay a winner $60. (States now generally pay out 500 to one). Of course, the actual chances of the bettor picking the winning number would be 1,000 to one, a fact that guaranteed the bookmaker a profit over time.

Some numbers were popular at various times and places, such as a three-digit exchange at the beginning of a phone number, or a three-digit route number of a heavily travelled road. During the 1950s the popular TV show *Dragnet* began every week showing a policeman's badge with the number 714, making it a frequently bet number.

At the height of its popularity, approximately one out of every three Washingtonians played the numbers and most knew at least one bookie.[4] And like the bootleggers before them, the numbers writers became cult heroes in many neighborhoods.

A bookie's identity was usually the worst-kept secret in the neighborhood. A relative stranger to the newsstand, bakery, or local grocery may not have picked up that the slovenly man behind the counter also was a bookie, but practically all those in the neighborhood were aware of his second profession.

Bookies often had colorful nicknames like "Sugar Pops" or the "Bread Man." The local numbers writer was someone who knew his regular customers' favorite three-digit numbers as well as he knew their names. He expected to see his regular players every day and would probably inquire about their welfare if they didn't come around.

Joe Gallagher, who became one of the all-time great high school basketball and football coaches in the entire country at St. John's College High School in Washington, DC, grew up in Foggy Bottom. As teenagers he and my older cousin, Frank Cady Jr. used to sit across the street from St. Stephen's Church at 25th and Pennsylvania Avenues and watch policemen and local bookmakers go into the church to secretly conduct business with Emmitt in one of the confessionals.

On one such afternoon, they composed a singsong medley about a hypothetical numbers writer, called Pete. At Joe's ninetieth birthday in 2011, he passed out copies of the song and asked almost 300 well-wishers in the St. John's gym to sing along with him to the following:

"The Numbers Game Song"
Lyrics and Medley by Joe Gallagher and Frank Cady Jr.
Now who's that coming down the street?
It's old Pete the numbers man, with a pencil and pad in his hand.
Got some extra cash today, so I think I'll give that guy some play.
Just to start off the fun, put me down for a nickel on 101.
Now if 101 sounds good to you, you better put a nickel on 202.
202 sounds good to me, you better put a nickel on 303.
303 is not so sure, but you better put a nickel on 404.
404 is full of jibe, better put a nickel on 505.
505 plays lots of tricks, got you for a nickel on 606.
606 I got from heaven, better slap a nickel on 707.
707 is at the gate, I've got you for a nickel on 808.
808 is always behind, going to put a nickel on 909.
If that's all the numbers you're going to play, I think I'll be on my way.
Hey wait a minute before you go, you better put a nickel on 000.

The local numbers man had replaced the local bootlegger as the provider of everyday diversions from the doldrums of the Depression. Many people were either out of work or were barely scratching out an existence in the job they did have. Playing the daily numbers gave them a welcome diversion from their dismal condition and hope for a partial escape from poverty.

As with alcohol consumption during Prohibition, the numbers game and other forms of gambling tested the government's ability to regulate behavior that it deemed harmful to citizens. Law enforcement found in both cases that if a significant number of people wanted to partake in the banned substance or activity, someone would meet the demand. Just like the bootleggers who came to think of themselves as businessmen with loyal customers and a weekly payroll to meet, those in the "numbers business" came to see themselves in the same light.

In order to provide their customers the daily pleasures that reform committees and politicians attempted to deny them, bootleggers and bookmakers had to secure the protection of "friendly" cops. These policemen certainly could rationalize their cooperation; it allowed them to concentrate on crimes that had real, unwilling victims and to supplement their low-paying jobs. Any end run around the enforcement arms of an intrusive government could be justified.

The men who provided the booze or an outlet for gambling were usually held in high esteem on the streets. These racketeers came from the same relatively poor backgrounds as their customers. They often showed more compassion than the government, providing their customers with food or coal for stoves during tough times. Many of my friends whose parents or grandparents had lived in Foggy Bottom or Georgetown during the '30s spoke to me of how they'd heard that the Warrings came around with coal during the winter for those who could not afford it.

The numbers game might have become the most lucrative racket in town, but bootlegging hadn't ended with the repeal of Prohibition. There was still a flourishing market in DC for illicit alcohol. It was cheaper than the spirits produced by the legal distilleries. The country was still in the throes of the Depression and drinkers had to also watch their pennies. Legitimate operations invested more to create a better tasting and safer product, and they had to pay for the licenses, revenue stamps, and other taxes. Their product always was more expensive than the illicit liquor.

While growing their numbers business, the Warrings were among the bootleggers who eagerly continued to fill the market demand for cheaper alcohol. Emmitt Warring's man for this operation was Samuel Montgomery. "Monty" was at least a decade older than the Warring brothers and most of the men who worked for them. That fact was reflected in his noticeably receding hairline, which he accentuated by combing his hair straight back.

A group of younger men worked with Montgomery, including Joseph "Sam" Bond and Jack Sweeney, who at age nineteen was the youngest of the group.

Bond was definitely the tallest in the gang, standing approximately 6' 3". He was referred to in newspaper articles as "Joseph F. Bond," "Joseph Samuel Bond," and "Joseph Barnes," which might have been his real name. I know that my father referred to him as "Sam Bond."

Jack Sweeney was cast with a florid complexion from his Irish heritage and rail-thin. Once, pursued by the police, he attempted to hide behind a telephone pole to avoid detection.[5] Although most of the men who dealt in illegal booze or bookmaking wished they could make good money in something "legit," none meant it as much as Jack Sweeney. If there was ever a reluctant rumrunner, it was Jack. A Foggy Bottom native, Jack was a master at calligraphy. Anyone who received a Christmas card from him knew without opening the envelope that it was from Jack because of his elaborate handwriting. Jack also had a ritual of sending his friends a crisp one-dollar bill in Christmas cards every year. Long after his bootlegging days, Jack tried to go "legit" by selling insurance. He was doing well before a jealous coworker who knew Jack's criminal past informed Jack's boss, who then had to let Jack go.[6]

Under Emmitt Warring's direction, Montgomery ran a distribution network out of 10 warehouses in DC, selling over 5,000 gallons of alcohol every week in bottles labeled "Alky," "High Moon" and "Green Country."[7] Montgomery managed a convoy of approximately thirty vehicles, driven by over a dozen men and purchased by Emmitt under various names, to haul the liquor from a large supplier in Trenton, New Jersey to the warehouse in DC. Ultimately it went to legitimate liquor stores or "hip pocket" distributors.

CHAPTER NINE

Things Heat Up

Washington lived up to its reputation of being a southern town in July 1936. The heat was practically unbearable. The July 10 edition of the *Washington Post* carried a lengthy story on how the weather was affecting the area and the nation.[1] The day before, the temperature in DC had reached 104 degrees and only cooled to 81 at 3:00 a.m. Three area residents died of heat-related causes. Many federal and city workers were sent home hours before the regular closing times. Because most homes lacked air-conditioning, literally thousands of residents retreated to the banks of the Potomac with their makeshift bedding to spend the night. Thousands more slept on their porches whether they were screened in or not.

But the heat didn't stop Washingtonians from enjoying the summer. A record crowd of 37,500 attended the Nationals -Yankees doubleheader on July 4. The Nationals' management lost count of ticket sales and sold more tickets than seats, so thousands were allowed on the playing field to watch the game. Some fans celebrated the 4th by throwing firecrackers on the field during the game. A ball hit into the outfield was caught by a fan before the Nationals' outfielder could get to it. To encourage fans to leave the stadium, the management announced over the loudspeaker that they had been notified of a death of a family member of someone attending the game, but they didn't have the heart to announce the name. The Yankees, led by Lou Gehrig and a rookie named Joe DiMaggio, won both games.[2]

Maybe it was the crazy heat of that summer that made three small-time bootleggers from southeast Washington brave enough to push their business into the Warrings' territory. They boldly hijacked a liquor-filled car belonging to the Warrings and then called Monty

Montgomery the next day with an offer to sell the car back, absent the booze, for $100. When Montgomery told Rags about the phone call, he decided to teach these brash young guys a lesson. A rough ride out of town might discourage any more trouble from this group.

On the evening of July 21, twenty-three-year-old Joseph E. O'Brien had just finished a meal at the Majestic Restaurant (now Le Bon Cafe) at 210 Second Street SE near the corner where Second Street, Independence Avenue (then called B Street) and Pennsylvania Avenue all intersect, just two blocks from the U.S. Capitol dome. O'Brien was with his girlfriend, Viola Josephine Jennings, and his two partners, Harry "Spike" Behrle and W.R. "Country" Carpenter.

After the meal, Behrle bid his dining companions good night and walked north up 2nd Street. Lingering outside the restaurant for a few minutes to enjoy the relative coolness of the summer evening, O'Brien noticed two carloads of men pulling up to the curb. In the two cars were Rags Warring, Monty Montgomery, George "Teddy" Tear, Sam Bond, Clarence "Cocky" Ware, and Jack Sweeney.[3]

O'Brien and company initially thought the men were partygoers looking for a late-night snack. But then Rags Warring walked up to O'Brien and told him at gunpoint to get into the car. Perhaps he didn't immediately recognize the youngest of the Warring brothers or the members of the reception committee standing next to the cars. He also may not have noticed that Spike Behrle was already in the backseat of one of the vehicles after being taken hostage. (He had been picked up by the gang on a corner at Second and East Capitol Streets.)[4] But as O'Brien approached one of the autos, he definitely recognized Monty Montgomery as the driver. He turned to run, but Rags struck him over the head with the butt of his revolver and sent O'Brien to the pavement at the feet of Sam Bond.[5] As O'Brien lay on the ground, young Sam Bond suddenly shot three bullets into O'Brien's legs, one of them shattering a kneecap.[6]

That Bond aimed only for O'Brien's legs indicated the gang did not want to kill O'Brien or his partners. It was a common practice to "send a message" to the victim by shooting him in the legs and not the torso. As a general rule, the law pursued and punished severely those who murdered—but not those who only wounded—another underworld figure. However, shooting him in front of a restaurant in the heart of town had not been part of the plan. This case would be different due to the extent of O'Brien's injuries and the public's disgust with the series of shootings in the middle 1930s.

Country Carpenter quickly decided that he was not going to be the next target. It took a moment for any of the Warring gang to realize that Carpenter had retreated back into the Majestic Restaurant, charged through the nearly empty dining area, then burst through the kitchen and out the back door into the night. The Warrings eventually released Spike Behrle unharmed, but warned him about talking about what happened.

Unfortunately for the Warring contingent, a Navy Yard employee who lived nearby witnessed the shooting and jotted down the first two digits of one of the tag numbers and a description of the car. Within hours, the Virginia State Police detained a car that fit the description in rural Dumfries, Virginia, about twenty-five miles south of Washington. They immediately arrested its occupants—Monty Montgomery, Teddy Tear, and Sam Bond—and returned them to DC.[7] Less than a half an hour after they were charged and bail was set, someone had raised $60,000 in bail money ($20,000 apiece). The man who arranged bail was Emmitt Warring.[8]

The shooting on Capitol Hill was exactly the kind of attention and negative publicity that Emmitt wanted his operation to avoid. The potential downside was much worse than losing one carload of alcohol. Even the cops on Emmitt's payroll would not be able to ignore the pressure from an outraged citizenry, inflamed by the sensational headlines that were to follow.

Within days, the *Washington Post* raised the specter of police corruption. On July 25, 1936, the paper reported that "it was rumored at police headquarters that there was an 'understanding' between persons close to the Police Department through which certain racketeers were to get a measure of protection from arrest."[9]

Three days later, the police tried to shift the blame. In a *Washington Post* article entitled "Police Blame Gang's Power On Lax Court," police officials laid the "failure to cooperate in ridding the city of the Foggy Bottom Gang" at the feet of the justice system. As stated in the *Post*:

Inability to purge the city of the last "pre-repeal" mob of bootleggers and "numbers" racketeers was admitted by police yesterday when they condemned the District courts for failing to co-operate in ridding the city of the "Foggy Bottom" gang.

Police said the Warring brothers are the last well-organized gang of racketeers in the city...

"These men should be run out of the city," a high police official was quoted as saying yesterday, "but the courts refuse to indict members of this gang and if they are indicted and convicted, the men are placed on probation."

On July 30, after a futile search for Rags Warring, Cocky Ware and Jack Sweeney, Chief of Detectives Bernard W. Thompson officially ordered the arrest of the three in connection to the shooting of Joseph E. O'Brien.[10]

Although Rags did not significantly curtail his travels around town, he decided to stay away from his sister Esther's house where he had been living. He figured the police were surveilling that house in hopes of apprehending him coming or going. Instead he spent his nights at the home of his longtime girlfriend, Mary Healy, who lived with her mom on Kansas Avenue in upper northwest Washington. Rags slept in one bedroom and Mary Healy and her mom slept in another. After looking for Rags for over a week, police detectives Clement Cox and Thomas McVearry surprised Rags as he slept in the Healy home and took him into custody. Ironically, one of the detectives had known Mary Healy since she was a young child living in poverty and had followed her quick rise through the ranks in the US Government to the position she now held as personal secretary to the executive officer of the National Archives. He knew about her relationship with Rags and did not approve it.[11]

On their drive downtown to police headquarters, Rags beseeched the detectives not to report the true location of the arrest. He knew of the embarrassment to Mary Healy and her mom once the newspapers learned where Rags was apprehended and realized the possibility that they could be charged with harboring someone wanted by the police. In the worst-case scenario, she could lose her job and her government career. Understanding the possible ramifications of reporting that the Healy home was the location of the arrest, the detectives agreed to select a busy location a few blocks from police headquarters, i.e., Seventh and G Street northwest—current location of the Verizon Center arena. The next day the newspapers reported that location as the site of the arrest.[12]

After his arrest Rags was immediately taken to Providence Hospital to stand before Joseph O'Brien's hospital bed. O'Brien quickly identified Rags as the man who slugged him before others opened fire. Rags was then questioned by the superintendent (chief) of police, Major Ernest W. Brown, and chief of detectives, Bernard W. Thompson. Twenty-five minutes later, the man described by police as the "co-leader of the Georgetown Warring mob" was charged with "assault with intent to kill" and released on bond of $20,000. [13]

The last two suspects, Cocky Ware and Jack Sweeney, still were at large. On August 9, detectives made a trip to Colonial Beach, Virginia, to search Emmitt's beach house for the two men. But the detectives returned empty handed, claiming that someone must have tipped off the pair to the impending raid.[14]

In mid-August, Lieutenant Little, chief of the vice squad, told the press that the police knew that the Warring numbers runners met every afternoon to turn in their number slips (bets) for the day in the shade of Rock Creek Park at 26th and L Streets NW. He went on to complain that the police were handicapped because under the existing law, it was not illegal to possess "numbers slips."[15]

Later that summer, Emmitt's fears that the O'Brien shooting would bring more "heat" were realized. As part of their continuing search for the last two suspects in the shooting, a special police squad arrested thirteen men in a gaming establishment at 2512 L Street NW that was "reputedly operated by members of the elusive Warring gang." The police confiscated a large quantity of gambling and horse race betting equipment. Although Emmitt and Leo were spotted in front of the place as the raiders approached, they escaped after recognizing what was about to take place. The police were prepared to use their sledgehammers and battering rams against the thick steel doors and the windows barricaded with wooden planks, but someone—perhaps thinking it was Emmitt and Leo wanting to come back in—mistakenly opened the door for them.[16]

Finally, on September 1, Cocky Ware and John Sweeney walked into the familiar Third Precinct station. The police attributed their surrender to the "heat" that had been placed on the District underworld. Sweeney explained that they had been on "vacation" and only learned that they were wanted by the police upon their return home.[17] But what was not reported was that some of that "heat" was directed at Mary Healy who was questioned if she knew where Sweeny and Ware were hiding. The day after the questioning, Sweeney and Ware gave themselves up.

Washington newspaper readers probably felt that the papers were publishing the weekly script of a radio gangster serial during these late summer months of 1936. The upcoming trials would seem like the second installment.

As the trial date approached, prosecutors felt confident they would obtain convictions of the six defendants charged with the shooting of Joseph O'Brien. While in the hospital, O'Brien had cursed his assailants by name and vowed, "I'll go to court and testify against those guys if I have to go in a wheelchair."[18]

Prior to the trial, the police and prosecutors were concerned for O'Brien's safety and that of his two partners, Spike Behrle and Country Carpenter. O'Brien had been guarded around the clock at the hospital since the night of the shooting. The department placed a 24-hour escort on Behrle and Carpenter, but neither wanted it. Perhaps the two men felt that the police had exaggerated the danger, or perhaps they wanted to return to their bootlegging activities. Whatever the reason, they secured the services of attorneys Myron Ehrlich and Joseph "Jiggs" Donahue, employed previously by the Warrings, to have the courts try to get rid of them. The attorneys argued in District Court that the constant surveillance was "embarrassing" and threatened to ruin Behrle and Carpenter's health and unspecified business. However, Justice Daniel W. O'Donoghue refused to prevent the Police Department from maintaining their twenty-four-hour-a-day watch over the two witnesses. He pointed out that the president of the United States has guards with him at all times, and he doesn't complain about it.[19]

All six defendants were charged with assault with a dangerous weapon and with intent to kill.[20] Although all the bullets had been fired from one gun, the grand jury had, in effect, placed the gun in the hands of all six defendants. Those indicted by the grand jury were the same men who had been arrested in the police round-up:

Charles R. "Rags" Warring: Alleged co-leader of the Foggy Bottom Gang;

Samuel "Monty" Montgomery: Chief operator of the Warring bootlegging network;

Joseph F. "Sam" Bond: The man who actually shot O'Brien;

John "Jack" Sweeney: The youngest of the defendants;

George "Teddy" Tear: Already behind bars for operating an automobile with a smoke screen and assault with a dangerous weapon.[21] The assault charge stemmed from his attempt to wreck a police car during a chase around the Ellipse (an oval-shaped park just south of the White House) as he blocked police efforts to catch another Warring roadster loaded with booze;[22]

Clarence "Cocky" Ware: Like most of the defendants, Ware had been born and raised in Foggy Bottom. He was called Cocky because his eyes were slightly crossed or cockeyed. Cocky often took afternoon naps in Frank DeMisa's barber shop at 25th and Pennsylvania Avenue, and teenagers would have fun arousing him by screaming "police coming" through the barber shop doors. He had large hands and was probably the most physically imposing of the gang. Emmitt frequently took Cocky along when someone needed to be "straightened out." Cocky resembled actor Victor McLaglen from the John Ford movies, a big, simple man who was happy if you just bought him a drink. Although not the smartest man in the outfit, he was the only person who wasn't a member of the Warring family but was allowed to enter the "money room" at their headquarters without being escorted by one of the Warring brothers.[23]

CHAPTER TEN

"I Forgot to Remember"

On Monday, December 7, the trial began with jury selection. Defense attorneys Harry Whelan and Charles Ford used peremptory challenges to keep women off the jury.[1] The prevailing thought was that women may have less tolerance for violence, even if it was just between bootleggers. The prosecution rejected all men who lived in Foggy Bottom, Georgetown, or Southeast Washington out of concern that they may have some direct or indirect connection to the defendants.

The first witness called by Assistant District Attorney Irvin Goldstein was Joseph O'Brien. The *Washington Times* described O'Brien as "husky" and "looking older than his 24 years." Appearing prosperous and dignified in a conservative blue suit, he entered the courtroom on crutches, apparently still recovering from the bullet wounds suffered the previous July.

All six defendants, sitting twenty feet from the witness stand, were "neatly, nattily dressed except 'Teddy' Tear, who wore a wrinkled blue [prison] sweater." As O'Brien took the stand, "he faced their battery of 12 unblinking eyes."[2]

Assistant District Attorney Goldstein asked O'Brien the opening question.

"Where were you on the early morning of July 21?"

O'Brien stared at Goldstein and answered mechanically, "I stand on my constitutional rights and refuse to answer that question on the grounds it might incriminate me."

The six defendants leaned back in their seats and shifted their eyes to the presiding judge, Justice Peyton Gordon.

Judge Gordon protested, "I don't think that is a good reason. Answer the question."

O'Brien finally admitted that he was in the 200 block of 2nd Street SE on the night in question. But he then turned to Judge Gordon and pleaded. "Your honor," he said, wringing his hands, "do I understand I have to answer all these questions—that I don't have any rights?"

Judge Gordon's face reddened above his black robes. "Yes, you have rights," Gordon said, "but I'll decide what questions incriminate you. Go ahead and answer."

Assistant District Attorney Goldstein, irritated with this surprising and unwelcomed turn of events, resumed his questioning. Calling each of the defendants by name, Goldstein asked O'Brien if he knew them. O'Brien reluctantly admitted that he knew each of the men, although he added, not very well.

Then Goldstein asked the most critical question: "Do you recognize anyone in the courtroom as one of the men who assaulted you?"

O'Brien eyed the defendants and then quickly pronounced, "I seen the men that shot me, but I don't recognize any of these men."

Suddenly, Goldstein saw his "locked" case begin to dissipate like smoke entrails from a cigarette.

Goldstein pressed on, but O'Brien kept waffling. "One guy got out of a car and came up to me. He had a gun and he said, ah—I don't what he said—" Then O'Brien added, "I was knocked down or fell down, and the shooting started."

O'Brien admitted that before the shooting started, he had been talking to his girlfriend and Country Carpenter. O'Brien explained that "Carpenter ran through the restaurant before the shooting started," perhaps laying the groundwork for any claim by Carpenter that he did not see the shooting take place.

Against the protestations of O'Brien's own attorneys and the defendants' attorney, Judge Gordon allowed Goldstein to cross-examine his own witness.

"Don't you recall telling Lieutenant Cox that 'Monty' Montgomery was at the wheel of the car with a gun in his hand when Tear and a tall fellow who looked like Bond attacked you on the sidewalk?" asked Goldstein.

"I remember talking to Cox, but I don't recall saying anything like that," responded O'Brien.

"When police brought Montgomery to your hospital room, didn't you say, 'That's Montgomery; I've known him a long time. He was the man in the car?'" questioned Goldstein.

"I might have said he was Montgomery, but I didn't say he was the man in the car," O'Brien replied.

Almost every question that Goldstein asked met the reply, "I can't remember," or "I don't recall."

O'Brien admitted he had been shot only after he turned to Judge Gordon and inexplicably asked, "Will that incriminate me?" Informed it would not, O'Brien said: "I was shot."

Defense attorneys Whelan and Ford pointed out to the jury that the Government had not produced "one scintilla of evidence" against the defendants. Whelan emphasized that the victim failed to identify any of the accused as part of the group that had assaulted him. Ford labeled O'Brien a liar and urged the jury to completely discount any weight given to the statement he made to police in Providence Hospital.

The prosecution, who once thought their case "iron clad," now awaited the testimony of O'Brien's two partners to see if their memories of the events were any better.

Country Carpenter and Spike Behrle suffered memory lapses as bad as O'Brien's. As documented by the *Washington Post*:

The crowded courtroom expected a thrill yesterday and it was not long in coming. First witness summoned was "Country" Carpenter. Broad shouldered and pleasant of face, there was little about his demeanor as he ambled to the stand to support his reputation in the underworld as a "bad man."

Carpenter began to lose his composure, however, when he faced the six Warring mobsters seated in a semicircle around him. Their eyes, cold and hard, sought to meet his.

"Did you see these men here," said [District Attorney] Goldstein, indicating the defendants, "when O'Brien was shot."

"Country" fleetingly surveyed the accused men, shuffled uneasily and with six pairs of eyes boring into him replied: "No sir, I did not."

"Country," under questioning, said that he did not remember hearing any shots at the time O'Brien was shot and was sure he had not seen "Monty" Montgomery at the wheel of one of the gangs' cars.

Goldstein then was given permission to impeach his own witness, and the prosecutor asked if he remembered a conversation in the District Attorney's office [the previous] Friday. To freshen "Country's" memory, Goldstein reminded the witness that he, Goldstein, Lieut. Clement Cox, and Carpenter were present at the time.

"Country" wracked his memory and recalled the meeting but said he couldn't remember anything about it.

"Do you mean to say," shouted Goldstein, "that you don't remember telling me only last Friday that 'Monty' Montgomery was driving one of the cars?"

Montgomery ... leaned forward in his chair.

"Country's" eyes shifted to the semi-circle of defendants and back to Goldstein. "No sir. I don't remember," he said.

"Didn't you say you heard Montgomery cry out "let him have it?" pressed Goldstein.

"I can't remember," said Carpenter.

Justice Gordon was sitting forward in his chair and his face was growing florid as the questioning proceeded.

The climax came when Goldstein produced a statement implicating the defendants and signed by Carpenter. "Country" studied the signature and said it was his alright and blandly added that he could not remember having made any of the assertions set forth in the statement.

"Lock him up," said Justice Gordon.

A look of hurt surprise came over "Country's" broad face as marshals led him away.

"Spike" Behrle, pasty faced, thin and nervous, came next. Red splotches appeared on his cheeks and even his forehead when he met the stare of the defendants.

"Spike" remembered his name alright and even remembered that on the night of the shooting, Montgomery picked him up in his car at Second and East Capitol Streets and drove to the scene of the shooting.

Goldstein was impressed and he asked: "Did you see anything happen or hear anything happen after you got there?"

"Spike" winced at the question and the flush on his face deepened. "No sir, not a thing," said "Spike."

After that, "Spike's" memory was almost as bad as "Country's."

Exasperated, Goldstein produced a statement Behrle had signed at police headquarters. It implicated all of the men on trial.

"Yes, I signed the statement, but I don't remember anything in it. The police kept me up all night. They made me sign it," said Behrle.

"Spike's" memory failed when he was asked the name of the policeman who had made him sign it, and Judge Gordon leaped forward:

"Lock him up," he said.

"Spike" seemed rather glad to get out of the courtroom.[3]

The prosecution then called their three remaining witnesses.

Lieutenant Cox of the DC Police Department took the stand and testified that he had taken Rags Warring, Montgomery, Sweeney, and Ware to Providence Hospital and that O'Brien had identified them as members of the gang that attacked him.

Virginia State Policeman Harry L. Robertson next testified to arresting Montgomery, Bond, and Tear in Virginia after receiving a description of the car that had fled from the scene of the shooting.

Finally, Washington Navy Yard employee Ralph May, who spotted the first two license numbers of the fleeing car, said he saw O'Brien knocked to the ground and shot after a voice from the car shouted, "Let him have it." But he could not identify the men.

Defense attorneys asked for a directed acquittal from Judge Gordon. After mulling over the matter for several minutes, he turned the request down and sent the case to the jury.

The first jury heard from on December 8 was the grand jury. They had responded to the urgings of Justice Gordon to hold Country Carpenter and Spike Behrle accountable for their gross and unexplained lapse of memory. Both Carpenter and Behrle were indicted for perjury.

The jury deliberating on the case of the six accused men in the shooting of Joseph O'Brien took approximately four hours to come to a verdict. The jurors had left the courtroom at 3:20 in the afternoon but word from the jury room required Judge Gordon to cancel a scheduled 7:00 lecture at a local law school in order to return to the bench.

The six defendants beamed as the jury foreman read the first six counts, ending each with: "Not guilty." But on the seventh and eighth counts (assault with intent to kill and assault with a dangerous weapon), all were guilty. Surprised and understandably disappointed by this outcome, the six defendants were immediately escorted back to jail.

"The verdict unquestionably is a victory for the orderly process of the court," said District Attorney Leslie C. Garnett.

"It will teach gangsters that the courts can't be trifled with," said Police Chief Ernest W. Brown.[4] After the killing of newspaper carrier Allen Wilson, the public would not have accepted any outcome that saw the gamblers go free.

The *Washington Post*'s editorial board observed; "Even if a jury is convinced that witnesses for the state are lying, it takes a tremendous responsibility upon itself by bringing in a verdict of guilty against defendants exonerated by the victim of the attack."

The paper further declared: "By this vigorous action, the district attorney's office serves notice that it is out to fight the local gangster problem on every front."

From that hot night in July in front of the Majestic restaurant on Capital Hill to the eventual verdict against the accused, the newspaper-reading public had been taken for a virtual roller coaster ride of sudden dips and turns. Therefore, it was not surprising when even the sentencing had a twist.

In early February 1937, the six men were returned to the courtroom for sentencing. The courtroom was packed with their relatives and curious spectators. Judge Gordon prefaced his sentencing by making an offer to the men. "If I could find out who shot this man [O'Brien]," he said, "I might not be so ready to impose heavy sentences."

"Your honor, I did the shooting," insisted Joseph "Sam" Bond.

"And who are you?" asked Judge Gordon, scarcely looking up from his records.

"Bond–Joseph Bond," said the tall prisoner.[5]

Without comment, the judge inexplicably continued with the sentencing, apparently unmoved by the admission.[6]

Justice Gordon then proceeded to sentence the six men to 18 months to two years in prison, with an additional year for Teddy Tear because he had been already serving a sentence on the smoke screen charge. The sentences were relatively light given the maximum sentences by law could have run from five to twenty-five years. All were moved immediately to the DC Jail for transfer to Lorton Reformatory in Virginia.[7]

As far as the fate of the three victims, O'Brien, Carpenter and Behrle were all convicted of perjury and sentenced to twenty-four to thirty months in prison.

O'Brien's simple defense to the perjury charge was based on his claim that he "forgot to remember" who shot him that July night.[8] But at the trial, a gas station attendant testified that he overheard O'Brien remark that he had been paid $3,500 by Emmitt Warring.[9]

ശ

Shortly after the defendants were sentenced for the O'Brien shooting, the DC police raided one of the Warrings' Foggy Bottom operations at 2423 Pennsylvania Avenue. Approximately $2,000 in coins was seized along with a coin counting machine worth $4,000. Arrested at the "counting house" were Ellis L. "Sugar Pops" Solet, Edward J. Juliano (brother of Toots Juliano) and Edward "Legs" Oliveri.[10] But Emmitt and Leo were nowhere to be found. Police had been tipped off that Emmitt usually showed up about 7:30 at night. They hoped to nab him, but apparently Emmitt was the last one to be tipped off because he was a no-show that night.[11]

Whether warranted or not, the gang quickly suspected that a cab driver named Clair A. Kensinger had informed the police. The cabbie lived at the same address, directly under the room used as a clearing house for the daily numbers receipts, so he could easily have observed the Warrings' operation. On the morning after the raid, Kensinger and his wife were awakened at 5:30 a.m. by an odd noise. Going to their window, they saw a car pushing Kensinger's cab towards Washington Circle. He later told police that he thought that his cab was being taken because of an overdue garage bill. He decided not to do anything about the matter at that hour but planned to straighten things out with the garage later in the day.

Later that morning, a government landscaper working on the banks of the Potomac near the Titanic Memorial—then located at the foot of New Hampshire Avenue—sighted a cab floating in the water with its dome light still shining.[12] The gang had pushed the cab six blocks from Kensinger's home down New Hampshire Avenue to where it ended at the banks of the Potomac (now the site of the Kennedy Center) and hadn't stopped until the cab was in the river. Police at the scene noticed tire tracks in the snow that indicated the cab had been pushed by a second vehicle.

Kensinger asked for police protection when he heard about the fate of his cab. "I'm certain those gamblers must think I turned them in," he said, "but I didn't know what was going on up there."[13]

Years later, my dad taught my brother and me that we should never tell on anyone else. He pointed out that Judas, the most loathsome figure in Christianity, was a stool pigeon in assisting the authorities in apprehending Christ. The gang apparently thought that Kensinger had committed the ultimate sin of becoming a stool pigeon.

The police got a solid lead on the culprits behind the waterlogged cab when they found a license plate on the ground where the cab had entered the river. Apparently, the plate had fallen off the car as it was being pushed against the rear of the cab. The license plate was traced to Maurice "Buddy" Sweeney, who admitted being a "numbers writer" but maintained he did not know Kensinger and was in bed hours before the incident.

Sweeney's roots were deep in Foggy Bottom and he and Rags Warring belonged to the same Boy Scout troop. One newspaper mistakenly stated he was a brother of Jack Sweeney, who was serving time for the O'Brien shooting.

Although Sweeney was indicted by the grand jury for the destruction of the cab, the charges were later dismissed.[14]

No direct evidence linked Emmitt Warring to the gambling operation at 2423 Pennsylvania Avenue. However, the next morning Emmitt was brought before United States Commissioner Needham C. Turnage, the DC commissioner who was responsible for "Public Safety," and was charged with operating a lottery.[15]

Emmitt never went to trial, and his case and those of the other gamblers "were ignored" due to insufficient evidence.[16] Without a change in the law, the mere possession of numbers slips was not enough to obtain a conviction. Emmitt and his men had eluded the police and the prosecutors again.

ꟹ

During the 1920s and early '30s, Sam Beard had been one of the biggest racketeers in the DC area in more than one way. Over six feet tall, the rotund Beard approached 300 pounds. Commonly referred to as the "Pickle King" because he owned a pickle factory, "Big Sam" set the standard for how to effectively organize liquor and gambling operations, including steady graft to the local police.[17] He operated gambling clubs from downtown DC to the Maryland suburbs.

In October 1934, discussing an upcoming raid with an assistant district attorney, DC police Lieutenant George M. Little mused, "Wouldn't it be funny if Sam Beard should be there? You know, I've never seen him."

"Don't worry about that," the assistant district attorney replied. "You'll never find him there."[18] Everyone in the district attorney's office knew how elusive this big fish had been.

As reported by the *Washington Post,* a raiding party of eight policemen proceeded to the Maher Building at 916-18 G Street NW, and battered down the heavily-bolted door of the National Amusement Company.[19] When Little entered the premises, he was approached by a well-dressed man.

"Won't you come in?" asked the man, extending his hand. "I'm Sam Beard."[20]

Initially doubting his good luck, Little stared at the large, well-dressed man in a light-gray suit for a moment and then shook hands. "Mighty glad to meet you, Mr. Beard, after all these years," he said. "I'm Lieut. Little. Won't you come with me to headquarters?"

Beard then ordered all of his men within earshot not to say anything. Little asked Beard if he was in charge. "I'd rather not answer that at this time," Beard replied.

Little then ordered Beard to put on his coat. Beard knew it was time to play his last card. "Lieutenant, you have a reputation for being a good fellow. Why not let me out of here?" Beard implored. Little's reply was short and clear. "Nothing doing," he said.[21] There was no way that Little was going to let this prize catch get away.

Despite the efforts of defense counsel John J. Sirica, who would later find fame as the judge in the Watergate case, Beard and his twelve accomplices were found guilty. However, days after the conviction, the defendants suddenly found grounds for an appeal. Three members of the jury publicly admitted that they had been "pressured" by the foreman to vote guilty.

The jury had been given a break from the rigors of the deliberations to spend a short time under supervision in Rock Creek Park. While riding the bus back down Connecticut Avenue to the courthouse, the jurors had seen a newspaper headline at a newsstand announcing "Gamblers Bet 10 to 1 Beard Will Go Free." According to jurist Geraldine Wilner, the foreman of the jury, Charles Hauf, had said, "I will take some of that" upon seeing the headline.[22]

Later in the jury room, Hauf accused the jurors who had voted for acquittal of being "plants" working for the defense. Although all three of the jurors denied the accusation, they reversed their votes to "guilty."

Beard's defense team, led by Sirica, continued to appeal the guilty verdict into 1936, but the United States Court of Appeals and the Supreme Court refused to reverse his conviction. Beard returned to court with his twelve co-defendants for sentencing. Former district attorney Leo A. Rover, who had been added to the defense team, moved that all but Beard—who was ineligible for parole—be placed on probation. Rover delivered a sincere but boilerplate defense of men driven to gambling by the Depression in order to make a living. "I think your honor should know what is in the heart of each of these men; why they succumbed to temptation; whether some of them—married and with families to support—were stricken by this blight of depression and forced to take this means of obtaining a livelihood." Rover went on to state that "Gambling involves no moral turpitude such as attaches to a crime of violence or stealing from widows and orphans." Rover concluded by claiming, "We are going to have gambling in the District as long as its residents want to gamble and that will be until time is consummated."[23]

In the end, the twelve co-defendants received probation, and Beard was ordered to immediately start a two-to-six-year sentence in the Atlanta Federal Penitentiary. The prosecution sought to send him far from Washington and any ties to his gambling contacts.[24]

From the way 1938 started, the Warring brothers should have guessed that it was not going to be a good year. In January, Rags was not yet half way into serving his eighteen-month sentence for the O'Brien shooting. He had been incarcerated in the Lorton Reformatory, approximately 20 miles south of DC in Virginia. It was the preferred federal prison for convicts from the District. Prisoners were allowed visitors two Sundays a month and could see their local attorneys at any time.[25] It was convenient for Charlie's brothers and sisters to visit, and "arrangements" could be made with certain guards to make his stay easier. But Rags was about to be caught up in a vortex surrounding where Sam Beard should be incarcerated.

In January 1938, Lorton made an arrangement with Atlanta to exchange thirteen prisoners. Lorton sent thirteen "desperate" inmates who presented "custodial difficulties," believing that they would be more secure in Atlanta. In return, Atlanta sent thirteen prisoners with Washington backgrounds who officials felt could finish their sentences safely at Lorton. One of the prisoners who made the bus trip from Atlanta to Lorton was Sam Beard, who had served twenty-one months of his two-to-six-year prison term for violating gambling laws.[26]

Beard's transfer to Lorton set off alarm bells in some quarters. Dr. James A. Nolan, the director of a crime-fighting citizen's group called the Washington Criminal Justice Association, announced that members of the association felt "in view of the gambling situation here now, Beard should be kept as far away from Washington as possible. We believe that Beard might be able to re-establish with his old contacts in Washington's gambling fraternity despite Lorton's strict rules governing visitors."[27]

A seemingly unrelated event was tied to "Big Sam," casting him in a suspicious light. On the day Beard arrived at Lorton, prominent local gambler "Nubby" Nuckols was found dead in his four-room apartment on Connecticut Avenue. The pistol that caused the gaping wound in his temple and a suicide note were found with the body. Nuckols had a long record going back to Prohibition but his luck finally had run out, and he was days from starting a stretch in prison for a gambling conviction.[28] Apparently, suicide was his means of escape.

Despite all evidence pointing to suicide, not everybody was convinced. Nuckols had ordered delivery from a restaurant an hour before he was alleged to have shot himself. When the delivery boy arrived with the food, he found the door partially opened and could see Nuckols dead on the floor.

He ran back to the restaurant where his father, who owned the restaurant, ordered him to keep his mouth shut and not get involved.[29] The death went into the books as a "suicide."

Dr. Nolan could not refrain from taking the opportunity to further inflame public opinion against Beard, thinking it would help send Big Sam back to Atlanta.

"Isn't it quite a coincidence," Nolan commented, "that Nuckols should have committed suicide—if he did commit suicide—on the same day Beard arrived at Lorton?"[30] The *Washington Post* added fuel to Nolan's fire by announcing on the front page that "Sam Beard May Reach Through Lorton Bars To Take Over Nuckols' Gambling Throne."[31]

Despite assertions by Washington Public Welfare Director Elwood Street that he was "confident that any prisoner at Lorton can be completely handled," Dr. Nolan and his Justice Association got what they wanted, plus some.

Perhaps because Beard was placed in the same cellblock as Rags Warring, Monty Montgomery and Sam Bond, District Commissioner Melvin C. Hazen was suddenly alarmed and upset that three of the six convicted of shooting Joseph O'Brien were allowed to serve their time at Lorton. (The other three, Teddy Tear, Cocky Ware and Jack Sweeney had been transferred to Leavenworth Federal Penitentiary in Kansas to serve their sentences.) Hazen quickly pressed Cummings to send Warring, Montgomery, and Bond with Beard to Atlanta where "they will be made to do more work and have less freedom."[32]

Officials at Lorton attempted to calm public fears by a show of getting tough with the prisoners by placing Beard, Warring, Montgomery and Bond in quarantine. They were not permitted any visitors or privileges and were confined to a cellblock usually reserved for incorrigible inmates.

But the attorney general was convinced these prisoners should be in Atlanta. On January 21, US Marshals herded the four men through the concourse of Washington's Union Station, using the presidential entrance. Beard met with his attorney, John Sirica, for a few minutes until the train to Atlanta arrived. The *Washington Post* described Beard as "pale and gaunt after 18 months in prison."

Some of Charlie's brothers and sisters were there to see him off. When the timing was right, Emmitt got the attention of John B. Upperman, a deputy US Marshal assigned to ensure the safe delivery of the men to Atlanta. Emmitt slipped Upperman a $20 bill to "take care of" his brother during the long train trip and to make sure that Charlie got "a juicy steak" from the train's dining car.[33]

Hundreds of spectators were on hand at the station to watch the Marshals accompany the prisoners on to the special Pullman car.

When it came time to board the train, the prisoners raised their collars high in order to hide their faces. This was not so much in disgrace or so as to shield their identity, but to degrade the quality of the photos taken by the newsmen. The prisoners felt the newsmen were taking advantage of the men's misfortune to advance their own careers. Sam Beard, unable to see well because he had pushed his collar over his face, slipped and fell beneath the car before being lifted up by the Marshals.

As the train sat on the rails waiting to depart, Emmitt decided to board the train to make sure that Charlie knew that Upperman had money to cover anything that he wanted. Against procedure, Upperman allowed Emmitt in the private accommodations for a few minutes.

Rags would later refer to his stay in the Atlanta Penitentiary as "when he was away in college." Although it was said light-heartedly, Rags's stay in Atlanta was undoubtedly hard on him. The Atlanta Penitentiary was known among criminals as the toughest of the federal prisons.[34] It was a commonly-held opinion that the Atlanta prison was extra hard for Yankees from up North because it was administered by Southerners and manned by "crackers" as guards. Al Capone was originally sent to Atlanta before he was transferred to the newly-opened Alcatraz.

Rags contracted gum disease while in prison in Atlanta. The prison's solution was to pull all of his upper teeth and most of his lower ones. He was left with only a few teeth in the middle of his lower jaw and forced to wear false teeth on formal occasions for the rest of his life.

Rags would later point out that "you never want to get one of those 'screws' [prison guards] down on you." He would acknowledge that "certain people do belong in prison, but it is usually not anything you should wish on somebody."

With Rags in Atlanta, he was now further away from his family and longtime girlfriend, Mary Healey, who worked as the personal secretary to the executive officer of the National Archives. Their romantic relationship would continue to be put on hold.

CHAPTER ELEVEN

Building a Case for the Bureau

In 1935, Emmitt Warring decided it was time to move out of the Bottom.

He purchased a new four-bedroom house at 3900 Macomb Street NW for $17,681.[1] The home was located in fashionable upper northwest Washington between Wisconsin and Massachusetts Avenues. Emmitt finished the basement and had a full-size bar installed with a large, decorative mirror as a backdrop. He installed a state-of-the-art security device on the front door of the house that allowed him to look onto his small, gray slate tile porch. If visitors attempted to look in, they would see only their mirror image.

The home was furnished in a modern motif with an expansive sectional sofa and two red leather chairs that sat in the living room immediately to the right of the entrance. The master bedroom had ash-blond furniture and a double bed. The back of the house and the backyard were concealed by a border of evergreen trees.

A few months later, Emmitt purchased another house around the corner at 3935 Massachusetts Avenue for about $23,500.[2] This house was also newly constructed, and the brick was painted white, giving it a stately look. The 3,500-square-foot interior featured five bedrooms. The basement, finished with linoleum floors, contained a second kitchen larger than the kitchen on the ground floor.

Emmitt purchased the home on Massachusetts Avenue for his sister Esther, who was now estranged from her husband Bill Cady. Their daughter Tibby and her husband Ralph would also stay there, although Ralph spent most of his time in the late '30s playing drums on the road with notable bands, including the Harry James Band when Frank Sinatra was the lead singer. A baby, Ralph Warring Hawkins, was added to the family in 1937. Until Charlie married in the late '40s, he too would call this house his home.

The house also served as temporary lodging for various Warring associates who needed a place to stay. Sometimes it wasn't very temporary. Jack Schley, who worked for the Warring brothers, came for a weekend but stayed for almost five years until his early death from tuberculosis. But even in death, he had no place to stay, so he was buried in the Warring family plot at Mount Olivet Cemetery, perhaps making this the longest weekend stay ever.

In 1936, Emmitt purchased four lots on the banks of the Potomac River in Colonial Beach, Virginia for $1,600. He then paid $3,450 to have a cottage built on one of the lots. Colonial Beach was a favorite vacation spot for Washingtonians before the bridge was built across the Chesapeake Bay, connecting vacationers with the Maryland and Delaware beaches on the Atlantic Ocean. Colonial Beach, located sixty-five miles southeast of Washington, just down the road from George Washington's birthplace, was a gambling oasis. Technically, there was no legalized gambling anywhere in the state of Virginia at that time; however, the boundary for the state of Maryland, which did allow slot machines, abutted the Virginia shores of the Potomac River. Long piers were built out into the waters of the Potomac, and casinos were established with names like Little Reno. It was "the poor man's Las Vegas."[3]

Emmitt bought several other Virginia properties in the mid-to-late '30s. For $34,500 he bought eighty-six waterfront acres in Fairfax County, about twenty-five miles south of Washington. For $12,000, he also bought ten acres across Chain Bridge near Pimmit Run close to an eleven-acre tract he had purchased two years earlier. These properties were not far from the Tysons Corner area of Virginia that became prime real estate in the 1960s.

In 1935, he bought a thirty-two-foot speedboat cruiser (christened *Playtime*) with a half-mile searchlight for $4,500 (over $45,000 in today's dollars). These purchases created a record of over $100,000 in cash outlays (over $1 million dollars in today's terms) over just a few years.

All of these purchases were to become fodder for the Bureau of Internal Revenue to build their case against Emmitt and his two brothers. Every time Emmitt bought a lot or built a home, he unwittingly helped the Bureau build its case. Were the Warring brothers claiming income and paying taxes that supported these significant expenditures?

Although the law had been unable to make gambling charges stick against the Warring brothers, the "green eyeshade" types in government were slowly making progress, hovering over paper documents and adding machines. A squad of so-called "untouchables" from the Internal Revenue Bureau was quietly working behind the scenes. They had sent Al Capone to Atlanta for tax evasion and convicted the other leading crime figure in DC, Sam Beard. According to a *Washington Post* article, federal agents were now checking the "hidden bank accounts of leaders of the Warring mob and other powerful figures in the rackets."[4]

If the Warring brothers were going to taste the fruits of their labors, the Bureau of Internal Revenue was going to make it a bitter experience.

By the spring of 1938, if newspaper readers in Washington were not yet very familiar with the Warring brothers, they soon would be. Yes, there had been references to the "Warring gang" during the coverage of the Joseph O'Brien shooting, but Rags received almost all of the print. From this point forward, Emmitt would receive attention from reporters like no other racketeer in Washington.

The newspapers quickly characterized Emmitt as the "brains" of the organization, Leo as the "hard worker" who spent eight to ten hours a day in the office, and Charlie as the one on the streets who was occasionally called upon to be the "triggerman."[5] Emmitt was often cast as an entrepreneur and leading businessman. He was alleged to be "the founder of a numbers business" and "reputedly directing one of the District's biggest numbers 'banks.'"[6]

The Internal Revenue Bureau was very interested in how the profits from the business were distributed. During the investigation for income tax evasion, Emmitt claimed that he had initially paid Leo and Charlie a salary, but later made them partners. Emmitt told the Internal Revenue Bureau that he, Leo, and Charles "shared and shared alike."[7] Leo had started to take bets on horse races on his own. He personally found the horse racing industry more interesting than the numbers business. But he had to financially back those bets on his own because Emmitt was leery of the possibility of horse racing results being manipulated by shady characters.

However, it was clear that Emmitt actually oversaw the cash and expenses of the numbers business. When the business and the related cash had been located at their headquarters in their Aunt Delia's house at 2510 K Street, any brother who took out cash was required to put in a slip of when, how much, and for what purpose.

Shortly after Emmitt moved to his home on Macomb Street in 1935, he purchased a strong business-style safe to hold the cash. Made of thick steel, the safe could withstand any attempt to open it by gunfire. The safe was so heavy that it remained in the Macomb Street home decades after Emmitt's death until the owner finally had it removed by a crane through a bedroom window.[8]

Now Leo and Charlie would have to go to see Emmitt at his Macomb Street home to get money for expenses. By 1937, Leo was married with two children and Rags was starting to serve his prison sentence for the O'Brien shooting. It made sense for Emmitt to assume the responsibility for and the risk of securing the significant amount of cash they had amassed.

Furthermore, Emmitt made the decisions when it came to most of the business expenses, i.e. who would be paid and how much. That included protection money paid to the police and gifts to family and patrons of their business.

After a few years of dealing with "mooching" friends, Emmitt tired of people coming to him for handouts. Once when being interviewed by investigators, Emmitt complained, "I run into them every day, people wanting money. When you are working and they are not, your friends always try to get money out of you, and I would rather put it down a sewer than give it to most of them."[9] But he did continue to be very gracious at times, usually at his initiation and discretion without being asked.

The government's strategy to get the Warring brothers was clear. The Feds had toppled Al Capone from his throne in Chicago by invoking the income tax law, and the same tactic was now being employed in the East Coast cities. The *Evening Star* reported that this would be the first time the government had made an income tax case against anyone who primarily earned their money from the DC numbers racket.[10]

This was also going to be the first income tax fraud case brought in Washington. Usually federal tax cases were tried in Baltimore, where income taxes from the District were sent at that time. But the prosecution of the Warring brothers was based on the theory that the alleged conspiracy occurred in Washington.

On April 4, 1938, the grand jury indicted the three Warring brothers on charges of conspiracy to defraud the government of income taxes. Indicted along with the Warrings was Gordon Sadur, head of the tax-accounting firm hired by Emmitt, and Sadur's brother-in-law and junior partner, Henry Scherr.

The indictment was mostly based on testimony from Internal Revenue Bureau agents who interviewed the Warrings and their tax accountants and a review of the records of their numbers business. The agents focused on establishing that what the Warrings claimed as net income (gross revenue minus payoffs to winners, their payroll, and other expenditures) was less than the sum of the Warrings' personal expenditures, including houses and cars. Therefore, according to the government, the Warring brothers had to have understated the net income on their income tax returns.

Immediately after the indictment was returned, Emmitt and Leo appeared at the courthouse with their attorney, Harry T. Whelan, and posted the required bond of $5,000 apiece. They then went to the office of Captain George M. Little at police headquarters and were booked.

"What's the charge?" the booking clerk asked Emmitt.

"I don't know," Emmitt replied. "Stealing from the government, I think."

An attaché of the United States District Attorney's office then cited the exact statute that Emmitt and Leo were charged with violating. The brothers chatted with policemen and appeared to be indifferent to the formalities taking place a few feet away. The newspapers pointed out that brother Rags was not present because he was still serving a prison sentence in Atlanta for the O'Brien shooting.

According to the indictment, in 1935 the Warring brothers falsely represented themselves as "commission brokers" and reported total incomes of less than $6,000. However, the indictment charged that for 1935, the Warrings' numbers business made a net profit of almost $85,000. For 1936, the brothers filed a partnership return showing total income of approximately $58,000, but the government stated it was actually twice that amount. The government's estimated income figures were derived from the brothers' expenditures for homes, cars, cost of living, etc. In reality, the income amounts charged by the government were probably lower than the actual income, given that the Warrings' own business ledgers showed $4,000,000 in bets taken over a two-and a half-year period.[11]

Five days later, Emmitt and Leo entered their pleas in the court. With hats in hand, the two brothers, more subdued than at their previous appearance, mumbled "not guilty." Arraigned with them were their accountants, Gordon Sadur and Henry Scherr, who also pleaded "not guilty."[12]

In early June, the government brought Rags up from the Atlanta Penitentiary for his arraignment on tax charges. Accompanied by attorney Harry T. Whelan, and wearing a dark gray suit with a light grey fedora, he characteristically joked with the guards while waiting for the judge. Not surprisingly, Rags pleaded "not guilty" as his brothers had in April. [13]

If the public thought that this would be mostly a tedious "numbers crunching" tax trial absent the drama of the O'Brien shooting case, they would soon learn that would not be the case. In mid-October 1938, it was announced that the Warring brothers' trial would begin on November 15.[14]

ɞ

The legal cast that was assembled definitely had local roots. Judge Bolitha James Laws was born in Washington and had graduated from Georgetown Law School in 1913. He was a Bible class teacher at the large Mount Vernon Place Methodist Church in downtown Washington.[15] After being nominated by President Franklin D. Roosevelt, he had been sworn in to a new seat on the United States District Court just weeks before the start of the trial.[16]

The lead prosecuting attorney was David A. Pine. Also born in Washington and also a member of the Georgetown Law School class of 1913, Pine possessed the stern looks to go with his prosecutorial duties. Years later he would become a judge best known for issuing an injunction against President Harry Truman's order for the federal government to seize and hold steel plants in order to avert a strike by steel workers during the Korean War.[17] The Warring trial would be Judge Laws' first major case and United States District Attorney Pine's first court appearance since taking over the position earlier in the year.[18]

Working with Pine was Assistant District Attorney John J. Wilson. Wilson had graduated from the National Law School (later part of George Washington University) at the age of twenty. He became a defense attorney in later years, gaining notoriety in the early 1970s by representing White House aides H.R. Haldeman and John D. Ehrlichman during the Watergate hearings.[19]

The Warrings' lead attorney was Harry T. Whelan who had earned a reputation of being the defense lawyer to hire when in a serious jam. Brooklyn-born, he served in World War I and later graduated from Georgetown Law School.[20] During the late '30s and early '40s, Harry Whelan represented a number of high-profile defendants.

Assisting Whelan was his law firm partner, William B. O'Connell, another Georgetown Law School graduate. O'Connell also served in World War I and had been stationed in General Pershing's headquarters in Chaumont, France. He lived in Georgetown and was a well-known and respected figure in the community.[21]

Leo A. Rover represented the Warrings' lead accountant, Gordon Sadur. Born and raised in Washington and a graduate of Georgetown Law School, Rover was known as "the little bulldog with a booming voice." The *Washington Post* noted that "his cross-examination techniques earned him the reputation of a 'lawyer's lawyer.'"[22] In his early years, Rover had shown a love of the law when he would sneak away from his father's delicatessen near the District courts to listen in on cases. It was said that "he hung around the courts like other kids hung around drugstores." Like David Pine, Leo Rover would go on to become a judge in the District.

Rounding out the defense team was Irvin Goldstein, who represented Sadur's junior partner and brother-in-law, Henry Scherr. Goldstein had prosecuted Rags and the rest of the gang involved in the O'Brien shooting. This time he was on the defense team.

CHAPTER TWELVE

The United States v the Warring Brothers

The first day of the Warring trial was front-page news, but the lead headline in the *Washington Times* concerned the fate of dozens of cherry trees given to the U.S. by Japan decades before. They graced West Potomac Park, adjacent to Washington's Tidal Basin. The work to remove some of them to make space for the new Jefferson Memorial had begun, despite protests by citizens. Even some within the Roosevelt administration were against placing the structure at its proposed site and current location. Secretary of Commerce and longtime DC resident Daniel Roper declared, "We have been witnessing assaults upon the liberties … of certain foreign states … and I believe that any assault upon our cherry trees is almost an assault upon something that has come to be, for us, an individual liberty – something that cannot be disassociated with ourselves."[1] After more bombastic rhetoric from citizens, including threats by the Daughters of the American Revolution to chain themselves to the trees, a general compromise was reached to transplant as many of the trees as possible. [2]

Even before the trial had begun, Judge Laws showed he was not going to sit back and wait until he had to rule on something. In an unusual ruling for that era, he excluded thirteen prospective jurors from consideration because they admitted to reading an advance news story on the trial.[3] In the end, eleven men and one woman were chosen for the jury.

The day before the trial, the *Washington Post* observed that, if the Internal Revenue Bureau's claim of unreported income was accurate, the brothers were making "more profits than President Roosevelt makes in salary."[4]

At the opening of the trial, all three brothers were present in the courtroom. Rags had been released from prison in September after Washington bondsman Meyer Weinstein flew to Atlanta and posted a $5,000 bond. Emmitt sat at the defendants' table with lawyers Harry T. Whelan and William B. O'Connell, and Leo and Rags sat in the first row directly behind the table. The Warrings' principle accountant Sadur and his junior partner Sheer, also sat with their lawyers. The tall, broad-shouldered, black-mustached Sadur sat at one end of the table with his attorney, Leo Rover, and Scheer sat at the other end of the table with his attorney, Irvin Goldstein.[5]

During the trial, the local newspapers often referred to Emmitt, Leo and Rags as the "Warring boys," and noted the brothers were well dressed, neat and gentleman-like.[6] Emmitt was usually seen leaning forward in his chair with a keen interest in every word that was spoken during the proceedings. On the other hand, Leo and Rags seemed at times to be only casual observers, sporadically acknowledging familiar courtroom spectators. This behavior reflected their usual attitude that Emmitt, or "Pudge" as they called him, was in charge.

In his opening statement, District Attorney Pine said the government would provide evidence of the Warrings' real income during the three years under scrutiny: 1934, 1935, and 1936. "We will show they had no other source of income than this illegal gambling business," Pine asserted. [7]

Pine went on to predict that the evidence would show that Emmitt Warring, "the head man, the brains of the business," started a numbers game early in 1934. The income tax conspiracy, Pine asserted, would "not be proved by some eavesdropper, but by acts, facts and statements."[8]

The first pieces of evidence that the government introduced were the Warrings' tax returns for the years in question as "Government Exhibits for Identification 1 to 8." Besides the figures representing the "commissions and salaries" paid out as expenses, the 1936 return surprisingly listed the seventy-five individuals who received the payments (fifty-six runners or pickup men and nineteen office workers), an increase from eleven employees in 1934 (six runners and five office workers). A few of the names listed were very nondescript, e.g. "Shorty, address unknown." But others were identified very specifically, e.g. Mrs. R. Saylor, 4521 Georgia Avenue, Apartment 506; and Donald K. Wallace of 1907 Pennsylvania Avenue NW; the same Don Wallace (who had been with Rags at the scene of the Joe Nalley shooting). Other familiar names were William Cady (Emmitt's brother-in-law), Ellis "Sugar Pops" Solet, Maurice "Buddy" Sweeney, Edward "Legs" Oliveri and Nellie Parish, one of Emmitt's earliest girlfriends. Clarence "Cocky" Ware's name was also on the return as a "commission" employee, listing his address as the District Jail. [9]

One of the government's first witnesses was H. Watson Leese, an Internal Revenue agent with almost twenty years on the job. A blond-haired, soft-spoken man of slight build, Leese took the stand and described an interview with Emmitt conducted by Internal Revenue agents in the law offices of Emmitt's attorney. Leese stated that Emmitt acknowledged paying out money for immunity from arrest for himself, his brothers, and others who worked for them. Emmitt claimed that he had paid $400 a month in 1934 and $1,000 a month in 1935 and took care of the protection payments himself. Later Leese stated that Emmitt told him the amount of protection money paid in 1935 had virtually doubled in 1936.

Based on the testimony regarding protection money, Melvin C. Hazen, the DC commissioner who oversaw police operations, ordered the police to determine the names of officers accused of accepting bribes. Hazen contacted the Chief of Police, Earnest W. Brown, and directed him to assign an officer to observe the court proceedings. Brown designated the head of the vice squad, Lieutenant George Little, to act in that capacity.[10] However, the only opportunity for the prosecution to delve into the details of the payments would be for Emmitt to take the stand, and of course there was little chance of that happening.

On the second day Leese stated that Emmitt said that he could always come up with the cash for any payoffs from the reserve he kept primarily for large payouts on winning numbers. Those in the courtroom seemed amused when the special agent gave the example of what he called the "Popeye Days," a two-day period in 1936 when the brothers had to pay out almost $42,000, after the Popeye newspaper comic strip mentioned a three-digit number. Amazingly, that number hit for two consecutive days after number players had bet extraordinary amounts on it.[11] The courtroom was packed with many curious spectators who were also in the numbers business, and many heads nodded in recognition of those "Popeye Days."

Later in the Warring trial, District Attorney Pine asked Internal Revenue agent John Cox, who headed the Internal Revenue Bureau investigation, "Did he [Emmitt] ever let you know the names of these policemen he was paying?"

"No, he never did," Cox replied. "I told him that I was working on another case involving this matter of police protection, and if he would cooperate with me, we could convict some of these crooked policemen."

Emmitt had replied, "What's the use? If they got rid of those policemen, they would put others on, and I'd have to pay them."[12]

Whether the admission of the protection money was based on professional advice or initiated by Emmitt himself, the revelation appeared to have dug a deeper hole than the hole that Emmitt and his brothers were already in. Now it would be harder for the court to allow this admitted corruptor of police to go free and unpunished.

Emmitt had likely taken notice a few years before of the most celebrated conviction Internal Revenue had obtained—that of Al Capone, who had sent no tax returns or payments to Uncle Sam.[13] Ironically, Emmitt's decision to file tax returns and keep accounting records of the business activity to avoid prosecution for income tax conspiracy now appeared to be working against him.

He realized that the government had gotten Capone on a felony charge of conspiracy to defraud the Treasury by evading taxes. Emmitt knew that the failure to pay enough taxes was technically just a misdemeanor, and by being relatively transparent with his records and cooperating with the Internal Revenue Bureau, he probably thought that he could defend himself and his brothers against any felony charge. But any serious review of the Capone case showed that the government's real intent was not to have Mr. Capone pay his fair share of taxes but to send him to jail for a long while.

Understandably, the Warrings' defense team never questioned the authenticity of the Warrings' books, now being used against them by the prosecution. On the contrary, the defense attorneys stressed repeatedly that the Warrings had cooperated during their dozen conferences with the Internal Revenue Bureau and had not intentionally withheld any source of income.[14] In fact, Special Agent Leese had testified that "He [Emmitt] brought in the books of his numbers business and said 'Here's the records—if you want any further data, call me up.'"[15]

The prosecution next called a special agent from the Treasury's intelligence unit, William H. F. Swain, who had interviewed Rags Warring at the Atlanta Federal Penitentiary earlier in the year.

Pine opened by asking Swain, "Where did you interview Mr. Charles Warring?"

Instantly Leo Rover, Gordon Sadur's counsel and a former district attorney, leaped to his feet. "May we come to the bench, your honor?" He was quickly joined by the other defense counsels who also rose to object to Pine's question.

The defense lawyers were joined at the bench by Pine and Assistant District Attorney Wilson. Leo Rover, speaking for the defense, whispered his objection. Judge Laws and attorneys on both sides continued to speak in hushed tones so the puzzled jury could not hear. Now Swain was invited to join the conference. When the huddle broke, Swain returned to the witness chair and the lawyer resumed their positions.

"In Atlanta, Georgia," Swain replied. He made no mention that the interview took place at the penitentiary in Atlanta or that the captain of the prison guard was also present during the interview, a disclosure that would have most likely prejudiced the jury.[16] Swain testified that "Charles stated that he did not have any money at the time the numbers business was started. I also recall that he told me to see his brother, Emmitt, who was the business manager, about the income. Charles didn't give me any idea of what the income was and he said that he did not know. He could not even give me an estimate, he said." Wisely deferring all questions to Emmitt, Rags ensured that he did not misspeak or say something that contradicted what Emmitt was telling the government.

Swain described how the agents pressed on, determined to know how much money Rags had put in the business. Using the double negative that was common with all of the Warring brothers, Rags replied: "I didn't have no money. Listen, you better talk to my brother Emmitt. He takes care of all that."[17]

When the Internal Revenue Bureau came to interview Leo, he also had little to say in regard to the business. However, Leo claimed that he had lost several thousand dollars from horse racing bets that he booked on the side and had to reimburse himself from the numbers business. He added that the Warring brothers had "a reputation of paying off on winning bets" which they had to live up to.[18]

On the following day, the prosecution introduced a transcript of an interview that the agents had conducted with Emmitt. The prosecution then began to read the transcript into the record with a certain "dramatic art." Assistant District Attorney John Wilson read the questions that agents had directed to Emmitt, while District Attorney David Pine sat in the witness chair and gave Emmitt's answers. Peering over his round wire-rim eyeglasses, Pine delivered Emmitt's replies in mock innocence.

After a few questions and answers, it was clear that Pine was having fun at Emmitt's expense. Emmitt's lawyers had finally heard enough and objected to the routine. The judge smiled and ordered the prosecution to stop reading the transcript in this manner.

Wilson then continued with the reading, playing the parts of both the agents and Emmitt.

Wilson read a number of quotes from Emmitt, all reflecting an image of a man who did not spend much and didn't partake in the finer things in life:

"I don't spend much money. I don't need much money for myself."[19]

Emmitt claimed, "My living expenses aren't as much as yours. You know where I am every night—at 3900 Macomb Street. I haven't been to a show for over a year. I don't go nowhere. I don't entertain. I don't have no expense with girls."[20]

Although these statements might have been mostly false during the early and mid-1930s, they had become close to the truth by 1938. Emmitt seemed to realize that his lifestyle and expenditures were going to be used against him, so he started to adjust his lifestyle accordingly. In addition, more cars, more clothes, and more new friends had not brought this natural introvert any sense of lasting satisfaction.

The Warrings' attorney attempted to convince the jury that by keeping business records, filing income tax returns, paying income taxes, and offering to pay whatever was due, the brothers had demonstrated they did not intend to evade taxes. But the prosecution quickly pointed out that the brothers had not been indicted for evading taxes but for conspiring to conceal from the government the income from which taxes could be levied.

That was the strongest beam in the construction of the government's case. The Warrings' expenditures reflected an income that was far greater than the income stated on their income tax returns.[21] As the prosecution had done in the Capone case, the Warring prosecutors put on the stand a parade of individuals who testified that Emmitt had made various cash purchases of real estate, new cars and one speedboat cruiser during the 1934-1937 period. The defense countered that expenditures were not direct proof of income.

After a lengthy argument by Henry Scherr's legal counsel, Irving Goldstein, the charges against Scherr were dropped. Judge Laws decided that the government had failed to produce prima facie evidence to support the charges against Scherr, who was basically an employee of his brother-in-law, Gordon Sadur. The fact that Scherr had signed an affidavit swearing that Sadur knew that the Warrings' accounting books reflected "protection" payments as deductions from revenue further helped influence the judge and the prosecution to look leniently upon him."[22]

ေ

The defense team had to wait until after the Thanksgiving holiday recess to present their case. In his opening statement to the jury, the Warrings' lead attorney Harry Whelan charged that the government had promised Emmitt immunity from prosecution if he agreed to turn over his business records to the Internal Revenue. Whelan claimed that Emmitt was given "absolute assurance" by Internal Revenue officials that they wanted the books and records solely for determining income tax assessments. Everything had been conducted in "good faith" as far as the Warrings were concerned, Whelan insisted, and they "cooperated and offered every support."

"The present conspiracy proceedings," Whelan told the jury, "were instituted not because the government was interested in adjusting the tax matter, but because Emmitt refused to talk and name the policemen to whom alleged 'protection' money was paid."[23]

Leo Rover, the defense counsel for tax expert Gordon Sadur, then finished the opening defense statement. Rover maintained that the evidence would show that Sadur was innocent of entering into any conspiracy to defraud the government of taxable profits from the Warrings' numbers game. The evidence also would prove that Emmitt Warring had hired Sadur to straighten out his difficulties, and Sadur had performed his services "honestly, faithfully and as a legitimate representative of a taxpayer."

When he took the stand on his own behalf, the thirty-nine-year-old Sadur admitted that he deducted protection payments listed in the Warrings' books from the taxable income. He contended that he thought that such payments were a deductible item from revenue generated by an illegal business.

"I considered such payments were necessary expenses in the Warring business," Sadur claimed with certainty, but barely loud enough to be heard.[24]

At that point, Laws took on the role of questioning witnesses about protection money. He asked Sadur: "In this protection matter, how much of an investigation did you make?"

"I asked him [Emmitt] if he had any records showing this [the payments] and he said that he had none," Sadur replied, "He said he would rather see the deduction disallowed than to name names."[25]

Sadur had been advised during the conference with Department of Justice officials that he had been recommended for indictment by the Internal Revenue Bureau along with the Warring brothers. Sadur said that he had expressed "great surprise" at this news.

"After giving 100% cooperation to the government in an effort to arrive at an accurate taxable income for the Warrings, I was naturally amazed at being drawn into the case in this manner," said Sadur.[26]

After the government rested its case, Harry Whelan renewed his motion for a directed verdict to the jury of acquittal for his clients. Whelan claimed that there was no evidence that Leo and Rags Warring had known of the existence of the business and tax records of their enterprise because they had left all business matters to their brother, Emmitt. And Whelan insisted that Emmitt did all he could to help the Internal Revenue agents, more than once offering to pay the tax owed, if they would just tell him how much.

Judge Laws denied the motion.

Both sides would now have one more chance to convince the jury during the closing arguments. Assistant District Attorney John J. Wilson wasn't far into his closing statement when he began resorting to hyperbole and name-calling.

"Don't be fooled by this Warring mob," Wilson warned.

The Warrings lead defense attorney immediately protested and asked for a mistrial.

Referring to Wilson's use of the term "mob," Whelan said, "That's a prejudicial statement. It implies many damaging things, when these men are charged only with failure to pay income tax." Whelan objected that the harmful effect on the jury could not be negated now by any corrective instruction from the judge "any more than a drop of ink spilled in a glass of milk could be removed from the glass."[27]

Judge Laws disregarded Whelan's contention. In denying the motion for a mistrial, he instructed the jury: "The word 'mob' is not to be taken by you as implying anything outside of the evidence in this case."[28]

Then Wilson fired his verbal arrows in the direction of the Warrings' tax advisor, Gordon Sadur, whose wife and young sons were in the courtroom. Mrs. Minerva Sadur emigrated from Russia during the pogroms against Jews and worked as a bookkeeper for her husband's business. She was now experiencing how unpleasant the American justice system could be.

Wilson warned the jury, "Sadur is a liar. Sadur is a cheat. Sadur is a crooked accountant. Don't be fooled by the soft-voiced representative of this Warring mob."[29]

Returning to the Warring brothers, Wilson said, "Don't be fooled into thinking that these Warring boys are babes in the woods who don't know anything about figures when they have built up a $2,000,000 business—these Warring brothers who have corrupted the District of Columbia police on a wholesale scale."

He ridiculed the "modest" taxable incomes reported by the brothers for the three years at issue—pointing to Emmitt's boat, house, and country home at Colonial Beach as "luxuries of a rich man."

It was then Harry Whelan's turn to give the closing argument for the Warrings' defense.

"So far as Leo and Charles were concerned," Whelan said, "there was no evidence that they ever saw the books or even knew they existed. Emmitt ran the business, but in his case, there was no evidence that he ever showed the slightest intent to defraud the government."[30]

Leo A. Rover, counsel for accountant Gordon Sadur, made the closing argument on behalf of his client. He asserted that the words of a government official did not, in America, send a man to prison.

Rover maintained that Sadur never knew of the Warrings' expenditures for a houseboat and beach property, and that he made his income tax estimates only on the books given to him. On the other hand, Rover said, Treasury agent Leese, had made his tax estimates for the Warrings on the basis of expenditures and estimated living expenses. Rover called this the "whimsical" Leese theory of accountancy.[31]

District Attorney David A. Pine had the last word for the prosecution. Pine floated the question: "They asked us why we didn't let the Warrings pay up their tax?" and continued, "You would think the government was dealing with a Bible class. The defense cited the cases of business executives, professional people and movie actors who were allowed to adjust large income tax claims. I know of no cases where the government let racketeers pay up to escape prosecution—that's the difference."[32]

❧

The jury began their deliberations after their Friday lunch. During the afternoon, the area outside the courtroom drew a surprisingly large crowd of defendants, their lawyers, numerous witnesses, and scores of spectators including loyal Warring employees.

The *Washington Post* reported that during the wait, "Rags Warring, dapper and genial triggerman of the gang, spent more than an hour in an earnest but amicable argument in the outside corridor with H. Watson Leese and William H. F. Swain, Internal Revenue agents, who were the star witnesses against him (and the other defendants)."[33] He was likely making a case that all this could have been straightened out over a few beers.

By Saturday night there still was no decision. Defense attorney Rover dropped by the courthouse on his way to a District Bar Association banquet at the Mayflower Hotel. Justice Laws was going to be the toastmaster at the dinner. After deliberating Saturday night, the jurors could not reach agreement on a verdict.

Sunday came and went without a decision. The *Washington Herald* noted that despite its apparent disagreement on a verdict, the "jury was in an amiable mood as it went to dinner under the guidance of Marshal John B. Upperman." He was the same deputy marshal who had accompanied Rags and Sam Beard to the Atlanta Penitentiary. Upperman had been responsible for the jury since the beginning of its deliberations. By 10:30 p.m. on Sunday night, they had deliberated fifty-eight hours without a decision. The longest session remembered by veterans of the US Marshal's office had been one in another case that had begun late on a Friday and ended early the following Monday.[34] The long deliberation gave the defense team a cause to be optimistic and the prosecution to start doubting an outcome in their favor.

At 9:30 on Monday morning, Judge Laws called in the jurors to read them instructions known as the "Allen charge." Under this charge, the presiding judge advises an apparently deadlocked jury that it is the duty of the jurors in the minority to try to reconcile their views with the majority. Because it is used to dislodge jurors from an entrenched position, the "Allen charge" is sometimes referred to as the "dynamite charge."[35]

At 10:00 p.m. on Monday night, Judge Laws called the prosecution, the defense, and the jury into the courtroom. The jury had now had the case for eighty-two hours.

"I assume you have reached no decision," Laws said to the jury. The foreman of the jury replied that they had not.

"That is true as to all defendants?" the judge inquired.

"It is," the foreman responded.

"After consideration," Judge Laws said, "I have decided to dismiss you from any further service, and you are free to go."[36]

The *Washington Post* reported that the final count stood seven to five for conviction after more than 400 ballots.[37]

Almost immediately District Attorney Pine urged the court "in view of the great public interest of the case" to schedule a retrial as soon as possible after the first of the year. After asking the lawyers a few questions about their calendars, Judge Laws set January 23, 1939, as the tentative date.

As Laws rose to leave the bench, Mrs. Gordon Sadur—seated in the courtroom with her two sons, Marvin, twelve, and Hillard, sixteen—screamed and collapsed. The thought of another trial overwhelmed her.

Mr. Sadur rushed through the three Warring brothers, who had turned towards the courtroom commotion, and took his wife in his arms. The Sadur boys assisted their dad in trying to revive their mother, the older boy fanning her with his handkerchief. John B. Upperman, the US Marshal attending the jury, brought Mrs. Sadur a glass of water.

After the courtroom was mostly cleared, Mrs. Sadur was able to stand. As she was leaving with her husband and sons, attorney Leo Rover tried to comfort her, urging her to "have courage and keep your chin up."[38]

It was during this time that Rags received a letter of encouragement from an ex-convict working for the US National Park Service who noticed news of the "long tedious trial." The letter stated, "I have never met you personally, but I am familiar with your kindness and with your tolerance and decency to your more unfortunate associates." He mentions that since his release he has found that "friends do not forget or forgive easily." He closes with "the best of luck to you and your brothers is my sincere wish."

CHAPTER THIRTEEN

"A National Disgrace"

On the first day of the new trial, Judge Laws presided over the selection of twelve jurors and two alternates. The selection was unusually long because many of those impaneled had prejudice either for or against gambling. Newspapers listed personal information about all the jury members starting with juror number one, Carl T. Denekas, forty-three years old, who lived at 106 Varnum Street NW and was an employee of the Potomac Electric Power Company.[1]

In order to ensure the jury would not be swayed by newspaper accounts, Judge Laws announced, they would be sequestered in a nearby hotel every night until they reached a verdict. The white-haired and portly US deputy Marshal John B. Upperman was once again given custody of the thirteen men, while two female deputies were assigned to the one female juror.

In his opening statement, prosecutor Pine labeled the Warrings "captains of this [numbers] industry" and said that Emmitt admitted to paying bribes that appeared to have exceeded their reported income.[2] Pine stated that the government regretted that the jury had to be locked up at night but said he would try to hasten the trial. Immediately, defense attorney Leo Rover protested that such a promise was improper and that the defense would also try to have a quick trial.

One of the first government witnesses was Internal Revenue Special Agent Leese, who had testified at the first trial.

"Who first brought up the subject of police protection in connection with the Warrings? You?" asked Whelan.

"No. It was another special agent," snapped Leese. "Prior to that time, I never knew cops took anything but apples and bananas."

Laughter filled the courtroom. [3]

Although they had the weekend off, the jury would be sequestered in the Continental Hotel until Monday morning. But by Monday afternoon, breaking news regarding the trial was screaming off the front page of the *Evening Star*.

ళ

On Sunday, Carl Denekas, juror number 1, started to act strangely at breakfast.

According to deputy Marshal John B. Upperman, Denekas had his head and arms on the table. He appeared extremely nervous, and complained of a headache and blurred vision. Denekas kept muttering the words "Fine" and "Blue Bell" over and over, and also said something about "those damn Warrings."

Upperman grabbed Denekas by the shoulders and tried to shake some sense into him. Later, Upperman found Denekas lying in bed fully clothed with a blanket over him and his head swathed in a towel and called a physician to the hotel.[4]

Dr. Christopher Murphy said his first impression was that Denekas was acting like he was "coming off of a [drinking] spree."

Denekas finally blurted out that he wanted to talk to Judge Laws and District Attorney Pine about the case.

The main headline in the *Evening Star* the following day reflected the consequence of Denekas' revelation to the district attorney: "Warring Bail Raised As Jury Tampering Charges Are Made." Earlier that morning, Justice Laws revealed that he had received word at his home on Sunday of the alleged jury tampering. The next morning, the *Washington Post* stated that "the florid, well-groomed number operators [the Warrings] heard Justice Laws with amazement. Wholly surprised seemed their [legal] counsel."[5]

Based on Denekas' statements, the individual bonds on the three Warring brothers were increased from $5,000 to $50,000 apiece. The bonds were among the highest ever posted in District Court, comparable to what was required of the accused in the Teapot Dome scandal.[6]

Judge Laws then declared a mistrial in the Warrings' [second] income tax case. Laws further noted that Gordon Sadur was not being accused of any involvement in the jury tampering.

Although four criminal contempt rules were served only on Emmitt, the bonds were raised on all three brothers until the District Attorney's office could determine what role Leo and Rags had played in the alleged jury-tampering. The criminal contempt charges submitted by District Attorney Pine read as follows:

> Criminal Contempt No. 98 asserts: Emmitt Warring, on January 15, [1939] at the Brown Derby Restaurant, asked Harry Fine to tell Carl T. Denekas, who was called for jury duty in the second Warring trial, that Warring would pay Denekas $600 [over $6,000 in today's money] if Denekas got on the jury and "would vote not guilty and see that things came out right."... Warring, on January 30, at the Brown Derby, asked Denekas what he was going to do to aid him. Denekas was seated on the trial as Juror No. 1. A contempt rule asked against Emmitt Warring and anyone else involved.

That the name of "Harry Fine" was cited in the contempt charge provided some clarity as to why Denekas kept muttering "Fine" during his anxious moments in the Continental Hotel.

> Criminal Contempt No. 99 asserts: Emmitt Warring on January 24, telephoned Thomas Harrison Quinlan [employee of the phone company] and asked Quinlan if he knew Edward D. Spedden ... and Robert L. Sayles ... [also phone company employees] who were called to jury duty in the second Warring trial. Quinlan said he did. Warring invited Quinlan to his home where he told Quinlan he was looking for somebody who could be fixed. A contempt rule asked against Emmitt Warring and anyone else shown to be involved.

It was probably no surprise that Emmitt Warring, the alleged head of a criminal gang, had been named in the first two charges. But the next two charges named a man thought to be beyond reproach: John B. Upperman. The affable deputy US Marshal was known for strictness in seeing that nobody approached juries under his charge while they were deliberating.

> Criminal Contempt No. 100 asserts: Deputy United States Marshal John B. Upperman on February 1, took the oath not to speak to the

> jurors in the second Warring trial or to let anybody else do so and was placed in custody of the 12 jurors and 2 alternates. That evening Emmitt Warring sent to Upperman at the Continental Hotel, where the jury was kept, 2 quarts of whiskey, which Upperman and some of the jurors drank. Two more quarts were sent and consumed February 3. Emmitt Warring on February 5 got in touch with Upperman at the hotel and asked whether Upperman wanted any more whiskey. Contempt rules asked against Warring, Upperman and anyone else shown to be involved.
>
> Criminal Contempt No. 101 asserts: Before the first Warring trial started (in the previous year), Emmitt Warring caused Upperman to be informed that if the verdict was satisfactory, Warring would take care of a $150 note Upperman owed, which was soon to be due. In the trial, Warring told Upperman he "would send something over to him." This meant liquor with which Upperman was to seek favor with the jurors. ... The first day the jury was deliberating, Warring sent Upperman 2 quarts of liquor, which Upperman shared with some of the jury. Similar packages were sent after that. "Upperman spoke favorably of the Warrings whenever the opportunity afforded to certain jurors." ... After the jury was discharged hopelessly deadlocked, Warring caused Upperman to be given $100. ...[7]

When Upperman learned that Denekas had admitted to drinking alcohol during the Warring jury deliberations, he knew that there was nothing for him to do but to come clean and admit to his role in providing the liquor. He told how Emmitt Warring had sent liquor to the jurors during both income tax trials. The prearranged packages were signed "Florence," the name of Upperman's wife. He confessed that he drank some of the liquor and the jurors drank the rest.[8]

The revelations contained in Criminal Contempt No. 101 (above) regarding the first Warring trial caused one of the prosecutors to comment, "We were shadow boxing." Looking back, the prosecution felt they'd been fighting an uphill battle during the first trial if Upperman was plying the jury with liquor and telling them that the Warrings were "not bad fellows."[9]

The *Washington Post*'s editorial board was quick to identify the national impact that this case was projecting:

> The accusations in the Warring case brought by the district attorney yesterday are a matter of importance to the entire United States. The underlying issue is of as much concern to Maine and California as to the District of Columbia. For it would be nothing short of a national disgrace if it were demonstrated that jurors can be bribed, and court officials seduced from their duty, at the seat of National Government.
>
> In the minds of thoughtful Washingtonians, the Warring case has come to assume symbolic qualities. The atmosphere surrounding it has begun to raise doubt whether racketeers can actually be brought under control in the District of Columbia...
>
> It now remains to ascertain the truth behind these shocking charges, to settle the Warring case once and for all, to let the people of America know definitely whether or not racketeering is a privileged and protected occupation in the Capital of the United States. Fortunately, the present accusations of jury tampering, if substantial, will place in the hands of the court a powerful weapon for demonstrating that the machinery of justice is not clogged in the District of Columbia.[10]

For months, extraordinary legal and also apparently illegal efforts had been made to extricate the three brothers from the government's charges. But the problems had multiplied instead of going away. One newspaper characterized the jury intrigue as the Warrings' jumping from "the legal frying pan to the judicial fire."[11] Emmitt had assumed the full risk of using underhanded methods to free both himself and his brothers. Now his plan had collapsed around him. Would he shoulder the full burden of the government prosecution?

ഗ

The day after the *Washington Post* called the jury tampering charges a "national disgrace," the paper reported the resignation of Emmitt's two defense lawyers, Harry Whelan and William B. O'Connell. Deputy Marshal John Upperman claimed to have received money directly from both men. The two attorneys immediately and adamantly denied any role in the jury tampering charges.

Emmitt's new lawyer was F. Joseph (Jiggs) Donohue. He had defended Joseph O'Brien, Spike Berle and Country Carpenter in the trial stemming from the shooting on Capitol Hill in the summer of 1936. Originally a New Englander, Donohue later became a key player in Democratic politics and later was said to be a poker-playing crony of President Harry Truman.[12]

Emmitt completely absolved his brothers of any involvement in the jury-tampering. Both Emmitt Warring and deputy Marshal John Upperman pleaded guilty to the charges. But each man had an opportunity to tell his side of the story in court before sentencing.

Like many of those in law enforcement in DC, Upperman apparently saw Emmitt as a decent man who provided daily diversions to common folk in the city and was willing to help those who could do him future favor.

Upperman had been a steady figure around the courthouse for over a decade. The amiable Marshal with a teddy bear-like figure now walked uncertainly to the witness stand. Many in the courtroom were moved to pity as the ashen-faced, watery-eyed Marshal spoke in a barely audible voice. Upperman testified that the Warrings' attorneys had given him money during and after the first trial.

"[During the first Warring trial] I went to see Mr. Whelan," said Upperman, "and told him I had to get $150. I had a note due. He said that he would see what he could do and if things worked out right, he would see the 'little fellow.'" It was clear that the "little fellow" was Emmitt Warring.

As to the other Warring attorney, Upperman continued, "Mr. O'Connell met me one night and asked me how I was making out at the [Continental] hotel and I told him 'all right,' and he gave me $10."

Upperman said that he saw Harry Whelan again after the first Warring trial ended.

"Mr. Whelan gave me the $100 and told me he was sorry that he couldn't get any more but that was all the 'little fellow' had," said Upperman. "It was the first time" that he, Upperman, had done anything of the sort, the Marshal insisted. [13] Later that day, attorneys Whelan and O'Connell released a statement denying all of Upperman's assertions and citing their lengthy and honorable record of practicing law in the District. Their statement noted their record could "be subjected to the closest scrutiny by anyone without any fear on our part."

Emmitt's new attorney Jiggs Donohue cross-examined Upperman, who said that he had only known Emmitt since the first trial. "Isn't it a fact," queried Dononhue, "that Emmitt Warring gave you money before?"[14]

Upperman thought about the question for about 30 seconds. "Mr. Upperman," said Judge Laws, "I don't think that you need to reflect to answer that question."

In a barely audible voice, Upperman admitted that Emmitt had given him money to look after Emmitt's brother, Rags, at Union Station before he'd accompanied Rags to the Atlanta Penitentiary.

"What were you supposed to do for that money?" asked Judge Laws.

"Look after Charlie, I suppose," said Upperman. "See that he got what he needed on the trip to Atlanta."[15]

Upperman admitted that he had spoken favorably of the Warrings to members of the jury at the first trial during the extended time the jury was deliberating. Upperman acknowledged he told the jury that the three Warrings were "not bad fellows."

Judge Laws then stated that he wanted to hear what Emmitt had to say about Upperman's testimony before he passed sentences on both men.

Upon taking the stand, Emmitt said that he knew Upperman before the trial. Asked if he had given the deputy Marshal money before the first tax trial, Emmitt said that he had, several times. "Whenever he said that he needed money, I never refused him," said Emmitt, "but never over $20 at a time."[16] Emmitt said that these occurrences generally took place in restaurants or wherever he happened to run into Upperman.

Laws then asked Emmitt with interest, "What I can't understand is why you and Mr. Upperman would carry out transactions like this right in public?"

"We thought nothing of it," Emmitt replied.[17]

Emmitt went on to recall how at the beginning of the second trial, Upperman reminded him that the jury was going to be sequestered in a hotel during the entire trial, and asked what was the chance of getting some liquor delivered to the hotel.

Emmitt added, "I asked him what kind he wanted, and he said any kind. I ordered two quarts from a liquor store."

Emmitt also contradicted Upperman's testimony that Emmitt's attorney, Harry Whelan, handed Upperman $100 after the first trial. Emmitt insisted that he gave Upperman the money and it was specifically a $100 bill. He said that he gave the bill to Upperman in the telephone booth in the lobby of the Columbian building where Whelan and O'Connell had their offices. Upperman had approached Emmitt and told him that he had lent money to his boss, the chief of the deputy Marshals, and had not been repaid. The chief had been dismissed for appropriating funds for his own use, and Upperman was out of the money to pay the debt on a note coming due.[18]

At the end of Emmitt's first day in the witness chair, it was clear that he was trying to portray himself a victim of a "shake-down" on more than one front.

❧

The following day, others implicated in the jury tampering charges were on the witness stand before Judge Laws. Those who testified included former juror number one, Carl Denekas, and Thomas Harrison Quinlan, who said that Emmitt Warring had called him about two jurors.

Carl Denekas testified that just days before the beginning of the trial, bookmaker Harry Fine came by his house and mentioned that he saw that Denekas was going to be on the Warring jury. Then according to Denekas, Fine asked him "How would you like to make $600?"

According to Denekas, the next night he waited for Fine in the Blue Bell Restaurant on Connecticut Avenue. When Fine arrived, Denekas said that Fine told him that he wanted him to meet a friend who was outside in a car. Soon Denekas found out that Fine's "friend" was Emmitt Warring. They drove up Connecticut Avenue to the Brown Derby nightclub in the Cleveland Park section of town.[19] A Douglas Fairbanks Jr. movie was playing at the cavernous Uptown Theatre on the other side of the wide avenue. One reason Emmitt chose the Brown Derby was that he silently owned a piece of the nightclub.[20]

The layout of the Brown Derby was somewhat unusual. It was long and narrow L-shaped room. There was only room for medium-size tables on both sides of a narrow walkway that extended about a hundred feet back from the front door to where the room took a ninety degree turn to the left. After the turn, there was additional room for a few semi-secluded tables. There was a small area for entertainment between the two groups of tables, so patrons could see the performance no matter where they sat.

Emmitt, Fine, and Denekas entered from the back door of the

Brown Derby and sat at one of the semi-secluded tables in the rear. Emmitt bought Fine and Denekas two rounds of Scotch and soda. Denekas said that when he went into the men's room, Emmitt followed him and asked, "What are you going to do for me?"

Denekas testified that he replied, "I won't do anything for you, but I'll do anything for Harry." The former juror testified that he did not receive anything as a result of his discussions with Emmitt and did not make any promises or offers to him.

Judge Laws reminded Denekas he was asked at the start of the trial if he knew Emmitt Warring, but he did not acknowledge that he did. Denekas told the judge that at the beginning of the trial he could not see Emmitt plainly and did not recognize him. Assuming that at some point during the trial Denekas must have realized that this was the same man that he spoke to in the Brown Derby, Laws asked him: "Didn't you think it was your duty to tell the court?"

"It ought to have been," Denekas conceded. He said that he intended to tell the judge several times but never got around to it. However, Denekas claimed that while locked up with the rest of the jury in the Continental Hotel, "it sort of came over me."[21]

When Emmitt testified, it was clear that he felt that he was being "shaken down" by Harry Fine. As had been the case when Upperman asked him for money, Emmitt feared the consequences of turning down those seeking money. He told how the small-time bookmaker Harry Fine had first telephoned him and then visited his house on Macomb Street. After arriving, Emmitt quoted Fine as having said, "You know, you've got a fellow on this jury that I know." He said that Fine claimed Denekas had been a friend of his for almost fifteen years. Emmitt testified that Fine told him that Denekas "would do anything in the world for me, and he's not the sort of fellow you would have to pay." Fine asked Emmitt where he should bring Denekas and Emmitt told him "not to bring him here."[22]

According to Emmitt, after Denekas had consumed two Scotch and sodas at the Brown Derby, he remarked, "There are a lot of people in this place, how long are we going to stay?"

Emmitt's testimony then contradicted Denekas story. He contended that Denekas wanted to speak to him privately, so he took the juror into the washroom. There, Denekas said, "I haven't got much time. What do you want me to do?"

Emmitt said he explained that he "would feel better if he knew he had a few friends on the jury who would give him a square deal."

Denekas kept asking him, "What do you want me to do?"

Emmitt thought Denekas was smart enough to figure things out, so he did not want to say anything more incriminating than he had to. Although willing to bend the law to the breaking point, he was reluctant to say something that could later be used against him. Frustrated with Denekas, Emmitt said that he finally told him, "Well, you know I don't want to get convicted."

Emmitt testified that the juror shook his hand and said that Harry Fine was a good friend and he'd do anything for Fine.

When Denekas was on the witness stand, he also confessed that he had told Fine that if the jury was locked up, he would like to have an occasional drink.

Judge Laws asked the witness: "Did Fine say that he would see that you got it?"

"No, he didn't," replied Denekas.

"But he did say you would get some liquor?" Laws quickly added.

"Yes, he did say I could get it," Denekas said. Fine implied that someone else might provide the booze.[23]

Thomas Harrison Quinlan was the next witness. Emmitt knew that he worked at the phone company. Apparently, Emmitt had asked for Quinlan's help in the past to determine whether his phone was being "tapped" by law enforcement. Emmitt had called him to inquire about two other telephone company employees who had been identified as prospective jurors.

Earlier in the day, another telephone employee testified that Thomas Quinlan had approached him and asked whether a fellow employee who was on the jury list could be "fixed." Emmitt's lawyer Jiggs Donohue then put Thomas Quinlan back on the witness stand and asked him, "Did Warring use the word 'fix'?"

Quinlan replied, "No."

Again, Donohue asked, "Did Warring ever do more than to ask you to find out the general character of those two men?"

Quinlan again replied, "No."

When Emmitt returned to the stand to give his version, he said that he feared that he might have made enemies of some of the prospective jurors and wanted to know if that was the case. He denied that he ever used the word "fix" in discussing the jurors with Quinlan.

"I don't use that word—'fix,'" Emmitt insisted.

"You want the court to believe that you merely wanted to know what kind of jurors they would make?" Judge Laws inquired. Emmitt said that that was his only purpose.[24]

During the two days of testimony, the courtroom was packed with onlookers, and there was a crowd outside waiting to get in as seats were slowly vacated.

A reporter found Rags outside and asked him why he wasn't listening to the hearing.

He answered, "They won't let me in. They say there are no seats left."[25]

But he didn't seem to mind. In a way, he was holding his own "court" among a mixture of police and fellow numbers men.

The circus-like proceedings drew to a close as Laws promised to soon sentence the men who had pleaded guilty to jury tampering.

ဢ

The United States Attorney General was not impressed by Emmitt and John Upperman's efforts to attach an almost benign explanation to their actions.

Attorney General Frank Murphy promised that, in the review of the actions of the US deputy Marshals, the people will not be satisfied "with confessions, suspensions or citations for contempt."[26] He announced plans for "sweeping reforms here and throughout the country."[27] All US Marshals were ordered to undertake an immediate review of personnel with a view of elevating standards for deputy Marshals.

Murphy characterized the disclosures of the Warring trial as "an outrage" and met with FBI Director J. Edgar Hoover, District Attorney David Pine, and top US Marshal John Colpoys.

A few days before Judge Laws passed sentences on those guilty of jury-tampering, Emmitt Warring announced through his attorney that he and his brothers were "through with the numbers for good."[28]

Emmitt's lawyer, Jiggs Donohue, released the following statement: "My client authorized me to deny emphatically the statement appearing in a local afternoon newspaper [The *Evening Star*] that he had sold his numbers business," adding that Emmitt had closed up his business because it didn't pay. He further stated that Emmitt had "thought in the beginning that it was a harmless business giving food-money to 400-500 [people]," apparently referring to the network of pickup men and small-time bookies that worked for him.[29] Although Judge Laws was not going to be sentencing him on any gambling charge, Emmitt felt that this "confession" might strike a sympathetic chord with the judge. (If Emmitt did step away from the numbers business, it was just for a short while. He would be clearly operating a numbers business by the mid-1940s.)

On Friday, February 24, Judge Laws handed down his sentencing on those involved in the case, labeling it an "ugly picture."

First, he exonerated Emmitt Warring's two former attorneys, Harry Whelan and Willam B. O'Connell, despite claims by deputy Marshal Upperman that the lawyers had individually given him money on two separate occasions. Emmitt's contention that he was the one who had paid Upperman on more than one occasion apparently convinced Judge Laws of the attorneys' innocence.

Then Laws addressed Emmitt's case. The man labeled as the "Little Napoleon of the numbers racket" entered the courtroom a "silent and crestfallen figure."[30] He made no statement on his own but let his attorney speak for him. As Emmitt stood next to his taller attorney, his small, slender body and youthful looks gave one the impression of a juvenile delinquent staring up at the bench, waiting to hear his future.

Lawyer Donohue said that he had heard Emmitt called "a hoodlum, a Jesse James, and an overlord of the rackets." He contended that these exaggerations, along with the publicity that Emmitt was making $2,000,000 per year, had set "leeches" on him looking for handouts. Donohue pointed out that although Emmitt was engaged in an unlawful business, he had tried to observe other laws. He read from a financial statement that showed Emmitt had paid both a Social Security tax and District unemployment insurance for employees who worked in his numbers business. Finally, Donohue picked up a stack of letters which apparently showed that Emmitt had "contributed liberally to orphan asylums, hospitals and convents" in the District and neighboring states.

Before he sentenced Emmitt, Judge Laws commented, "While I feel compelled to give you a severe sentence, one of the severest I have found has been given in this type of case throughout the country, I believe that there is good in you. It is my hope that when you are released you will try to build a different empire."[31] He then sentenced Emmitt to two years and two months.

As a "broken" John Upperman stood before Justice Laws, the judge observed, "It is apparent to me that this affair has been a bitter experience to you." As the white-haired Upperman cowered before the bench staring at the floor, Laws continued, "It is hard for me to punish any person, especially of your age, who heretofore has sustained a good reputation. You have suffered. It may interest you to know that I have suffered also." Laws then sentenced Upperman to one year in jail.

Harry Fine, Carl Denekas and Thomas Harrison Quinlan were all given relatively light sentences.

Emmitt was initially taken to the District Jail in downtown Washington to start serving his sentence while the final decision regarding his home for the next twenty-six months was determined. The *Washington Post* chronicled his activity during his first couple days in jail reporting that "he commented favorably on the food" and went to the "jail church service" on Sunday. When Emmitt learned of John Upperman's sentence of one year in jail, he "sent a message to Upperman telling him he was sorry to hear the news."[32]

The events surrounding the jury-tampering charges give some insight into the mindset of my uncle. In the world in which he moved, everybody seemed to have their hand out, and everybody had a price. He often resented paying that price. Whether he was dealing with one of those "leeches" on the streets, a beat cop, or even the United States government, his attitude was, "So how much money do you want so you will leave me alone?"

Emmitt, his brothers Leo and Charles, and Gordon Sadur now waited and wondered when the third income tax trial would begin. This time the Warrings would seek a quick and entirely legal conclusion of the process.

∽

As the third trial opened, the prosecution lined up the same witnesses who had appeared previously, including Internal Revenue agents H. Watson Leese and William H. F. Swain. For the most part, the questions posed by the attorneys and the witnesses' answers mirrored the testimony in the first two trials. However, defense attorney Jiggs Donohue was able to break some new ground during his cross-examination of Leese.

Donohue induced Lease to admit that the idea of a deduction reflecting protection money was first suggested to Emmitt by one of the government's agents before Emmitt mentioned anything about paying off the Washington police. In other words, Donohue said, the Internal Revenue agents had set the bait for Emmitt, and he had taken it.

Donohue then tried to establish that Emmitt was being prosecuted regardless of whether or not he paid the correct tax.

"Did you ever send him a bill for his taxes?" the attorney asked.

"I didn't," said Leese.

"Did anyone else at the Internal Revenue Bureau?" asked Donohue.

"Not as far as I know," replied the agent.

"Didn't he [Emmitt] offer to pay whatever he owed?" asked Donohue.

"Yes, he mentioned that if he had made any mistake in his tax returns, he would be glad to correct them," Leese acknowledged.[33]

Perhaps it was Donohue's cross-examination, but suddenly talk of a possible "tax settlement" was in the air. The next day the three Warring brothers reportedly changed their plea to "guilty."[34] An agreement with the Internal Revenue Bureau had apparently been struck.

The long legal process against the Warrings was finally coming to an end. At the bottom of the front page of the Washington Post that day was the headline announcing that "2 Warrings Pay Fines, Go Free; Emmitt Gets 3 to 9 Months."[35] Judge Laws was especially lenient on Leo and Rags. He sentenced them to three to six months in jail and fined them $2,500 each, but he also ruled that the jail time would be revoked upon the payment of the fines. Judge Laws supported his decision by noting, "After diligent and lengthy investigation, the government could not prove that the brothers, Charles and Leo Warring, made any large expenditure or drew any large sums."[36] In addition, there had been very little evidence that Leo and Charles knew of or participated in any income tax conspiracy, despite changing their plea to "guilty." (The Government dropped the charges against Gordon Sadur the following year.)

In addition to jail time for evading his taxes, Emmitt could "settle" his debt with the Treasury by paying $10,000.

In announcing his decision, Judge Laws made several more points:

Despite the fact that testimony was introduced that indicated that Emmitt admitted bribing police, no formal charge had been brought before the court. To factor in the apparent bribery in the sentencing of Emmitt would set a dangerous legal precedent.

It was clear that Emmitt had expressed his willingness to the Treasury to pay whatever they felt to be the correct amount. Judge Laws declared, "Inasmuch as it then was apparent that the strong arm of the government was lifted against them [the Warrings], I am constrained to believe the defendants were willing to make a fair [tax] return and to pay whatever tax they might be told was due ..."[37]

Laws brought the trial to a close and Emmitt spoke to his brothers briefly before starting his walk back to the cellblock. As Emmitt left the courtroom, he called out to prosecutor John Wilson to come back to the cellblock.

As Wilson walked past the jingling of keys and the clicking of locks, he wondered what a defendant who had just been sentenced would want with the prosecutor.

When Wilson caught up with Emmitt, the prisoner extended his hand and said. "John, I just want to thank you for a fair trial."[38] Perhaps Emmitt was moved to this gesture because the prosecution did not present any serious objection to Judge Laws' rather lenient sentences.

Emmitt had assumed the primary responsibility for any attempts to evade taxes and took complete responsibility for the jury-tampering. This allowed his two brothers to go free while he headed to jail. The only remaining uncertainty was where he would do his time.

A confident-looking Emmitt Warring leaves the District Court after being arraigned on Federal tax evasion charges.

Even at play Emmitt (center with white shirt) could be a serious leader of the group.

Young Emmitt Warring wearing the ring that was stolen from his safe during the home invasion in 1950 .

rom left to right: "Rags" Warring, "Toots" Juliano, attorney Myron Ehrlich, and Don Wallace as the ree suspects turned themselves in after the killing of Joseph Nalley.

Leo Warring with son Leo Bruce and daughter Audrey Lorraine in front of sister Esther's home circa 1940.

Leo Warring had a fascination with horses (mostly the racing kind).

Seated: "Rags" Warring, Mr. Smith (owner of Pete the Goat), Standing: Jack Sweeney, Buddy Sweeney, unidentified, bartender Jack "Murphy" Levy at Pete Dailey's (circa 1960).

mmitt Warring is sworn in to answer questions from the US Senate Committee Investigating Crime Washington, DC.

From left to right: Jack Sweeney, "Rags" Warring, "Monty" Montgomery, "Cocky" Ware and Joseph Bond outside courtroom during trial for Joseph E. O'Brien shooting.

Charlie "Rags" Warring (left) and Emmitt Warring (right) during the brothers' tax evasion case.

"Vince" Mary Warring while dating "Rags" Warring.

Mr. and Mrs. Charles "Rags" Warring not long after they were married.

Charlie "Rags" Warring and son Leo at Pete Dailey's .

Charlie "Rags" Warring

ꓤichard “Bo” Warring (the youngest son of “Rags”) and his “motorcycle gang” drew Emmitt’s ire
ıonths before his death.

CHAPTER FOURTEEN

Lorton Reformatory

Judge Laws gave Emmitt two breaks: a comparatively short sentence and a convenient place in which to serve it. Instead of sending him to the Atlanta or Leavenworth penitentiaries, Laws allowed Emmitt to serve his sentence in nearby Lorton, VA, approximately twenty miles south of Washington. Laws had come to know the man who had sat in his courtroom through three tax trials and one jury-tampering trial. During the last trial, Emmitt had even taken the witness stand and been questioned by Laws. The judge must have acquired a sense of the man who sat a few feet from his bench during those weeks and months. From that exposure, he may have concluded that Emmitt was not the kind of criminal who needed to be incarcerated in a maximum-security prison hundreds of miles away from DC.

Years later, the *Washington Post* quoted one of Emmitt's former defense attorneys. The unnamed "noted criminal lawyer" stated, "Of all the gamblers that I have ever represented or known—here and throughout the country—I sincerely believe that Emmitt Warring is the most modest, most courteous, most charitable, most respectful and most respectable."[1] Laws probably saw the man the lawyer described.

In May 1939 Emmitt entered the Lorton Reformatory and was assigned number 7701. Within hours of his arrival, word spread throughout the prison that he was there to do a "stretch" because he had "taken the rap," allowing his two brothers to go free.[2] Any prisoner who took a selfless action of that type immediately earned special respect from his fellow inmates.

Prisoners' lives at Lorton were tightly controlled, as they were in most prisons at that time. Visitors were only allowed two Sundays a month. Their names and other personal information had to be submitted to the warden for approval in advance. The prisoners could write to and receive mail from only a select and limited number of pre-approved people, and of course any packages mailed to prisoners were thoroughly inspected.

The fact that his brothers, Leo and Charlie, had criminal records probably prevented them from getting on Emmitt's approved mailing list. Instead, Emmitt wrote most of his letters to his niece, 23-year-old Esther "Tibby" Hawkins, his sister Esther Cady's daughter. Emmitt apparently felt that his niece was the best person to pass on any instructions and would promptly respond to him when necessary.

It took some time for Emmitt to get his potential mailing list approved by Lorton officials, but that did not prevent Emmitt from immediately initiating messages to the outside. Many of the letters Emmitt sent Tibby from prison were found among her belongings by her son, Ralph Warring Hawkins, after her death in 1989. The earliest one appears to have been sent in May of 1939 by a guard or other prison worker who could get letters out. It read in part:

> Dear Tibby,
>
> I received a note from Emmitt this afternoon and he asked me if I would write to you—so here goes—First, he wishes you to know that he feels swell as he gets plenty of fresh air and sunshine and is permitted to have a good walk each day. The food is much better than at the [D.C.] jail and he has a good bed and clean sheets instead of a hammock and a couple of dirty blankets. In his note, he wishes me to tell you that he wants Harry [Whelan] and "Jiggs" [Donahue] to come down here. He had their names underscored so I assume he wishes them [his lawyers] to get here as soon as possible. ... He wishes you to extend his love and good wishes to all of the folks at "2528" [the L Street address of his parents]. He says to tell Leo and Charlie to keep their chin up. ... He hopes this letter finds everyone in good health and happy. Hello and best wishes to any of his friends you meet.
>
> P.S. Tibby, please do not mention this letter in the event anyone writes him.

The mysterious author did not sign the letter. But it seems to reflect a certain familiarity with both Emmitt and Tibby. Soon, a second letter arrived from the same correspondent. The letter was again unsigned by the "ghost" writer and contained a warning to "not mention this letter when you write him" in fear that the prison officials would discover that Emmitt was already receiving assistance from the inside. It read in part:

> Dear Tibby,
>
> I had a note from Emmitt asking me to write you. And in the meantime, I see that he has succeeded in having your name placed on his correspondence list. … He wishes you to ask Sister Alfreda, the nun at St. Ann's, and all the rest of the Sisters that used to write to him to now write to him here, as it will make a very good impression on a certain party here. When you send packages put an itemized list in them. [Emmitt apparently wanted to be able to ascertain what was being confiscated by the prison officials before it reached him]. … He also wishes you to know that he uses about three cartons of cigarettes and a box of cigars each week. [It is obvious Emmitt is not smoking that much tobacco but is using it as gifts to fellow prisoners and perhaps prison workers]. He extends his love and best wishes to all and a special kiss for you and Esther.
>
> P.S. In the event that he wishes you to know anything, or do anything that cannot be sent in a regular letter, I will see to it that he gets in touch with you. Please do not mention this letter when you write him.

When the letters that Emmitt actually wrote began to come from Lorton, they began with a simple "Hello," rather than the more personal salutation of "Dear Tibby" used by Emmitt's "ghost" writer. This simple "Hello" better reflected Emmitt's impersonal nature.

The initials of the official who reviewed and approved the letters were stamped or written at the top of all Emmitt's correspondence. The letters rarely ran more than one side of an 8½ by 11-inch piece of paper.

In a June 1939 letter, Emmitt made sure family members knew that they were welcome to go to his Colonial Beach cottage. He wrote: "you go down for the summer and make the best of it because I'm alright now and its nothing they [the family] can do up in Washington."

In a July 1939 letter, he mentions that "There's two colored fellas from the '[Foggy] Bottom' just got down here in the kitchen as waiters named Pridgin and King. If this keeps up, I'll think that I'm back home." In another letter, he shows his general lack of trust of people. Referencing some hustler who apparently stopped by to visit Tibby, he warns her to not trust him because "he would steal air if it wasn't free." Also, in an October 1939 letter, he mentions that he read about a "Mr. Burns" dying and asks, "How many days did Leo stay at the wake?" He obviously was concerned about Leo's drinking at the wake [a common Irish practice of the day], and asks if "they had to carry more than one body out the morning of the funeral like they did at Jimmie Flanagan's funeral?"

In a letter dated November 9, 1939, he tells Tibby to pass on birthday wishes to his brother Charlie [Rags] whose birthday had been two days before. In a letter written after Christmas of 1939, Emmitt conjectured: "This Christmas was a lot better than what a person on the outside would think a person on the inside could spend one." With words reflecting the effects of strict confinement, he almost gloated that "after breakfast, we walked wherever we wanted to go until lunchtime." He conveyed that the prisoners were entertained by a band in the afternoon before watching the B-movie that was shown to the prisoners at night, *The Girl From Mexico*, starring the "Mexican spitfire," Lupe Velez. Perhaps starved for any entertainment or diversion, Emmitt seemed to thoroughly enjoy his first Christmas behind bars.

In all his letters, Emmitt never complained of any problems in serving his sentence. He often wrote of how fast time was passing. In one letter dated September 11, 1940, he wrote that he "saw some birds flying north and if the Jewish Holidays are about two weeks away, it means that time is moving right along."

I have heard my father generally speak of a convict who "could really do time." It was almost a badge of honor to endure confinement without suffering physical or psychological damage. It was to a convict's credit to make the most of the situation and not to pine for the outside with its privileges and amenities.

Of course, Emmitt brought his ability to manipulate the system on the outside to inside the prison walls. He found other prisoners and even guards willing to do his bidding. On designated Sundays, "friendly" prison guards would show up at Emmitt's sister's house on Massachusetts Avenue to be paid and receive certain items that could not otherwise get to him through the regular prison channels.[3]

On most Fridays, Emmitt would have crab cakes from one of his favorite Georgetown restaurants, Martin's Tavern, delivered to him through a special network.[4] Emmitt was friendly with the owner, Billy Martin, whose restaurant opened in 1933 and still operates in Georgetown.

In 1940, prison officials somehow found out that Emmitt had received three packages that had not been first inspected by guards. He was immediately placed in a "control" building and his locker was searched for contraband. Prison officials found a new pair of shears, a pair of clippers, and a large quantity of medicine not issued through channels. Emmitt admitted to working with two other prisoners, whom he paid in cigarettes, to obtain clippers and shears from the prison hospital.

Authorities later discovered that Emmitt had acquired a set of expensive dentures. An investigation revealed Emmitt had arranged for the prison dentist to be paid before making a special set. Emmitt was placed under stricter supervision and deprived of credit for 210 days of "good time."

Otherwise, prison officials described Emmitt as "even-tempered and agreeable," a good worker who "performed his work in a highly satisfactory manner" while handling bakery accounts.[5] He also worked for a while in the carpenter's shop.

Emmitt was always mindful of the watchful eyes of prison officials, especially when it came to letter writing. He often wrote cryptically without mentioning specifics. In one letter, Emmitt wrote in almost coded fashion concerning a recent visit by one of his lawyers: "Myron [Ehrlich] was down and we had a long talk. I told him 'alright' if what he said about what that man told him is true. I don't think that man would go back on his word. Those people usually keep their word."

Perhaps to convey he was not totally locked away from worldly happenings, his letters often referred to events on the outside. Knowing that Tibby's husband, Ralph Hawkins, was a drummer in the Harry James Band, Emmitt often wrote about big bands that he heard on the radio while in prison. He mentioned the Harry James and Benny Goodman bands and hearing Count Basie "lay it on the piano." In one letter, Emmitt even questioned whether his "Papa" was still listening to that "Gay Nineties" music.

During 1940, the "Warring" name seldom appeared in the newspapers. One positive exception came in October when a photo of Girl

Scouts standing around a wooden barrel appeared in the *Washington Post*. The scouts were collecting shoes for the British War Relief Society. The short description of the photo noted that the barrels used for collection points were donated by Bruce T. Warring of 3256 K Street [address of the barrel shop.] Fortunately, there was no mention of his three youngest sons whose names had been plastered on the front pages of newspapers for much of 1938 and 1939. According to an older cousin, our grandfather, Bruce, and the siblings who stayed in the family business, Lillian and Bruce, thought it was "disgraceful" that the Warring name was regularly associated with lawlessness. They did not stop loving the three young brothers as a father, sister and brother might, but were greatly disappointed that the brothers had chosen a life of crime.

CHAPTER FIFTEEN

Departures and Arrivals

It seems that my dad, Charlie, had only two truly steady girlfriends.

The first was Mary Healy, whom my dad went with for most of the 1930s. She was employed at the National Archives in Washington and moved up to the position of personal secretary for Collas G. Harris, the executive officer of the Archives.[1]

During 1939, the United States Civil Service Commission—the precursor of today's Office of Personnel Management—conducted an investigation of Harris' suitability after certain claims of impropriety came to light. Harris was accused of "advancing and promoting friends and associates, and condoning grievous faults of a particular group while condemning less serious infractions and conduct on the part of others." There was also a charge that he "protected Mary E. Healy, his private secretary, a consort of one Charles 'Rags' Warring, a notorious gambler and racketeer in the District of Columbia, for a number of years."[2]

A carbon paper copy of an interview that Joseph G. Welch, assistant to the chief, Investigation Division, Civil Service Commission, conducted with Harris on June 14, 1939 was among my dad's papers at the time of his death. The document included a question-and-answer exchange between Welch and Harris regarding Mary Healy. The grilling of Harris, one of the top administrators at one of the government's most respected agencies, is noteworthy. Some of the more significant exchanges between Welch and Harris are as follows:

Welch: When did the connections of Miss Mary E. Healy with Charles "Rags" Warring first come to your attention?

Harris: The detectives came to my office on the same day that they went to her house and the story [of Rags' arrest] appeared in the paper the next morning and Miss Healy came in to tell me about it.

Welch: What did she say?

Harris: That if it was going to cause any embarrassment to the National Archives, she would tender her resignation. ... I told her that her continued employment in the National Archives will have to cease unless she ceased her relationship with Charles Warring.

Welch: Did you receive her promise to break off connections with Warring on that date?

Harris: No, on a later date.

Welch: Why not that date?

Harris: I don't recall. It was all news to me.

Welch: What date was it that you received the promise?

Harris: Sometime later.

Welch: When?

Harris: I can't recall exactly.

Welch: A year later?

Harris: Not as much as that.

Welch: Didn't employees mention her relationship with Warring?

Harris: No sir.

Welch: What was the conversation with the detectives?

Harris: They were looking for two members of the Warring gang [Cocky Ware and Jack Sweeney] and couldn't find them, and wanted me to use my influence and speak to Miss Healy and find out where they were hiding. That's all.

Welch: Did the police officers tell you anything about Miss Healy?

Harris: Not any more than one of them who said that he had known her since she was a little girl. That she had come from a poor environment in southeast Washington. That she had shown spunk by climbing her way up over her environment. But he couldn't understand why she was going with Warring. And that she had been going with him for six years.

Welch: When did you get the first definite promise from Miss Healy that she would break off her association?

Harris: I don't remember exactly.

Welch: Some months after the appearance of the newspaper article on Warring, you sent one of your assistants to the police department to check up on Miss Healy.

Harris: Yes, I told him to go to see if she was involved.

Welch: What precipitated that visit?

Harris: Over-cautiousness

Welch: Are you sure of that?

Harris: That's all.

Welch: Was it because of the fact that mail was going through the National Archives addressed to the Atlanta Penitentiary?

Harris: No sir.

Welch: Did you know of this matter?

Harris: Somebody said that she had sent a letter, but I don't remember anything about it.

Welch: Was it because of the fact that she attempted to visit Warring in the Atlanta Penitentiary?

Harris: No.

Welch: Did these incidents as to the letter and the visit to the Atlanta Penitentiary follow the promise by her to sever connections with Warring?

Harris: I don't remember exactly. I think as I remember the facts—she said that she wanted to see him once more and tell him that she was severing their relationship.

Welch: When did she say she had seen him?

Harris: When he returned to Washington after getting out of prison. She said that she wanted to see him and tell him.

Welch: Why?

Harris: Well, it was the better way to do it. Anyway, she wanted to think it over. To see him and to speak to him was the only decent thing to do.

Welch: Do you know whether she has severed connections?

Harris: I've taken her word for it.

Welch: But in the two years since then, you didn't check up on her?

Harris: No, we don't employ snoopers to go around looking into the personal life of employees, setting up a Gestapo. Her statement was sufficient.

Welch: During these two years did you give any thought to the National Archives and the embarrassment that might result from the association of this woman with Warring, especially in view of the fact that she was your secretary?

Harris: I don't believe that if a person makes a mistake, they should be condemned for it if they are willing to rectify it. I imagine that she gave a great deal of thought to it. She went with him for a long time. I imagine she liked him.

Welch: You have no evidence that she has rectified this "mistake," as you call it?

Harris: No, only her word.

The questioning was documented on almost forty legal-size, single-spaced pages, inquiring more about Miss Healy and other matters under Harris's responsibility.

Collas G. Harris withstood the investigation and remained with the National Archives. He later helped develop special display cases that would help preserve such documents as the Declaration of Independence. Harris served as an intelligence officer in the South Pacific during WWII, which led to a career in the Central Intelligence Agency (CIA) until his retirement in 1968.[3]

Despite being described by Collas as having "one of the quickest and alert minds of any person I have had the privilege of working with," Mary Healy was held back like many women at that time by the proverbial "glass ceiling" which was in place even in government. Although Collas admitted that Mary Healy had "intimate knowledge of the National Archives Building that would have taken any other employee years to accumulate," she was not named Chief of the Building and Grounds Section when the job became available because "it was a job for a man." Collas supported his decision because of the need for the chief to periodically inspect restrooms. Instead she was transferred to a position where she assisted the less qualified chief. [4]

Mary Healy eventually broke up with my dad. She apparently never married. She moved to Foggy Bottom and remained there for years, becoming a civic activist in the community. Her childhood in poverty probably influenced her decision to choose a solid career in federal government to ensure financial security for her and her mother over a continued relationship with my dad. Fortunately, someone else came into my dad's life shortly after they parted—my mom.

∽

Baptized Vincentia Maria Bellucci, my mom was the oldest child of Urbano and Josephia Bellucci. My mom was the product of an arranged marriage. Her father, Urbano, had immigrated to the United States from Troia, Italy, early in the twentieth century along with his brother, Eleuterio. Not long after they settled in Washington, DC, an Italian marriage broker convinced them that two sisters back in Italy named Josephia and Angiolina Ciuffreda would be the perfect marriage partners for the two brothers. They agreed to the proposal by only looking at a photograph of the sisters. The sisters came from a mountain village close to the Adriatic coast named Monte Sant Angelo, which is not far from Troia.

Urbano had a long career with the Washington Gas Company and lived a simple but comfortable life with his family raising two children, my mom and her younger brother, Louie. My great-grandfather on the Bellucci side must have been named Vincento, because in addition to my mom, her female cousin was also named Vincentia, and a male cousin was named Vincento. While attending the local public school, my mom's name was shortened to Vince by teachers and American friends. She accepted the name and used it for the rest of her life, even on formal documents.

My mom's earliest recollection of my dad was watching him descend the stairs of his sister Esther's house on Massachusetts Avenue. She had met my dad's niece, Frances "Tanky" Cady, at a downtown business school where they were studying to be secretaries. They both discovered that they would rather skip class and attend one of the many movie theatres in downtown Washington at the time. Tanky may have purposely brought my mom up to the Massachusetts Avenue home to meet my dad. Esther had the largest home in the family, and with Esther's daughter Tibby married to a world-class drummer, the house was a bee hive of activity and the place to be for young people looking for a good time.

Their meeting must have occurred around the time that Mary Healy broke off her relationship with my dad because of the pressure the Civil Service Commission was putting on her and her supervisor. My dad was thirty-two and my mom was twenty-one when they met.

My mom was a full-blood Italian and looked the part, with long-flowing dark hair and solid brown eyes. She was tall for girls of her day at about 5' 9" and was so thin when she met my dad that Emmitt asked in a letter from prison, "Does Vince still look like she is starving?" If she was thin in her twenties, it was not because she did not love food. She came from the typical Italian family where food was a religion and to miss a meal was blasphemy. Years later I told more than one person that if I went to my mom and said, "I got fired from my job, my wife left me, and the house burnt down," she would probably say, "That's terrible. Now sit down and have something to eat." My mom was a great cook and used that skill to give others enjoyment.

My mom always had fine taste when it came to clothes and fabrics. Probably with the ulterior motive to see my dad more, she took a job at the Warring brothers' office booking bets on horse races. With her salary, she now could shop at some of the best department stores in Washington and it showed.

For my mom and dad, the fact that they were seriously dating was met with a mixed reaction from their families. My dad's family expected him to find another Irish girl or wait for Mary Healy to change her mind. As far as my mom's family—yes, my dad seemed to be able to support my mom for now and he was fun to be around, but he wasn't Italian and did not have a steady, secure job. Although my mom and dad were both Catholic, their respective in-laws did not initially accept them because of their ethnic differences.

They went on dates, mostly to the movies (both my parents were big John Wayne fans) or out to eat at some restaurant where my dad knew the owner and was well received by the staff and other patrons. But many times, their date consisted of nothing more than my mom accompanying my dad as he made his nightly rounds claiming to "need to see a man about business."

☙

Through the pressures of operating bootlegging and a numbers businesses, and the constant threat of going to jail, Leo maintained his marriage to Audrey and raised a family. They had two children, Leo Bruce and Audrey Lorraine. As a young teenager, Leo Bruce was sent to Charlotte Hall Military Academy in southern Maryland. He was not a problem child, but his parents thought it best that he be removed from the turmoil of the family income tax trial of the late 1930s. Sending sons to military schools was somewhat common for those in the rackets.[5] After graduating from Dartmouth College, Leo Bruce started a twenty-nine-year naval career that included command of destroyers. Among the ships he commanded was the USS *The Sullivans*, named after the five brothers who had died together on the USS *Juneau*, which was sunk by a Japanese submarine during the naval battle of Guadalcanal.

But Leo had demons that led him to drink for days at a time. No one understood what drove Leo to drink. Was it an unhappy marriage? Or was it playing second fiddle to his younger brother, Emmitt? Did the fact that he had to turn back over the reins of the numbers business to Emmitt after running it smoothly for the two years while his brother was in jail trigger his latest drinking binge? No one seemed to know.

He was coming off one such drinking episode on the morning of December 6, 1941 (the day before the Pearl Harbor attack), when he slipped on a slick Washington street and hit his head on a curb. After a few days in a Washington hospital without regaining consciousness, he was transferred to Johns Hopkins Hospital in Baltimore to be treated by some of the nation's best doctors. Sometime during his stay, one of the physicians gave my Aunt Esther, who was closer to Leo than her other siblings, some encouragement by telling her that with the right care and a bit of luck, "he should be home by Christmas."

Four days after the accident, surgeons at Johns Hopkins operated on Leo to relieve pressure in the part of his brain injured by the fall, but the surgery did not save him. He died December 13, 1941, exactly a week after his accident. According to the death certificate, apparently Leo had suffered a previous head injury, and the recent fall (or the surgery) triggered bleeding from an area damaged by the first trauma.

Leo's death was a terrible blow to his family and the siblings closest to him. Esther was especially affected by Leo's death. Years later, whenever she would visit our home during the Christmas holidays, we were instructed not to play any Christmas music in fear of making her melancholy, given that Leo's death occurred shortly before Christmas 1941. The Christmas classic "I'll be Home for Christmas" was especially difficult for her to hear, given the unfulfilled encouragement from the doctor at Johns Hopkins that he would have Leo home by the holidays.

My dad thought enough of his older brother to name his first child after him, and dad gave me my uncle's full name: Leo Paul Warring.

The family would also lose their patriarch some five years later. Bruce Warring was suffering from the latter stages of cancer when he fell out of the third-story window of his home and died. The effects of the illness and pain-killing drugs apparently caused him to become disorientated, leading to his fall.

A man of the nineteenth century with roots in the Virginia countryside, Bruce was already a middle-aged man with ten children by the time the first Model T Ford rolled off of the assembly line. He worked hard at his barrel business, and he never accepted the illegal businesses that his three youngest sons adopted.[6]

In his will, Bruce rewarded the two children who had remained with him in the barrel shop, Lillian and Bruce. They assumed the management of the barrel shop until their mother, Julia, died in 1958. At that time, consistent with Bruce's will, the remaining estate was divided between the two siblings "in grateful remembrance and appreciation of the many years of business and other assistance, loving care, and kindness ..." shown to their mother and father. The year 1947 would usher in other changes, especially for my dad and mom. Much to the dismay of both my dad's and mom's families, my parents eloped to Manassas, Virginia one fall afternoon in 1947 and were married by a rural parish priest. They found two local children who were willing to stand as witnesses.

My parents lived at my Aunt Esther's home on Massachusetts Avenue at the time of my birth. My dad had been living there since his release from prison in 1939. My Aunt Esther loved my dad but sometimes did not appreciate his interference in matters under the rule of her house.

She once came home from the beach and noted that something looked different in the backyard. Suddenly, she realized that a beautiful weeping willow tree was gone. My dad, ever the superstitious one, had chopped down the tree because he believed in the ancient folklore that it caused bad luck. A bad day in the numbers business spelled the end of the tree. Needless to say, my aunt was not pleased.

After a year living at Esther's, my dad and mom found a new three-bedroom house about a mile from Georgetown Hospital selling for less than $30,000 dollars. My dad went to see Emmitt and showed up at the settlement with cash—almost unheard of in those days.

The 1940s would be a time of relative calm for the Warrings as they managed to stay off the front pages. The number business flourished, apparently under the protection of friendly police. This was especially true when one of Emmitt's good friends on the police force, Robert J. Barrett, became the chief of police in 1947. Due to the combination of payoffs and legitimate police attention to other, more serious public safety issues, there were few arrests of those in the Warring network and no serious legal problems for Emmitt or Charlie.

My dad enjoyed being married and having a family. My brother, Richard, came along four years after I had been born. I gave him the nickname of "Bobo," a nickname that stuck with him until he changed it to the more conventional "Beau" after moving to Maine as a young adult.

With a wife and two kids, my dad never had to be alone. Unlike Emmitt, who seemed content with solitude at times, I don't think my dad ever wanted to be alone. He would always encourage my brother or me to sit down and watch television with him. When he had to go out for a while, he always wanted us to come with him, if the situation warranted. Of course, we would be willing because my dad usually showed us a good time.

However, when my dad sought adult-male companionship, there was Pete Dailey's.

CHAPTER SIXTEEN

Pete Dailey's

Pete Dailey's, commonly referred to singularly as Pete's or Dailey's, was a Foggy Bottom neighborhood tavern that was more an old-time barroom than a restaurant bar. Owned by George "Pete" Dailey, who was regarded as the unofficial mayor of Foggy Bottom, it was situated a few steps from the intersection of New Hampshire and Virginia Avenues, at 2500 G Street NW (The Royal Embassy of Saudi Arabia stands there today, just up the street from the Watergate complex.)

An old newspaper article described Pete Dailey's as a bar where "members of the sporting [gambling] fraternities rubbed elbows with the social elite who found the atmosphere relaxing and informal."[1] For most of the members of the "Foggy Bottom Gang," Pete Dailey's was a favorite hangout. Besides gamblers and racketeers, Pete's customers included policemen, cab drivers, socialites, actors from nearby Arena Stage, and White House personnel. One old-timer who used to frequent Pete's recalled that once when entertainer Mickey Rooney was in DC, he asked his driver to find a good neighborhood bar. The driver brought him to the one he knew best—Pete's.

It was strictly a beer and hard liquor joint. Bartenders wore traditional white aprons. Unless you were a good-looking lady, they would laugh at you if you ordered any fancy cocktail. You were lucky if you could get a ham sandwich. The standard bologna and cheese sandwich was the only fare for a hungry patron. Pete's was the second home to many local Irishmen. The walls were "Irish-green with paper shamrocks all around."[2] And yes, they had green beer on St. Patrick's Day. My dad loved being Irish and enjoyed the ways of the Irish. So, St. Patrick's Day at Pete's was a special day for him.

Pete's most notable character was a four-legged one. "Pete the Goat" made his home at the nearby Edgewater Riding Academy. There he fulfilled a long-standing calling of goats, keeping nearby horses calm. The riding stable, located a few doors from Pete Dailey's, provided horses for those who rode in nearby Rock Creek Park. Although the goat's owner, William "Hat Rack" Smith, was a faithful customer, the goat did not depend on Hat Rack to bring him to the bar. For years, he just ambled over almost every day and butted the front door open. Unlike most of the bar's patrons, Pete the Goat would not drink but just eat—mostly crackers and cigarette butts. When he arrived, the bartender would ignore drinking customers to serve Pete the Goat his crackers. After that, Pete would be left to forage the floor of the bar for discarded cigarette butts that apparently pleased his palate. On St. Patrick's Day, his horns were painted green. Once Pete the Goat went missing, and Foggy Bottom was in turmoil. But he was eventually found on the other side of the Potomac River in Arlington, Virginia, gnawing on a steel pipe.[3]

Maurice "Buddy" Sweeney worked as manager and bartender at Pete's for years. Buddy also worked for the Warrings and had been indicted for pushing the cab of suspected snitch Clair Kensinger into the Potomac River. He grew up with the younger Warrings and was especially close to my dad, who was his age.

One morning in the late 1950s, a man came to our house to tell my dad that a body had been found in the Potomac and they thought it was Buddy Sweeney. I think that was the only time that I saw my dad cry.

It turned out Buddy Sweeney showed up alive for work at Pete's later that morning. All was well in Foggy Bottom.

My favorite bartender at Pete's was a roly-poly man named Jack Levy. But I didn't find out his real name until decades later. I only knew him as "Murphy," or "Murph" for short. The Jewish bartender was so liked by the predominantly Irish clientele at Pete's that they gave him the moniker "Murphy" to make him one of their own. A slightly balding, short and stout man, he was missing a couple of teeth on one side of his mouth that became noticeable when he smiled. And being of good nature, Murphy smiled often.

Murphy was by no means a tough guy, but he did not need to be one as long as my father was around. Besides serving up endless Cokes to me when I got stuck with my dad at Pete's, I remember him as the one constant guest to our house for dinner on Christmas and Easter Sunday. Because the bar was closed on those two days and Murph didn't have a wife or family, he was invited over to our house on those holidays. He had become like family for those two days of the year.

Legend has it that on one Sunday around noon, an out-of-town gentleman wandered into Pete's and ordered a drink. Buddy Sweeney politely explained that because of the District's liquor laws, he could not serve him until 2:00 p.m. on Sundays. The gentleman went to leave but then noticed a group of men sitting in a booth with alcoholic drinks in front of them. He pointed it out to Buddy Sweeney, but he again was refused anything to drink. Exasperated, the man lost his temper and threatened to be at the chief of police's office first thing Monday morning to inform him of this obvious violation of the liquor laws. But Buddy Sweeney politely advised the gentleman that he did not have to wait until the next morning. The chief himself was enjoying a drink in the same booth that had gotten the gentleman's attention.[4]

A lot of characters frequented Pete's. One of my favorites was an Irish immigrant who had been in America for a number of years but still spoke with the thickest brogue. He worked at a funeral parlor in Georgetown. The story was that many people in Georgetown were buried without the expensive shoes that their loved ones had left at the funeral parlor along with the other clothes to be worn by the deceased. The Irishman made sure that the shoes would not be wasted on the dead but were used by the poor back in his native Ireland.[5]

Occasionally, one of the guys would be brave, or foolish, enough to bring a girl into Pete's. The ladies usually weren't impressed. My dad had a regular line that he would always deliver to a guy upon meeting his girl for the first time, no matter what the gal looked like: "If I go blind, you can pick them for me." Of course, this would win over the guy and his date instantly.

Whenever Emmitt visited Dailey's, it was almost always about business. He took whomever he wanted to see into the backroom and left shortly thereafter. Whereas my dad tended to linger. But it was more for the company rather than the alcohol. Strangely, the same folks who were quick to point out how well they knew Rags would admit to hardly knowing Emmitt. My dad lived amongst the common folk while Emmitt rarely came out of his house and then only to perform an errand and return home without delay.

Dailey's was like a second home to my dad. He felt at home there around his predominantly Irish friends. He was totally accepted for who he was. Once, stopping at Dailey's after a funeral, he finally left the bar and was about five miles away when he suddenly blurted out a drawn-out curse: "Goddamn it. I left my teeth on the bar at Dailey's."[6] (His dentures never fit him properly and he would slip them out at the first chance.)

After decades at the G Street site, Pete's had to close its doors in 1957 to make way for development. The bar relocated a block away to 2532 F Street before closing forever in the mid-1960s to make way for the construction of the Kennedy Center for the Performing Arts. Knowing their eventual replacement, a small ad ran in a local football game program in 1964 that promoted "Pete Dailey's Cultural Center."

CHAPTER SEVENTEEN

A Dangerous Delivery

By 1950, Emmitt Warring was a familiar figure to his upper northwest Washington neighbors. They described Emmitt to inquiring newspaper reporters as a "fine neighbor" who invited kids into his home to watch his television set before other homes had purchased the new electronic marvel.[1] He was also known to drag his garden hose to a neighbor's home to water their yard while they were on vacation in the summer.

Lane Phillips grew up on 39th Street just down the street from Emmitt's corner house on Macomb Street. He remembers that on one day during World War II, Emmitt noticed that the Phillip's family car was running on tires that were worn to the point that they were dangerous to drive on at high speeds. The family had not replaced the tires because they did not have the required certificate issued by the government as part of a rationing program during the war. Emmitt squatted down next to one of the wheels to ostensibly get a better look at the condition of the tire, but he was also reading the tire size. The next day Emmitt called the Phillips' home and told them to go outside. They found new tires leaning against their garage door. Undoubtedly, Emmitt had gone to a black market source to acquire the new tires for the Phillips' family.

Lane Phillips also recalls that as a youth he learned firsthand of Emmitt's influence with local police. One day he and a friend were spotted by police officers as they were shooting Lane's BB gun across the four lanes of Massachusetts Avenue into the adjoining woods. The cops, after spotting them and scolding them for their reckless behavior, confiscated the BB gun. When Lane told his mother what had happened, she advised him that he had to tell his father as soon as he came home from work. Late that afternoon, Lane spotted his dad talking to

Emmitt in Emmitt's front yard. Lane's dad passed Emmitt's house on his daily walk from the bus stop on Wisconsin Avenue to his home and stopped to speak to Emmitt as he watered his lawn. Lane walked up the street to Emmitt's house to confess to his father. As Lane told his dad how his BB gun had been confiscated by the police, Emmitt continued to water his lawn indifferently. They left Emmitt without discussing the matter with him. But within the hour, while at supper, someone knocked on the Phillips' front door. It was a sergeant from the Eighth Precinct with Lane's BB gun. The sergeant returned it to Lane and mumbled to the boy that "it was all a mistake."

The neighbors also knew Emmitt as "the little man with the big dog." For seven years, Emmitt shared his home with a huge Great Dane named Duke, which he had raised from the time the dog was a three-week-old puppy. Duke usually got his exercise in Emmitt's spacious backyard. Whenever Emmitt decided to take Duke for a rare walk around the neighborhood, the diminutive Emmitt looked like he was walking a pony.

Emmitt, a bachelor, was now set in his ways. He rarely went out at night and was usually in bed by 1:00 a.m. His breakfast was limited to coffee. He took his one full meal around 3:00 in the afternoon. Emmitt's favorite spots were Martin's Restaurant or Britt's Cafeteria, both in Georgetown. At times, he would return to Martin's for a bowl of soup or sandwich after 9:00 p.m. He would occasionally drop by one of Georgetown's retailers before returning home in the afternoon. Word would get around if Emmitt shopped regularly at one of the shops on M Street or Wisconsin Avenue. Soon number writers and bookies would refer to it as one of "Emmitt's places."

Before returning home around 6:00, he would pick up the day's betting receipts from the "office." Usually the large and imposing—but completely trustworthy—Cocky Ware would meet Emmitt on a street location that varied from day to day. He would just walk up to Emmitt's car and drop the money bag onto the passenger seat. Before "bucket seats" were standard in cars, Emmitt kept a pistol squeezed into the crease that formed where the bottom of the front seat of the car met the back rest, and he would slip his small right hand into the crease and on the gun while the money transfer took place.[2] Emmitt tried to avoid going into the office since the DC law had been changed that now considered paper containing betting information as incriminating evidence of gambling. The police could not make a gambling charge stick if he were stopped and found only in possession of money. A significant portion of the money that Emmitt picked up was made up of coins used by the everyday low-income bettor. In the summertime during the 1940s before most homes were air-conditioned, neighbors could hear Emmitt's automated coin sorter emanating "clicking and clanging" sounds from the Macomb Street house.

When Emmitt was out, he would customarily ask his brother-in-law, Bill Cady, to stay at the house for security reasons. Cady had been separated from Emmitt's sister Esther for years, but he remained Emmitt's close friend and confidant. Emmitt's trusted African American maid, Louise Enos, would usually be in the house during the day performing regular housekeeping chores and sometimes screening calls.

One of Emmitt's true friends in the rackets was Joe Nesline. Emmitt knew and admired Joe because of his business-like approach to the rackets. Nesline was cited several times in the 1930s for alcohol and gaming violations. In 1937, the District police charged Nesline with holding the largest cache of illegal liquor in D.C. since the repeal of Prohibition four years earlier.[3] In the 1940s, Nesline traveled to Las Vegas, building a reputation as one of the best craps players in the world.

As a favor to Nesline, Emmitt hired George Harding who had grown up with Nesline in a northeast Washington neighborhood near 6th and Massachusetts Avenue. Harding did not seem to fit the mold of the kind of guy Emmitt wanted working for him but the hiring was probably a favor to Nesline with whom Emmitt had developed a close relationship.

The olive-skinned, slender Harding had a string of almost twenty arrests by 1950.[4] In the 1930s he had been convicted of manslaughter for the death of his employer, Harry "Doc" Davis. Harding claimed the killing was "accidental."[5] He was pardoned by President Truman, along with all other "convicted persons" in the armed services who received an honorable discharge after serving in World War II.[6]

But more recently Harding had attracted the kind of negative publicity that Emmitt usually steered away from. In 1947 Harding was charged with kidnapping and assaulting twenty-nine-year-old Alsace Lorraine McCormick. Although she had previously dated Harding, McCormick said Harding forced her at gunpoint to get into his car. While driving towards Silver Hill, Maryland, Harding repeatedly slapped the pretty brunette and battered her forehead with his gun until she promised to marry him.[7]

The three-hour abduction ended when Harding delivered the bloodied woman to Providence Hospital in DC. The following day, Harding brought flowers and candy to her at the hospital, but that night, he sneaked into the hospital at 4 a.m. and slapped her as she lay in bed after he found out she planned to press charges. Her screams and the screams of her hospital roommate caused Harding to flee. The *Washington Post* entitled their story of the abduction and assault "'Caveman' Wooing Tactics Lead to Indictment Here."[8] Harding was later found innocent of the more serious charges of kidnapping and assault with intent to kill, and found guilty only of simple assault and carrying a deadly weapon and served a prison term.[9]

Upon Harding's release from prison with no job, Emmitt hired Harding as a favor to Nesline and even allowed Harding to stay at his house on Macomb Street. Nesline, who was splitting his time between DC and Las Vegas, believed that Harding would be forced to control his emotions if he was working for Emmitt. Given Emmitt's aversion to negative publicity, especially as it relates to violence, Nesline knew that this was no small favor that he was asking of Emmitt.

But changing Harding's ways seemed to be too big a task for anybody. In August of 1949 he was charged with shooting fellow gambler Bernard "Yorkie" Del Negro in both legs outside a restaurant in Maryland. Earlier that same evening, Harding knifed a Georgetown clothing merchant during an argument for an unspecified reason.[10] The run-in with the Georgetown merchant was too much for Emmitt to bear. Emmitt always wanted to stay in the good graces of the shopkeepers of Georgetown and Foggy Bottom. Emmitt soon dismissed Harding and kicked him out of his Macomb Street house.[11]

ග

Nothing was out of the ordinary on Monday afternoon of January 9, 1950, when Emmitt went to Georgetown and left Bill Cady and housemaid Louise Enos at the Macomb Street home. But shortly after Emmitt left, there was a knock at the front door. Bill Cady went to the door, looked through the one-way mirror, spotted a man on the doorstep holding a crate, and inquired, "Who's there?"

Someone dressed like a deliveryman shouted through the thick door, "I got a crate of oranges for a Mr. Warring."

Esther and her daughter Tibby were on a rare out-of-town trip to Florida and had not yet returned to Washington, so this appeared to be a gift from them. Cady took his eyes away from the one-way mirror, unlocked the door and pulled it opened. The deliveryman stepped through the opened door with the crate and offered it to Cady. "Big Bill," so called because of his six-foot, 250-pound frame, took the crate from the smaller deliveryman.

As he started to turn to find a suitable spot to place it, without warning, two more men who had been standing out of view on the side of the small porch suddenly barged through the door and aimed their guns at Cady. The gunmen had gotten the drop on him. The Great Dane, Duke, barked loudly but did nothing to discourage the uninvited trio. They seemed to know that Duke, despite his menacing size and baritone bark, was a gentle giant.

Louise Enos came up from the basement and took a couple of steps down the narrow hallway leading to the foyer, but stopped when she saw the scene and raised her hand to her mouth to stifle a scream. The intruders ordered Cady to put the dog away, or they would kill it. Knowing Emmitt's love for the dog, Cady immediately grabbed Duke by the collar, dragged him to the garage door off of the hallway, and yanked the dog into the garage, closing the door behind the canine.

The men clearly knew that Emmitt was not home. They ordered the husky Cady and the slender Miss Enos up the stairs off of the foyer to Emmitt's bedroom. The intruders apparently were aware of the location of the safe in the bedroom closet. They made Cady and Enos sit on the bedroom floor while they proceeded to bind and gag them.

These men were no amateurs. All of them had made their reputation away from the Washington area.

They were led by burly Sidney "Big Sid" Stromberg (alias Sidney Max), kid brother of Harry Stromberg, alias "Nig Rosen," the Philadelphia mobster. The older Stromberg had had his sights on getting a foothold in Washington gambling circles back in the 1930s until the unintended killing of Allen D. Wilson, the innocent newspaper deliveryman. Accompanying Big Sid in the invasion of Emmit's house were two professional holdup men, Arthur Pelkisson (alias Arthur Miller) and

Malcolm Epstein, both dangerous men. Pelkisson was described by a Bronx assistant district attorney as a "vicious criminal" who "brutally and unnecessarily assaults his victims."[12] Epstein was wanted for the execution-style murder of a man in Wilkes-Barre, Pennsylvania in 1948.[13]

They first tried to see if Cady knew the combination of the safe. As Emmitt's closest confidant, Cady spent many hours in the house. When Cady said he didn't know the combination, the trio pistol-whipped him and threatened to do worse. After they had bloodied Cady's head and face sufficiently, they concluded that only Emmitt knew the combination.

But Cady was not a passive prisoner. Realizing he was next to a bureau that contained a loaded gun, Cady quickly opened the drawer with his tied hands and grabbed the weapon. But while attempting to pull it out, he lost his grip on the revolver and it fell onto the bedroom carpet. One of the holdup men spotted Cady's move and smashed his shoe on one of Cady's outstretched hands, breaking three bones.[14]

Meanwhile, the transfer of the day's receipts with Cocky Ware went without incident, and Emmitt headed for home, driving up Wisconsin Avenue. He parked at the corner of 39th and Macomb, and apparently intending to go out again, did not put the car in the garage. He thought it unusual that Cady had not picked up the afternoon papers from the front porch and brought them into the house to read. Opening the door enough to peer into the foyer, he noticed a crate of oranges on the floor. When he was through the door, he felt the cold steel of a gun pressed against the nape of his neck.

Emmitt was immediately rushed up to his bedroom. Ascending the steps, he worried about his close friend and his longtime maid. As he was pushed into the bedroom, he was relieved to find them still alive but distressed to see them sitting on the floor, both bound and gagged, and Cady bloodied. The blood from the cuts to Bill Cady's scalp had left a large stain on the carpet.

Ordered by Big Sid to open the safe, Emmitt stalled by responding, "I can't remember the combination."

"Mr. Warring, if you don't open the safe, we will blow your fuckin' brains out," Stromberg countered, placing his gun to Emmitt's temple.

"Go ahead," was Emmitt's brief and bold response. Louise Enos trembled and raised her eyes to the ceiling. The gag placed in her mouth muffled an incoherent cry.

Emmitt's defiance momentarily befuddled the robbers. Stromberg had not planned for any killing and was even distressed by the sight of Bill Cady's blood.[15] He knew that killing Emmitt wouldn't accomplish anything and would only hang a murder rap on his head. He also could tell from Emmitt's countenance that further threats would be useless. Then Stromberg had a better idea.

"If you don't open that safe, we'll blow his fuckin' brains out," he said, placing the gun inches away from Bill Cady's head.

This was different. Emmitt was confident that the gunman would not shoot him because he was the only one who knew the combination, so it would be pointless to kill him. But would they be willing to shoot Bill Cady? He wondered if they just might be up to that. He had to resign himself to the fact that he could not risk another's life, especially the life of his close friend.[16]

Emmitt opened the safe. Once the safe was opened, one of the men pushed Emmitt aside and pointed a flashlight into the cavity. He grabbed the cash and blew a soft whistle when he inspected Emmitt's six-carat diamond ring. The men then relieved Emmitt and Cady of the cash in their pockets. Later, Emmitt would reluctantly state that the thieves made off with approximately $25,000 dollars. Decades later, family members would speculate it might have been close to $225,000.

Emmitt immediately suspected the men were out-of-town professionals. But what he really wanted to know was who, locally, had "fingered" him for the job.

Emmitt did not report the robbery to the police through official channels because he did not want to invite questions from them or the media. What good could the police do at this point? The stolen money was probably stashed away, and arresting the robbers would not get it back. He did call his friend, Police Chief Robert Barrett, off the record, to see if the top cop had any insight into who may have pulled the job. About six weeks earlier, a floating crap game in northeast Washington had been held up for about $25,000, most of it coming at the expense of DC gambler Robert "Ryebread" Shulman. Barrett tipped off Emmitt that the portly convict, Sidney Stromberg from Pennsylvania, was the leading suspect in that case.

Word of the holdup leaked out in a day or two. When the newspaper reporters came to Emmitt's home to ask questions, they were greeted only "by the barking of a dog."[17] Emmitt did open the door to detectives from the gambling squad but emphatically denied that he had been robbed. Chief Barrett claimed that he was on the case himself "because these alleged victims are so un-cooperative."[18]

When reporters learned that Bill Cady had been beaten in the robbery, they went to the Massachusetts Avenue home of his estranged wife, Esther Warring Cady. When Esther's longtime African American maid, Gracie, answered the door and was asked whether Bill Cady lived there, she followed her general instructions to "know nothing" if someone asked questions and dutifully responded, "I really don't know who lives here."[19]

Within days, even the newspapers were focused on the "finger man," i.e., the insider who had passed on critical information to the men who actually committed the crime. Four days after the holdup, the *Evening Star* ran an article reporting that "Warring Holdup Search Centers on Ex-Friends."[20] The article stated that the burglars knew when Emmitt would be away from his home and when he would return in order to surprise him. They also knew the location of the safe and that the dog "Duke" was "all bark and no bite." Soon dozens of underworld informers entered the game by offering police (and probably Emmitt) tips on who might have been the "finger man" and what "out-of-town professional mobsters" might have carried out the robbery.[21]

A few months later, police broke the case. First, Malcolm Epstein was arrested in Pennsylvania for the execution-style killing of Harold "Red" Rowe in Wilkes-Barre in 1948. A few weeks later, Sidney Stromberg was arrested in Pottsville, Pennsylvania as an accomplice in Rowe's murder. Both Bill Cady and Louise Enos were brought to Pennsylvania and identified the men who pulled off the January robbery in Washington.[22]

When Emmitt finally admitted he had been robbed, he strangely maintained that he had not seen the faces of the gunmen. He claimed a towel had immediately been slipped over his head when he entered his home that evening. He insisted that the towel had remained over his head the entire time and that he only saw the feet of the robbers. Of course, Emmitt's claim raises questions as to why the trio would go to the trouble of hiding their identity from Emmitt when Cady and Enos had seen their faces. Even more puzzling was how Emmitt had opened the safe with the towel over his head. There was no real need for Emmitt to identify the robbers since Cady and Miss Enos would provide all the identification that was needed. It appears that Emmitt was keeping to the unspoken code of the underworld to never "rat anyone out."

About the time that Bill Cady and Louise Enos had identified the holdup men, Emmitt was spotted by a *Washington Post* reporter in a coffee shop and asked his opinion on the current Washington crime wave.

"It's awful," he told the reporter. "It shows that hard times make hard people. There are too many guns. The war is over and there are kids with guns," apparently referring to a recent case in which teenagers unintentionally shot and killed a man while carrying out a holdup.[23]

Shortly after Stromberg realized he had probably been picked out of a line up, he asked police to bring Emmitt to the prison so the robbery case could be "adjusted."[24] He told one of the investigating detectives from Washington, "Listen feller. I want no part of this Washington rap. There is only one thing that Emmitt Warring is interested in and that's the finger man. I don't want Cady, Enos or Warring to identify me [in court]."[25]

The fact that Stromberg was still concerned about Emmitt testifying against him in hindsight makes Emmitt's story that a towel was placed over his head during the entire time of the robbery seem even more suspicious. There is no documented account that Emmitt met with Stromberg in prison. However, a story has circulated over the years that a meeting did take place at which Stromberg revealed to Emmitt the name of the "finger man." Emmitt never did identify Stromberg, but Cady and Enos would identify him during his subsequent trial for the robbery and assault.

Soon word began to spread around town that George Harding was the man who had "fingered" Emmitt Warring.

Ironically, at the time of the robbery, the city directory listed Harding's address as 3900 Macomb Street, Emmitt Warring's home address.[26]

Many in the underworld had already suspected Harding was the "finger man" behind the robbery of gambler Ryebread Shulman. Now Harding was worried that his former employer, Emmitt Warring, would find out that he "fingered" the robbery and assault at Emmitt's house.

Once Emmitt knew who "put the finger" on him, it took all of his brotherly influence to keep his brother Rags from settling the score with George Harding. Emmitt assured his brother, who was now married with a baby boy, that he did not need to get involved. This thing with Harding would take care of itself.

Despite their childhood friendship, George Harding and Joe Nesline had a falling out sometime in 1950 after the robbery at Emmitt's house. If mutual friends knew the basis of their sudden animosity, they were not talking publicly. Nesline would later swear that he lived in fear of Harding. He claimed that ten to fifteen people had approached him and told him that "Harding said that he is going to bury me."[27]

The evening of January 9, 1951, the first anniversary of the robbery at Emmitt's home, began with both Harding and Nesline separately making the rounds of various drinking and gambling establishments with one or two friends. The blond-haired Nesline had a noticeable receding hairline but always wore a fashionable hat and expensive clothes that met his reputation as a dapper dresser. That night Nesline was carrying a .45-calibur semi-automatic pistol. According to Joe, he had just begun to carry it around with him after learning about the threats from George Harding. Some would later question the veracity of Nesline's claims of threats from Harding.

After a night of restaurant and bar hopping, Nesline and friend "Jabber" Corsi dropped by a Greek coffee house, Blackstone's, on 9th Street to watch a "card game." According to Nesline, after the house card game concluded, John Morisi, who was keeping the running score of the game, suggested to Nesline that they go to the Hide-Away Club, a Georgetown after-hours club. The club was located on K Street under the newly-built Whitehurst Freeway, just a block from the Warring barrel shop. In the 1960s, it would be called the Bayou and feature Dixieland music before showcasing more contemporary groups in the 1970s to attract the Georgetown University students.

After-hours clubs, sometimes called "bottle clubs," drew customers after the bars closed and could no longer serve alcohol. Patrons and club members brought their own liquor and were charged for set ups, (e.g., ice, soda) and usually assessed a cover charge. They got around the District's curfew regulations for bars and restaurants by a District law that allowed for the clubs to be operated as corporations for "benevolent, charitable, educational, literary, musical, scientific, religious or missionary purposes." Some of the other clubs called themselves names like "the United Nations Social Club, the Mechanical Print Craft Club (located a few blocks from the *Washington Post*) and the Gold Key Club."[28]

George Harding's evening was not so uneventful. Earlier in the evening at the Chesapeake House in Maryland, Harding had accused a bartender of giving him knockout drops. He fired a shot between the man's feet and then pistol-whipped him.[29] Later, he slapped a woman across the face at the Crossroads, another Maryland nightspot. Sometime in the early morning hours, he and his traveling companion, George "The Greek" Clainos, decided also to drop by the Hide-Away before calling it a night. Strangely, neither Harding nor Nesline was known to frequent the club.

It is unclear who arrived at the club first, but all accounts agree that Harding and Clainos were sitting at a table just across from Nesline's party. Relatively few people were in the dimly-lit nightspot, only eleven men and six women. Somebody was still feeding coins into the jukebox at 4:30 a.m. Wednesday morning when two police officers from the Seventh Precinct dropped by for a cup of coffee. One of them had been transferred to the precinct just eight days earlier.[30]

Nesline and Harding had been exchanging bitter words and glances for almost an hour. A waitress in the club, Mrs. Juanita Gilbert, would later say that Harding had been drinking heavily and boasting about the pistol-beating he had given to a bartender earlier in the evening at the Chesapeake House. George Clainos left the club but returned a few minutes later. Mrs. Gilbert said that she saw Clainos pass a revolver to Harding.

"He slipped it into his pocket," she would later tell investigators.[31] She said that Harding then remarked, "I'm going to take care of Nesline now." After passing the gun to Harding, Clainos left the club and did not return.

Shortly thereafter, about 4:50 a.m., Nesline left his table and went up the stairs to the second-floor balcony where the men's room was located. Because of the sparse crowd, the balcony was closed and no one was sitting at the tables situated there. The lights were off and only a fraction of light and drifting cigarette smoke escaped from the first floor to fill the air of the balcony. Into this near darkness Harding followed Nesline up the balcony steps. A few seconds later, a single, loud shot rang out.

The two policemen, sipping on their second cup of coffee, sprung from their table and ran up the balcony stairs. They could barely see a figure coming towards them down the stairs. They drew their weapons and shined a flashlight into the face of a man. It was Joe Nesline. He had fired a single round from his .45-caliber pistol into George Harding's chest from close range. One of the policemen pointed his flashlight towards Nesline's hands. The light fell on the pistol he held.

"I just had to do it," Nesline confessed as he offered the gun to one of the cops.[32] While one of the policemen stayed with Nesline, the other proceeded up the stairs. Only a few feet from the top of the stairs, he found George Harding facedown and gasping for his last few breaths of life. When the policeman rolled him over, a loaded .38 pistol slipped out of his right hip pocket. Clearly, he had not drawn his gun before Nesline shot him. Harding made it to a hospital emergency room but died without saying anything.

The two policemen, George "The Greek" Clainos, waitress Juanita Gilbert and a few others who were in the club that night testified to the grand jury a few days later. The jury returned an indictment of first-degree murder against Joe Nesline.

ↀ

Two trials in 1951 captured Emmitt Warring's interest. The first was the murder trial of his friend, Joe Nesline, and the second was the trial of "Big Sid" Stromberg for robbing the Warring home.

Emmitt had urged Nesline to hire the lawyers that he was now using exclusively, i.e. Charles E. Ford and H. Clifford Allder. Ford was a legend in law circles in Washington. By the late 1940s, he was known not just as a criminal attorney but as "the criminal attorney" in DC. The word around town was that "if Charlie Ford defends you, it's 3 to 1 you're guilty, and 6 to 5 you'll be acquitted." Most criminal law offices were on 5th Street NW near the courthouse, and Ford's reputation for oratory in defense of his clients earned him the moniker "The Fifth Street Cicero." When speaking before a jury, his voice would roar like a lion one minute and drop to a whisper the next. He was a close friend of the Chief of Police Robert J. Barrett, and the lawyer most policemen used when facing charges of misconduct. Many prosecuting attorneys found that Ford knew more about the details of a case than they did. Ford boasted that no client of his ever "burned" (in the electric chair which was still a legal punishment in DC). Although one murderer was found hung in jail, Ford's record remained intact.[33]

The Nesline case posed a stern test of that record.

Fate was unkind to Joe Nesline and his defense team when they drew Judge Alexander Holtzoff to preside over the trial. Born in New York and educated at Columbia University, the "bald, bantam-sized jurist" was known for his physical energy and voracious mind. Later in life, he challenged his body by taking long walks through the city and his mind by learning Italian into his eighties. He was also considered as a "pro-prosecution" jurist, known for meting out long sentences to those convicted of violent crimes. He once opined that he could not "understand why the so-called liberals are always leaning toward protecting the criminals … instead of leaning towards protecting the public."[34]

A jury of eight men and four women were empaneled in April 1951 to try Nesline, the former bootlegger, for the nightclub murder of "gangster" George Harding.[35] In his opening statement, prosecutor Arthur McLaughlin told the jury that evidence would show that Nesline ambushed George Harding in the dark of the second floor of the Hide-Away Club and shot him with deliberate malice. Deputy Coroner Dr. Richard Rosenberg testified that powder burns on Harding's shirt indicated the fatal shot must have been fired at point-blank range. Rosenberg stated that the bullet entered on the left side of Harding's chest and traveled downward.[36]

The two policemen who were at the Hide-Away testified the club was "unusually quiet" that night before the shooting. They chronicled how they rushed up the stairs after hearing the shot and how Nesline immediately said, "I had to do it."[37]

The policemen were followed to the stand by "pretty" Hide-Away waitress Harriet Harding (no relation to the dead man) who testified that Harding pushed her aside and shouted, "Get out of my way, baby," before ascending the stairs to the second floor. The "pert little blonde waitress with a 'Betty Boop' voice" stated that Harding was drinking, but he was not drunk at the time of the shooting.[38]

The final witnesses for the government were Detective Sergeants Lionel Couture and Arthur Webber who had interrogated Nesline shortly after the shooting. One of the detectives testified Nesline told him that he "was asking too many questions." But both stated Nesline had said, "Harding came toward me with both hands in his pockets."[39]

Attorney Ford was concerned about how the jury would react to his defense. He decided to do something criminal lawyers rarely do, especially in a first-degree murder case: put his client on the witness stand. Despite the risk, he felt that Nesline had the temperament to withstand the cross-examination of the prosecutor and the personality to impress the jury.

Nesline took the witness stand wearing a blue, double-breasted suit and with his blonde hair slicked and combed straight back. He said he was carrying a gun that night only because "I was afraid of George Harding, afraid that he was going to kill me." Nesline claimed that he was talked into going to the Hide-Away that night against his better judgment since he feared he might run into Harding. He said that when Harding walked into the club, he told those with him, "Oh, my God, there's Georgie."[40]

Nesline said that he went upstairs to use the men's room but, "On my way back—I don't know how far away—I saw George Harding. He was standing at the head of the steps facing me. He put both hands into his pockets."

"Then what happened?" Nesline's attorney, Ford asked.

"He…I said…he started walking around the railing. I said, 'Please,' that's all I said, 'Please, Georgie.'

"He was coming towards me, a step or two. He called me an awful name and a stool pigeon, and said to me, 'I don't want your money, I want your—'. He had taken his hands out of his pockets and was grabbing his coat. He had his coat open, as if he were reaching for something. I believed that he was going to shoot me, to kill me. I had this pistol between my pants and my shirt, and I reached out and pulled the trigger. The gun went off."[41]

Upon cross-examination, Nesline admitted that he had carried the gun in the glove compartment of his car for several days before the shooting because "I was afraid of George."

"You carried it to shoot Harding, if necessary, didn't you?" District Attorney Arthur McLaughlin asked.

"The purpose was," Nesline responded, "that I was afraid of George and it would give me a little security in the dark. I never had any intention of shooting him. I always prayed that it would never happen."

"But you did shoot him, didn't you?" McLaughlin pressed the defendant.

"Yes sir," Nesline responded in a low voice, "I did."[42]

Nesline claimed that he had never handled a gun before. "I didn't even know it was loaded. I just took it for granted there would be a shot in the chamber." Courtroom observers probably wondered if Joe had overplayed his innocence with that claim.

When asked about his criminal past, Nesline admitted mistakes. But he told the court that he now was an officer in a newly-formed oil company, Wash-Tex, Inc. He said that the president of the company, ironically, was his defense attorney, Charles E. Ford. Nesline stated that he was the secretary of the company and had made trips to Texas to examine how the company's one oil well was coming along.[43]

In his summation to the jury, prosecutor McLaughlin asked the jury repeatedly: "Did someone want to get rid of Harding for a reason we don't know? Is there something more behind this case? Was it a gang killing? Nesline was killing Harding for some purpose. He had murder in his heart and murder on his mind," the prosecution declared.[44]

McLaughlin went on to criticize the two policemen who were in the club the night of the shooting. He tossed an open question regarding the policemen to all those in the courtroom: "Did they close their eyes to certain things that existed there?"

Assuming somehow it all was a "setup," many in Georgetown and Foggy Bottom speculated that Emmitt had the cops positioned there to witness Nesline's immediate explanation of the shooting.

Attorney Ford, in his final argument, countered McLauglin's assertions by insisting that "Mr. McLaughlin is trying to horrify you. When you are full of fear someone's going to kill you, you can't think straight. Mr. Nesline had no choice at that moment except to defend himself."[45]

Ford concluded: "Call him a gambler, call him what you will, but he is still entitled to the laws of God, of nature and of the District of Columbia."

After the prosecution and defense rested their cases, Judge Holtzoff addressed the jury: "We want to get this case to you this afternoon. Undoubtedly, some of you will want to attend the [General] MacArthur celebration tomorrow," referring to a celebration for the hero of World War II and the Korean War that was to be followed an address to Congress.[46]

The jury deliberated for less than an hour and a half, a quick decision, generally a good sign for the prosecution.

Nesline stood expressionless as the foreman read the jury's verdict: "Not guilty," to the charge of first-degree murder. The jury found Joe guilty only of carrying a deadly weapon. Judge Holtzoff did not hide his displeasure with the decision. He immediately gave Nesline the maximum sentence possible under the law, one year in jail, plus a $1,000 fine.[47]

After pronouncing the sentence, Judge Holtzoff had more to say. When Ford requested credit for his client for the three months he had spent in jail since the shooting, Judge Holfzoff exploded. Peering down from the bench through petite eyeglasses held in place only by means of a clip over the bridge of his nose, Holtzoff exclaimed:

"Neither as a matter of law nor justice is the defendant entitled to credit for time served. The court feels it would be improvident and unjust [to grant the request]. ... This defendant is a dangerous individual. He is a racketeer and professional gambler and has been for 15 years or more. He carried the most vicious weapon. For the protection of the community, this defendant should be deprived of liberty for as long as the law permits, which unfortunately, is not very long."

Charlie Ford's record of saving every defendant from the electric chair remained intact.

Many on the Georgetown streets felt Harding's demise had to be connected to the robbery that had occurred at Emmitt's house exactly one year before the shooting. That Joe Nesline would become Emmitt Warring's closest friend for the next twenty years only reinforced that theory in the minds of many.

ꕥ

Five months after the Nesline case was settled, it was Sidney Stromberg's turn to face the jury. He had been charged with two counts of robbery and two counts of assault with a deadly weapon in connection with the theft from Emmitt Warring's safe and the related pistol-whipping of Bill Cady in January 1950.

Judge Holtzoff was back on the bench, and District Attorney McLaughlin again led the prosecution. Stromberg was represented by Baltimore attorney, R. Palmer Ingram, who amused court-goers with his use of a British swagger stick, a short stick traditionally carried by a high-ranking military officer.

Emmitt was one of the first called by the prosecution. He stuck to his story that he could not identify the robbers. Emmitt claimed, "Someone put a towel over my head and told me not to move. I could see he was a big guy by his feet. They told me to go upstairs. There was one in back of me, and I could see the other's feet. They took me in the front bedroom and told me to open the safe. I told them I didn't know the combination."

Emmitt spoke in a slow, steady voice and did not look in Stromberg's direction. He continued, "somebody put his fingers on my throat and asked 'Are you going to open the safe?' I felt like I was fainting."[48]

Upon further questioning by McLaughlin, Emmitt said that he resisted the robbers for about a half an hour before opening the safe.

I am sure that Emmitt purposely did not reveal the real reason why he opened the safe. My father told me years later it was because Stromberg and his partners threatened to kill Bill Cady. Emmitt must have known that if it got out on the street that he'd acquiesced to their demands to save Bill Cady's life—it might endanger Cady in the future and make both of them subject to threats of kidnapping or extortion.

When it came to a cross-examination by the defense, Stromberg's attorney stood and announced, "No questions." Emmitt ended his short time in the witness chair and stepped away from the stand.

When Bill Cady took the stand, he had no qualms about pointing out Big Sid Stromberg. "They busted my head open and wouldn't even take me out of the puddle of blood I was lying in," said Cady.[49] Almost Stromberg's size but twenty-five years older, Emmitt's white-haired brother-in-law pointed to the defendant and said in a husky voice, "That guy right there. I'll never forget that face if I live to be a million. I could pick him out of a crowded ballpark." [50]

The next day the defense pulled a surprise move and called Stromberg himself to the witness stand. It did not prove to be wise. As the dark-haired defendant sat uneasily in his dark blue pinstripe suit, the prosecution almost immediately asked if he knew the "finger man" for the robbery at Emmitt Warring's house. Stromberg stated that if he knew the "finger man," he would turn him in, "even if it was my own mother."

The courtroom was quiet. McLaughlin paused for effect. Then he asked, "Did I understand you to say that you would turn in your own mother?"

"Why certainly, to get out of this I would," Stromberg said.

Although he tried to be polite and proper under questioning, periodically using phrases such as "Oh, pardon me, counselor," Stromberg would occasionally shout out his denials to McLaughlin.

"Did you know George Harding?" prosecutor McLaughlin asked

the witness. With the mention of Harding's name, the defendant became excited and nervous.

"No, sir—what was that name again? Oh, yeah, I met him," was Stromberg's answer.

"Did you ever 'case' the Warring home the day of the robbery or at any previous time?" McLaughlin asked Stromberg. "Isn't it a fact," McLaughlin pressed, "that from January 5 to January 9, you were casing Emmitt Warring's house?"

"No, that is not a fact," Stromberg screamed. "It's a lie, it's a despicable lie."

"Didn't you have someone in Washington who lived here and who was giving you information about gamblers or people in Washington who had money?" McLaughlin shouted at Stromberg.

"No sir," Stromberg responded forcefully.

Then McLaughlin shot a volley of rapid-fire questions at the defendant:

McLaughlin: Did you know George Harding?
Stromberg: Yeah, I met him.
McLaughlin: Weren't you getting information from Harding?
Stromberg: He never gave me no information about nothing.
McLaughlin: Did you ever visit his home?
Stromberg: Might have. I don't recall.
McLaughlin: Did you ever have dinner at his home?
Stromberg: I might have.
McLaughlin: Don't give me that "might have" stuff. You were friendly enough to eat with him. You know that George Harding used to live at Warring's house?
Stromberg: No.

Stromberg went on to deny Cady's pistol-whipping and Emmitt's choking. He further denied telling the Washington detectives about the robbery while he was in jail in Pennsylvania for manslaughter. After about an hour of McLaughlin's cross-examination, Stromberg suddenly announced, "My head is hurting today—you're giving me a headache."

After Stromberg was excused from the stand, McLaughlin then introduced two witnesses to identify a registration card for the Ambassador Hotel in Washington, showing that Stromberg registered there under the name of Sidney Max on January 5, 1950, and checked out on January 9, a half-hour before the robbery.

When the jury convened to weigh Big Sid's fate, it took the six men and six women less than ninety minutes to find the "hulking hoodlum" guilty on two counts of robbery and one count of assault with a deadly weapon. Three weeks later, Judge Holtzoff sentenced Stromberg to ten to thirty years in prison for his role in the Warring robbery.[51]

CHAPTER EIGHTEEN

Congress Investigates

During 1949, a number of newspapers and national magazines ran sensational articles about organized crime. Many of these articles exposed how sophisticated criminals had corrupted the political process. On January 5, 1950, Tennessee Senator Estes Kefauver introduced a resolution allowing the Senate to investigate organized crime. A Senate Special Committee held fourteen hearings across the United States during the latter half of 1950 and early in 1951, subpoenaing mobsters such as Frank Costello, Mickey Cohen, Jake "Greasy Thumb" Guzik, Meyer Lansky, and Paul "The Waiter" Ricca. The televised hearings coincided with the introduction of television sets into most American homes. Frank Costello famously—and successfully—demanded that only his hands be shown on camera.[1]

Although the Senate Special Committee did not specifically address crime in Washington DC, the District did not escape Congressional scrutiny and investigation.

Ever since the beginning of the country, the United States Congress has held jurisdiction over the District, as granted by the Constitution. In 1950, the House of Representatives exercised its oversight powers and created a special committee to investigate crime in the District.

The committee chairman was Representative James C. Davis, a Democrat from Georgia, who would later make a name for himself as a staunch states' rights advocate and a signer of the "Southern Manifesto," which expressed opposition to integration.[2] Other committee members were Olin E. "Tiger" Teague, Democrat from Texas; Howard Smith, Democrat from Virginia; and Sidney Simpson, Republican from Illinois. The committee's legal counsel was Hyman I. Fischbach, a lawyer brought in from New York to lead the investigation.[3]

Part of the committee's investigation focused on Robert J. Barrett, the District's chief of police from 1947 to 1951. Barrett was known as a "cop's cop."[4] Upon his retirement from the force, the *Evening Star* once described him as "bullet-scarred and fist-battered, the rough and ready Irishman fought his way up through the ranks to see his beloved department achieve an outstanding crime solution record under his command."[5] During his tenure as chief, police department morale was said to be high despite the low pay. (The starting salary: $3,077). Barrett was a great believer in relying on the "beat cop" to prevent street crime. To his credit, he improved the communication system in the department and hired a record number of women to "release able men for beat duty."[6]

Barrett had received over one hundred commendations as an officer, though his record was tainted by charges of mistreating violent crime suspects. "Battling Bob" boasted that he had "arrested as many murderers as anybody who has ever been on the police force."[7] A newspaper article described Barrett as "forthright, fiercely loyal, antagonistic and grudge-bearing," and said he "thrives on criticism."

However, there were charges that he looked the other way, and profited by it, when it came to gambling. Barrett countered by citing the assistance gamblers often provided in solving violent crimes.

In January 1950, the counsel for the House District Crime Investigating Committee, Hyman I. Fischbach, advised Barrett that the committee wanted to know why there had been only one gambling arrest in the Third and Seventh Precincts combined during fiscal year 1949. The Third Precinct covered Foggy Bottom to the White House, and the Seventh Precinct encompassed Georgetown. These were the precincts, of course, where the Warring operation was located.[8]

Even before the committee could call their first witness, the former captain of the Third Precinct, Anthony Richitt, publicly accused Barrett of having ties with Emmitt Warring. Richitt claimed there was a hidden reason why he'd been recently transferred from the prestigious Third Precinct (where he'd accompanied President Harry Truman on his well-known morning walks around the White House grounds and the surrounding neighborhood) to the quiet, residential Eighth Precinct in upper northwest Washington. Though the official reason was that Richitt was disrespectful to his supervisors and had failed to carry out orders,

Richitt called a press conference at his home and claimed the real reason for his transfer was that he'd been unwilling to accept the arrangements Barrett was making with Emmitt Warring regarding gambling in the Third Precinct. Richitt also insisted that his efforts to crack down on gambling operations in the precinct were being frustrated by the lack of cooperation from Lieutenant Roy Blick, the head of the vice squad, which was supposed to initiate raids of gambling establishments.[9]

In addition, Richitt claimed that Emmitt telephoned him on January 31, 1950, and asked if he would meet him at Pete Dailey's. Richitt refused but directed Emmitt to come by the Third Precinct if Emmitt needed to talk to him. During the press conference, Richitt detailed how Emmitt said that Chief Barrett had advised him that the congressional committee was concerned about the lack of gambling arrests in the Third and Seventh Precincts. Richett claimed that Emmitt suggested he could help Richett in addressing the committee's concern about the lack of arrests in his precinct. In addition, Richitt said, he had refused Emmitt's offer to "take care of him."

Barrett was the first witness called by the committee. He denied calling Emmitt Warring to tell him about the committee's curiosity regarding the lack of gambling arrests in the Third and Seventh Precincts. He stated that on the day in question, January 31, 1950, he had given a speech in Richmond, Virginia at noon and did not return to the District until 10:00 p.m.

Richitt was the second witness, and he repeated the gist of what he'd said in his press conference and later told to Fischbach.

The next witness was Emmitt Warring. H. Clifford Allder, Charles E. Ford's junior partner and also a Georgetown Law School graduate, was by Emmitt's side at the committee hearing. Allder would have a sixty-year career as a criminal attorney and would eventually serve as the executor of Emmitt's estate.

Fischbach opened his questioning by asking the witness, "What is your business or occupation, Mr. Warring?"[10]

Emmitt immediately conferred with his attorney, H. Clifford Allder, and after a moment, replied," I refuse to answer that question on the grounds that I may tend to incriminate myself."

"In what respect?" Fischbach shot back.

Allder immediately objected to Fischbach's question, and Davis, the committee chairman, ruled that Emmitt did not have to answer.

Emmitt was then asked how long he had known Captain Richitt. Emmitt replied that he had known the captain for "two or three years." He also admitted to Fischbach that he had called Richitt but did not remember the exact date.

Fischbach asked Emmitt if he had given any indication that he "would take care of" Richitt.

"I positively did not say I wanted to take care of him," Emmitt replied.

"Have you ever given any money to anyone on the police force?" Fischbach then asked.

"No, sir."

"Has anyone on your behalf ever given money to anyone on the police force?"

Emmitt paused briefly, glanced at Allder, and then said, "No."

Fortunately for Emmitt, the committee was unaware that an Internal Revenue agent had testified in 1939 that Emmitt admitted to incurring expenses for "police protection."

Emmitt told the committee that he first learned of the committee's interest in the lack of gambling arrests in the Third and Seventh Precincts from the captain of the Seventh Precinct, Beverly Beach. Beach would later deny sharing that information with Emmitt.

In hindsight, Emmitt was amazingly glib about his contacts with police officials. His attorneys seemed to be preoccupied with steering Emmitt clear of any "contempt of Congress" charges if the committee felt he was trying to thwart the investigation. (Later in March, New York mob bosses' defense attorneys would counsel their clients during the Senate Crime Committee hearings to take the Fifth Amendment against self-incrimination in answering almost all questions.)

Fischbach and the committee members probably felt this entire investigation—with its cast of bickering cops and a gambling kingpin who seemed to be aligned with the police department to stave off embarrassing questions from the committee—was surreal. One can imagine the faces of the congressmen as they learned of Emmitt's admitted willingness to help his "friends" on the police department answer the committee questions

In the end, the committee decided not to get involved in internal operations of the police department but felt that further exploration into gambling in the District was called for. Committee Chairman Davis said, "With the right sort of investigation, we would be able to explain where Emmitt Warring got his information about the committee and a lot of other things we do not know now."[11]

ഗ

When the committee reconvened six months later, their focus was on the invisible workings of gambling kingpins, their lawyers, and the bail bondsmen who seemed to have frustrated the government's efforts to enforce the District's gambling laws. After a string of lawyers, gamblers, and bondsmen testified, the findings were that lawyers were not sure which clients they had represented, gamblers were unable to state who paid their legal fees, and at least one bondsman could not tell who had paid him for his services.

Ben Bradlee of the *Washington Post*, who would go on to become the paper's executive editor, reported, "Committee members shook their heads in dismay while the audience smiled as Committee Counsel Hyman I. Fischbach tried to pin down each witness."[12]

One of the first witnesses was Samuel Green, a convicted numbers writer. Fischbach opened his line of questioning by asking,

"You've been in the numbers game since about 1947, haven't you?"

"Yes, sir."

"Who did you turn in to?"

"We don't know the man. They always keep that man hidden from me. We just put the money in the bag with the [numbers] slips and leave it in a car on the corner."

Fischbach then reminded Green of his arrest earlier in the year. Bondsman Meyer Weinstein had arrived to bail him out.

"Did you know the bondsman before?" Fischbach inquired.

"No, sir."

"Did you pay for any bond?"

"No, sir."

"Did the bondsman ask you to pay him?"

"No, sir."

After Green identified James Hughes as his attorney in the case, Fischbach asked him how he had met his lawyer.

"He came up to me in court and said, 'Are you Green?' and I said 'yes,' and he said, 'I'm your lawyer,'" Green testified.

"Did you know him before?" Fischbach asked Green.

"No, sir."

"Did your lawyer ask you to pay him?"

"No, sir."

Bondsman Meyer Weinstein was then called. He testified that his records showed that he had written the bond for Green and had been paid $37.

"Who paid you the premium?" Fischbach asked Weinstein.

"I haven't got the vaguest idea," Weinstein replied.[13]

Earlier in the day, attorney Charles E. Ford had been called by the committee as a witness. He acknowledged that Emmitt Warring, "a fair and honest gambler," was a client of his. He said that he knew no Warring employees but admitted knowing two Warring "associates." Upon a request from the committee to reveal the "associates'" names, Ford refused. Ford said that he was reluctant to name these men because "the general public has no idea that they are gamblers." He claimed that the confidentiality of the attorney/client relationship prevented him from revealing their names.[14]

It is evident that these "associates" would not have welcomed the publicity that would come if their names had been broadcast at the investigative hearings. But that publicity would pale in comparison to the publicity Emmitt Warring was about to receive.

CHAPTER NINETEEN

"To Flood with Publicity"

After the second round of hearings concluded, the House District Crime Investigating Committee published its report declaring the crime situation in the nation's capital one of "shocking enormity." The report claimed that gamblers led a "charmed existence" in Washington because of the "ineptness" of the police and other law enforcement agencies. It labeled after-hours clubs a "breeding place of crime."[1]

The heart of the report, submitted to the House of Representatives by Chairman Davis, declared the following:

> Granting the difficulty of securing evidence necessary for successful prosecution, it would appear that little, if anything, has been done to scratch the surface. This probably explains in large part why it is that as notorious a character as the alleged 'fair and honest' gambler [Warring] who, by his own admission, for 20 years had followed no business about which he could testify without incriminating himself, can circulate freely, not alone without fear of the police, but also mentally disposed to friendship with important police officials.[2]

If attracting the interest of Congress wasn't enough publicity, actor and radio commentator Robert Montgomery, the father of future *Bewitched* TV star Elizabeth Montgomery, suddenly shared his view of the District's crime scene with his national radio audience. Montgomery, star of the original *Mr. and Mrs. Smith* and *Here Comes Mr. Jordan* films, was a Republican supporter and used his radio broadcast to label Washington DC as "a mecca for criminal racketeers." During his weekly show, the Hollywood actor and director asked why Emmitt Warring had not been arrested. Seemingly in response to Montgomery's charges, Chief Barrett offered a promotion to any policeman who could make a good gambling case against Emmitt. But Barrett observed that Emmitt Warring was "very, very cautious."[3]

In mid-September 1951, the *Washington Post* ran a week-long series on the "Mystery Man of Washington's Numbers Racket." The paper's ads promised to "turn the spotlight on the life of Washington's mysterious gambler—Emmitt Warring—a man who has led a charmed life!" The *Post* further urged its subscribers to "read about Emmitt Warring—who's been called everything from a philanthropic Robin Hood to a gangland Machiavelli!"

Each daily chapter of the week-long series was accompanied by an "Editor's Note" advising the reader of the following:

> This is the story of a man of importance and influence in Washington. He is a financial success in a multi-million dollar local business; a contributor to many worthy causes; the employer of hundreds of workers; the first name intimate of policemen, lawyers and leading citizens. His illegal numbers game is patronized daily by tens of thousands.
>
> The purpose of these articles is not to smear with ignominy nor gild with glamour, but to flood with publicity. He has been a hidden power and a secret force in this city. Citizens need to know those who, for good or evil, influence their daily lives.[4]

The lead reporter for the series was the *Post's* legendary police reporter, Alfred E. Lewis, who had served as the paper's primary crime reporter since 1935. Only a stint as a decorated combat correspondent in World War II interrupted his time at the *Post* until his retirement in 1985. Affectionately known as "Uncle Al" by those on the paper and in the police force, he tutored young reporters, once advising a young Ben Bradlee that "being a nice guy never interfered with the job." He bonded with policemen, going as far as to almost dress like one with his "white socks, and blue regulation Metropolitan Police sweater buttoned at the bottom over a Star-of-David buckle." He would later help Carl Bernstein and Bob Woodward break the story of the Watergate break-in in 1972. The lengthy September 1951 series on Emmitt Warring would win Lewis and his co-writer, Richard Morris, the annual grand prize award by the Washington Newspaper Guild.[5]

Although he was tight with the police, Lewis also had a way of gaining the trust of those on the other side of the law. Emmitt, who liked and respected Lewis, knew that Lewis would not try to do a "hatchet-job" on his character so allowed him to ask non-incriminating questions during an interview. Yes, Lewis would chronicle Emmitt's criminal past, but he would also be willing to show the real man who was the object of those allegations and charges.

Although the first chapter of the series detailed Emmitt's criminal past and holdings of cash and real estate, the second delved into the man behind the headlines:

The "Little Man" as he is called behind his back, has hundreds of friends in his bailiwick … yet is a lonely bachelor.

He drives a hard bargain. Yet he is a "soft touch."

He is a wealthy man. Yet he has few pleasures.

He is known to every policeman in Washington. Yet he eludes their grasp as if he were a wraith [a visible spirit].[6]

Emmitt opened up to Lewis so the reporter could share the details of his daily life with the Post's readers. They learned what time Emmitt woke up every day (10:00 a.m.) and what time he went to bed (1:00 a.m.), learned that he usually just had coffee for breakfast but ate his largest meal of the day around 3:00 p.m. Among other details of Emmitt's life, readers learned:

·He occasionally had a beer at home, shunning hard liquor. ("The smell of it makes me sick now.")

·He smoked moderately (Chesterfield's—and a few years later, he would quit altogether because of bouts with emphysema).

·He dressed conservatively in dark suits with a "flash of color being provided by his neckwear."

·He cared deeply for his pets and had recently purchased a German shepherd, Mark, to replace his beloved Great Dane, Duke, who had passed away. (Pictures of both dogs were featured in the articles.)

·He was generous to charities. Emmitt once bought a hundred books of raffle tickets at $5 apiece from a neighborhood boy. He contributed to a range of charities including the Little Sisters of the Poor, St. Ann's Orphanage, Kesher Israel (a Georgetown synagogue), and various youth groups.[7]

❧

The chapter even offered a favorable reference from Roy E. Blick, the only police official ever to place a formal charge of gambling against Emmitt Warring. Blick said that Emmitt was "a quiet, mild-mannered man, not like the other hoodlums and gamblers you pick up."

"He wasn't tough and didn't try to act tough. He spoke with respect and was gentlemanly," remarked Blick on Emmitt's demeanor when the policeman locked him up. The Warring brothers had always been keenly aware that hostility directed at the police was stupid and counter-productive.

But not all of the *Post's* readers were impressed. Ruth H. Lane from Arlington, Virginia, wrote a one-sentence letter to the editor facetiously pointing out that "you forgot to mention what deodorant Emmitt uses." Mrs. Thomas Pendleton from Bethesda, Maryland, wondered why the newsboys who "get up with the chickens" every morning to deliver the paper through all kinds of weather were not glamorized like this gambler.[8]

During the week that the series ran in the *Post*, readers were also reminded—or first learned—of the exploits of Emmitt and his brothers, Rags and Leo, from Prohibition to 1951. The series chronicled the shootings, arrests, trials, prison time, and recent congressional hearings that featured the Warring name.

One of the chapters concluded with a question that someone had once directed at Emmitt: "What accounted for his 'charmed life?'"

"They can't hang anything on you when they haven't got anything," was Emmitt's matter-of-fact response.

But the end of the daily chapters of the Post's expose on Emmitt did not end the publicity. Emmitt's next turn in the spotlight would be through the newest medium—television.

CHAPTER TWENTY

From the Bottom to the Hill

The Senate Crime Committee headed by Senator Estes Kefauver concluded its investigations in the spring of 1951. Many felt it had been little more than a theatrical show. The hearings were successful in publicizing the influence of crime in the major cities, but the televised show was closing because "I refuse to answer on the grounds that it might tend to incriminate me" was its most repeated line.[1]

Senator Kefauver, a Democrat, bowed out and resumed working on his presidential aspirations. Senate Republicans pushed for more hearings because of the political damage the investigations seemed to have on the Democratic machines that ran most big cities. In fact, many observers felt that the investigations of police scandals in Chicago led to Republican Everett Dirksen's upset victory over Senate Democratic Majority Leader Scott Lucas. Dirksen went on to have an illustrious career in the Senate.

In addition, the Republicans, led by Robert A. Taft of Ohio, urged a Senate probe of crime in the District.[2] The *Washington Post* editorial board also pushed for an investigation of DC crime:

> Especially because Washington is the home of Congress, the Kefauver Committee ought to take extra pains to expose unsavory conditions in this area and find out any links there are between Washington and the national crime pattern.[3]

But the Senate's answer was to create an entirely new investigative committee to look into crime in the District and to pick up where the previous House investigation had ended. The Senate's District Crime

Committee was chaired by Matthew M. Neely, a Democrat from West Virginia, who was the only West Virginian ever to serve in both houses of the Congress and as governor of West Virginia.

The leading Republican on the committee was Herman Welker from Idaho. He was known as the politician who advised the Washington Senators to sign a young player in his hometown by the name of Harmon Killebrew. (Killebrew went on to become a Hall of Fame player.)

The rest of Welker's legacy was not so commendable. He became a staunch defender of Wisconsin Republican Joe McCarthy and McCarthy's controversial tactics in pursuing those in government he thought were communists or homosexuals.[4]

Welker also was a party to one of the ugliest episodes in American politics. It involved a senator who was also a member of the District Crime Committee, Lester C. Hunt. Welker collaborated with Joe McCarthy to attempt to pressure Hunt, a Democrat from Wyoming, to give up his Senate seat. The pressure started in 1953 when Welker became aware that Hunt's twenty-year-old son had been arrested for soliciting prostitution from a male undercover police officer in Lafayette Square across the street from the White House. Welker warned Hunt that if he did not immediately retire or announce he would not seek re-election in 1954, they would ensure that his son was prosecuted and would publicize the arrest. Hunt would not be moved to vacate his Senate seat. His son was prosecuted, and the affair found its way into the newspapers. The pressure, combined with health problems, was eventually too much for the elder Hunt. In June 1954, he shot and killed himself at his desk in the Senate office building.[5]

When it came time to select the chief counsel and lead investigator, the Senate District Crime Committee reached up to New York City to pluck Arnold Bauman, who had learned racket-busting under New York prosecutor Thomas E. Dewey.[6] He worked with Dewey on the vice-ring case that led to Charles "Lucky" Luciano's deportation to Italy. A tall, thin pipe-smoker, Bauman was given the Senate offices of the disbanded Kefauver Crime Committee in the fall of 1951.[7] When asked by a reporter about the possibility of looking into the activities of Emmitt Warring, Bauman responded, "I'll go after anybody if the evidence leads in that direction—anybody!"

The committee first requested that DC police officers, including the chief of police, complete a twenty-seven-page questionnaire on their asset holdings. Chief Barrett attempted to fight the "request" by hiring Charlie Ford, the popular lawyer of both police and racketeers (including Emmitt Warring). But Barrett acquiesced when his boss, District Police Commissioner John Russell Young, ordered Barrett and the rest of the police force to complete the questionnaire.[8] Shortly after losing his fight against the form, Barrett retired from the police force.

In addition to police officials, the committee subpoenaed those on the list of "usual suspects" in the District crime world including Emmitt Warring, Abe Plisco (alias "Jewboy Dietz"), Sam "Pickle King" Beard, Roger "Whitetop" Simkins and Alfred "Puddinhead" Jones.[9]

When the hearings began in mid-January 1952, the four Washington television stations cancelled their regular programming in order to cover them. But the television cameras were turned off on the first day of the hearings after the committee agreed to a request by the first witness, former Chief of Police Barrett, who had resigned just a few months earlier. With help from his attorney, Charles E. Ford, Barrett successfully persuaded the committee that the "confusion" created by the cameras would have the effect of subjecting him to the "third degree" and might cause him to misstate facts.[10] The balding, bespectacled Barrett looked awkward in public without his police uniform, which had become part of his public persona. Puffing on one cigarette after another, Barrett defended his record as chief. He provided ambiguous answers to pointed questions about past transfers of police captains. He also had no plausible answers to the frequent drop in gambling arrests after the new captains were inserted in the respective precincts. Senators Neely and Welker reprimanded Barrett several times for not answering with a simple "yes" or "no" and for his habit of consulting with his attorney before answering many questions. He admitted knowing reputed gamblers such as Emmitt Warring and Whitetop Simkins for years but denied having any social relationship with them.

Committee Chairman Neely from West Virginia pressed the former police chief to explain how gambling had apparently thrived in the District over the last few years.

"Everyone who knows anything about this situation," said the senator, "knows that gambling on such a scale as exists in Washington cannot possibly happen unless the police officers are crooked and are in league with the gamblers and have knowledge of their operations."

"That could happen anywhere, even in West Virginia," retorted Barrett. "There has been gambling since the beginning of man. They even gambled over Christ's clothing."

"We won't hold you responsible for that," the senator jokingly responded. [11]

When it came time for Emmitt to testify, Charlie Ford resumed his spot in the counselor's chair. Ford attempted to have the cameras turned off again, but the committee refused his request. Emmitt did not seem bothered by the television lights. He looked relaxed and smiled freely before the questioning began and the television lights and cameras went to work. He had come a long way—from humble beginnings driving a mule team in Foggy Bottom to the television lights of Capitol Hill. But Emmitt changed his demeanor once the questioning began. As in most public appearances, Emmitt was impeccably dressed. That day he wore a modest grey suit with a white shirt and a grey-and-plum-striped tie. The *Washington Post* described Emmitt as responding to the questions "with a deadpan expression."[12]

Emmitt was willing to answer the first few questions regarding where he lived and when he moved into his house on Macomb Street. But when special prosecutor Arnold Bauman asked how much he had paid for the house and if he had paid cash for it, Emmitt responded, "I would like to decline to answer on the ground that it may tend to incriminate me because of an income tax case in court."[13]

Bauman then presented a series of questions that Emmitt also refused to answer:

- Is the nature of the [Internal Revenue] matter pending against you a criminal proceeding?
- Have you been indicted for any income tax evasion?
- Do you own property at 3935 Massachusetts Avenue NW in the name of Esther Cady?
- Who is Esther Cady? (Emmitt did answer this question, saying that Esther was his sister.)
- I believe that you have stated many times that you own property in Colonial Beach, Virginia. Do you own four lots there? Did you pay for that property in cash?
- Have you ever been in 4518 Brewer Place NW [later renamed Q Place]? Is that owned by your brother, known as Rags Warring? Did you contribute any cash toward purchase of that house?

Of course, Charlie and other family members stayed far away from the hearings for fear they would be recognized by the press and subsequently questioned by the committee. He was home watching on television when his name came up in a question about the purchase of his home.

Bauman asked similar questions regarding properties in Fairfax, Virginia, that the committee suspected Emmitt owned. Emmitt declined to answer any of them.

Bauman then asked whether Emmitt knew Chief Barrett. After Emmitt counseled with Charlie Ford, he was ready to answer.

"Yes, sir. I do know of Major Barrett," answered Emmitt.

"I didn't ask you if you knew of Major Barrett," Bauman quickly corrected the witness. "I asked you if you knew Major Barrett."

Emmitt curtly replied, "Yes, sir."

Bauman then asked if he knew the former chief "personally."

"I decline to answer that question, sir," responded Emmitt.

"Have you ever given Major Barrett a gift of over $500 in value?" quizzed Bauman.

"I decline to answer that question, sir," answered Emmitt.

At that point, committee member and former state attorney general Senator John Pastore (Democrat – Rhode Island) interrupted.

"On what grounds?" Pastore asked Emmitt.

"On the grounds that I am in fear I may tend to incriminate myself. The first part of the question may lead to other questions," Emmitt offered in reply, apparently voicing the explanation given to him by his attorney.

Bauman then questioned Emmitt about the unlikely coincidence that both Emmitt and Chief Barrett had summer homes not far from each other at Colonial Beach. Emmitt refused to answer Bauman's question as to whether he had ever seen the chief on the beach. Bauman then became facetious in his questioning.

"Have you ever seen the police chief swimming at one end of the beach while you were swimming at the other end of the beach?" the prosecutor wanted to know.

Of course, Emmitt refused to answer. Although this question appeared to be benign, Emmitt's refusal to answer it laid the foundation for a contempt of Congress charge against him.

In addition, Bauman asked Emmitt about his apparent inside knowledge of the workings of the police department.

"Now, Mr. Warring, it has come to the attention of the committee that on one certain occasion, you had a certain clairvoyance about certain transfers that were not made for about two weeks after you predicted their coming about?

Emmitt at first said he could not understand the question, so Bauman said it involved Emmitt's apparent knowledge of the impending transfer of three police captains to different precincts. When Emmitt understood what Bauman was driving at, he refused to answer.

Clearly, the committee had information that provided a foundation for all of the questions that the counsel was directing at Emmitt. But Emmitt and his counsel decided to risk a contempt of Congress charge rather than answer their questions.

In total, Emmitt took the Fifth Amendment in reply to approximately 200 questions. At the end of the questioning, Senator Welker could no longer contain himself. As an attorney, he said, he couldn't see how answering some of the questions could incriminate the witness. He contended that Emmitt did not have the legal right "to sit there hour after hour and decline to answer those questions."[14] He warned Emmitt that he was in contempt of Congress for not answering questions about such things as real estate holdings, which were a matter of the public record.

Emmitt who had only an eighth-grade education attempted to school the legally-trained senator. He said the questions would be all right if they didn't lead to others, but he was certain they would. There would be links—"I think it would be a good link, sir, not a weak link," Emmitt explained to Welker.[15]

ෆ

Emmitt surely had frustrated the senators on the committee with his lack of answers. But he would not be the only witness to do so. The "sick notes" had started to come in from doctors even before the senators had an opportunity to question any of the reputed gamblers.

Abe Plisco, alias Jewboy Dietz, timed cataract surgery to coincide with the hearings. Confined to the Episcopal Eye, Ear and Throat Hospital when the hearings convened, the reputed gambler sent a letter to the committee from his doctor that said the success of the operation would be jeopardized if Plisco were asked to appear.[16]

Sam Beard had his attorney, Denny Hughes, submitted a letter from Beard's doctor stating that Big Sam was suffering from hypertension (high blood pressure) and could not be a witness at that time.

One of the men subpoenaed who did appear was Roger Whitetop Simkins. He was the biggest of the African American numbers backers in DC and arguably one of the most well-known people in the city among both black and whites.[17] Upon his death the *Washington Post* noted he was regarded as a "dignified gentleman even by police." In 1973 when the District contemplated legalizing a numbers game, a DC city councilman suggested they should "get 'Whitetop' Simkins to design it for them." Simkins was a large man with sleepy, dark-circled eyes and a full head of white hair that served as the basis for his moniker. Simkins' territory started around the Capitol Building and ran uptown, including the busy Government Printing Office. I believe that among his fellow numbers backers in Washington during that time, Whitetop Simkins was Emmitt's best friend. When Simkins died suddenly in 1973, Emmitt expressed as much sorrow over someone's death as I had ever seen.

Room 457 of the Senate Office Building was packed as Simkins strode to the witness stand before the committee dressed in an expensive blue suit. He unbuttoned his vest and "slouched into his seat in a leisurely manner, appearing quite unconcerned."[18] Simkins nursed a cigarette and gave the committee a deadpan expression as he was questioned by lead investigator Arnold Bauman.

"What is your business occupation?" asked Bauman.

"I refuse to answer on the grounds that may incriminate me," replied Simkins.

"Have you ever been described as a speculator?" Bauman asked. But Simkins gave the same reply. Bauman thought he would try a less threatening question.

"Have you ever been described as 'Whitetop?'"

Simkins again declined to answer but after some prodding by Senator Welker and a short conference with his lawyers, Simkins confessed,"they call me 'Whitetop' sometimes, yes."

There was one light moment in the proceeding. At one point Bauman started a question with "Have you ever been aware over the years—" Simkins interrupted Bauman with the "I refuse to answer—" in his same monotonous tone before the investigator could finish the question.

If the television audience was bored by Simkins' limited responses, they were about to be entertained by the next witness, a woman who had worked for five years in Whitetop's numbers office, Mrs. Sarah "Dimples" Hall. Wearing a mink-trimmed Persian lamb coat, the chestnut-haired African American took her place in the witness chair. She was a "star" witnesses and the committee was anxious to hear from her. Dimples claimed that she not only worked for Simkins, but that she was his girlfriend and had allowed her dining room to act as the office for his operation from 1940 to 1945.[19]

Hall also testified that the police had never raided her home at 2056 Georgia Avenue during the five years it had served as headquarters for Simkins' operations. Even more damning to Simkins and the District police, Dimples testified that certain police officers would visit her home after the day's work was done. She also named other colorful characters who were involved in the Georgia Avenue numbers game, including Jack the Bear, Sporty Johnson, Lefty Winston, Piggy Leake, Odessa Madre, and Sunshine Boldware.

When Dimples was asked why she left Simkins' employment, she looked slightly startled by the question. She didn't leave, she said; "he left." Before she left the witness stand, she reluctantly admitted she had heard Simkins speak of paying for "protection" and also revealed to the committee the term that Simkins used in referring to those payments—"Ice."

The senators also received testimony from a police captain that Whitetop had been a small fry in the gambling world until Robert J. Barrett became chief of police.[20] Whitetop may well have parlayed his friendship with Emmitt Warring and found cover under the same umbrella of protection that seemed to shield Emmitt from police harassment and prosecution.

The political cartoonist at the *Evening Star* used the revelations about protection payments as the basis of a front-page drawing depicting an individual in colonial dress with "DC" on his coat holding a newspaper announcing "Crime Committee Told Gamblers Buy Police Protection." The thought attributed to the figure in the cartoon read "... And All The Time I Thought I Was Th' One Who Was Paying For Police Protection!"[21]

Because many of those called to testify were African American, many of the black-owned newspapers in the country also covered the hearing, including the *Afro-American* and the *Chicago Defender*. A writer for the *Afro-American*, Louis Lautier, accused the committee of digging more vigorously into the background of "colored" gamblers than they had into those of white operators such as Emmitt Warring, Sam Beard and Jewboy Dietz. He added in his column that "White gamblers have the same type of organization, but none of their henchmen and girlfriends have been dragged before the Senate committee."[22]

By the end of the hearings, the head of the District's anti-gambling squad tried to polish the department's image by announcing that his "undercover men have found that Emmitt Warring, Sam Beard and Roger 'Whitetop' Simkins have 'gone out of business.'" However, he admitted that the organization run by Jewboy Dietz remained in business but was reduced significantly.[23]

When it came to Emmitt, this probably was the truth. With such high-profile attention and his friend, Chief of Police Barrett now retired, it was time to get out of the numbers business.

In the month following the hearings, the committee made good on its threat and cited Emmitt Warring and Roger Whitetop Simkins with contempt of Congress.[24]

In July 1952, Emmitt found himself again in front of US District Judge Bolitha J. Laws, who had presided over the Warrings' income tax cases and Emmitt's jury-tampering case over thirteen years before. This time he was before the judge to enter a "not guilty" plea on the charge of contempt of Congress. Whitetop Simkins did the same when it came to his turn to enter a plea.[25]

In October, Judge Edward M. Curran dismissed the eleven-count indictment against Emmitt Warring for failing to answer certain questions posed by the committee. The judge explained in his ruling that "while the questions may have seemed innocent enough in themselves, they may have been proved to be links in 'a chain of evidence' which might have led to Federal prosecution of Warring on other charges."[26] It seems ironic that Judge Curran used the same term, "links," that Emmitt had used in defending his right not to answer certain questions posed by the Senate committee. The judge added that a witness cannot be required to state why he fears prosecution as a result of the answers he may give. Four days later, all of the contempt charges against Whitetop Simkins were also dismissed.

In the end, the committee's hearing proved, to borrow from Shakespeare, to be full of sound and fury signifying nothing.

CHAPTER TWENTY-ONE

Opening the Box

The contents of a safe deposit box are usually considered confidential, but the contents of the box that Emmitt Warring maintained at the Hamilton National Bank would forever be publicly associated with him.

When Internal Revenue agent Samuel Ford visited Emmitt on the morning of Friday, July 2, 1948, Emmitt was not aware of how his image with the Bureau and the public was about to change. At the meeting in Emmitt's home, Emmitt produced "little black books" that he claimed supported his income tax returns. Agent Ford (no relation to Emmitt's lawyer), asked Emmitt to accompany him and his partner to the Hamilton National Bank in downtown Washington to examine the contents of a safe deposit box maintained under the names of Emmitt and Charles Warring. Emmitt immediately called his attorney, Charles Ford, to ask if he should comply with the agent's request. Charlie Ford figured the agents would seek legal action to force Emmitt to open the box if he first refused. He advised Emmitt he would meet him at the bank, and then Emmitt could allow the agents to examine the contents of the box.

When the agents examined the contents, they found 240 $1,000 bills and one $10,000 bill. Agent Ford and his partner initially miscounted the contents of the box to be in the amount of $241,000. Proud of his possession of the $10,000 bill, Emmitt told the agents to "take another look at the bill on the bottom of the pile." When they did, the agents found they had initially counted the $10,000 bill as a $1,000 bill.[1]

After the correction, Emmitt immediately told the agents that the money represented income for several years with $110,754.68 from the first five months of 1948.[2] Since the tax filing deadline for that year was months away, Emmitt would have time to claim that income for 1948 and mitigate any claim that the presence of this money proved that Emmitt had committed fraud in his previous tax returns.

But the Internal Revenue Bureau smelled blood. The Bureau must have felt they had a piece of sensational evidence that would impress any jury. They picked one tax year to focus on—1947. That year Emmitt had reported income of only $29,559 and paid taxes of $12,005, but the Internal Revenue Bureau calculated his real income to be over $100,000. The Internal Revenue Bureau requested the Department of Justice's Criminal Tax Division initiate the prosecution of Emmitt Warring for fraud related to his 1947 income tax return. Since tax returns of DC citizens were filed in Baltimore at the time, the Justice Department sent the case to US Attorney Bernard J. Flynn in Baltimore for presentation to the grand jury.[3]

But despite the attention of the Bureau of Internal Revenue, the Criminal Tax Division at the Department of Justice, and the US Attorney's Office in Baltimore, over two years passed with no action taken by the government since the opening of the safe deposit box.

But on March 13, 1951, the Department of Justice filed a $159,917.89 tax lien against Emmitt Warring. The Internal Revenue Bureau said the lien represented unpaid income taxes of $95,239 for 1947, plus $47,631 in assessed penalties and $17,048 in interest.[4] However, Emmitt still was not indicted for fraud.

Bettors, who were always looking for a sign of what three-digit number to play each day, were drawn to "159," the first three digits of the tax man's action against the "numbers kingpin." The story on the lien ran in the afternoon newspaper on March 13. And wouldn't you know it—those alert bettors were rewarded when the daily number for the day came up "159."[5]

In early June, Emmitt turned over $159,917.18 to the Internal Revenue solely in order to stop the accrual of more interest and penalties.

Despite the payment, Emmitt and his lawyer still contended that he owed the government nothing. However, the government begged to differ. The Internal Revenue Bureau claimed that Emmitt had revenue of $122,245 in 1947 that he had failed to claim on his tax return.[6]

In September Drew Pearson, the nation's most-read syndicated columnist—who was known for ruining reputations—told to his readers that the delay in prosecuting Emmitt Warring lay at the feet of the US

District Attorney in Baltimore, Bernard J. Flynn. In an article entitled "Warring Tax Prosecution Tabled," Pearson stated that the Criminal Tax Division in Washington had become restless waiting for Flynn to act, but still nothing had happened.[7] At one point, Flynn had sent the case back to the Tax Division for more evidence. He apparently felt that the existence of the safe deposit box in both Emmitt's and Charlie's name was insufficient evidence of tax fraud by Emmitt. Also, who could say that none, some, or all of the contents of the box represented income from years prior to the 1947 tax year?

In any case, Emmitt was not indicted for a year, despite the negative publicity during the Congressional hearings in 1951 and 1952 and a long-standing recommendation to prosecute him from the Internal Revenue Bureau. (The disclosure of the contents of the box was not made to the congressional committees investigating Emmitt.) Finally, on February 16, 1954, less than a month before Emmitt would have become immune from prosecution under the statute of limitations, the federal grand jury in Baltimore indicted him for attempting to evade $92,082 in income taxes.[8]

Emmitt's lawyers immediately attempted to have the case moved to the District of Columbia. They felt there was a better chance of getting a sympathetic jurist in DC who directly or indirectly had experienced the Warrings' goodwill over the years. In court they argued that their client was a resident of DC and had allegedly committed the crime there. However, Judge W. Calvin Chesnut turned down their request. He said that under the law, tax violations committed anywhere in the collection district could be tried in the judicial district where the collection headquarters was located.[9]

While waiting for the case to go to court, the Internal Revenue Bureau took additional measures by filing another tax lien against Emmitt's assets, claiming that he owed $11,858 on his 1951 taxes. Emmitt's lawyers filed a counteraction seeking an explanation for a check the Internal Revenue Bureau had sent to Emmitt for $12,601 dated June 15, 1951. Emmitt had not cashed it. Not pointing out the obvious mixed message of sending a taxpayer a check while indicting him for non-payment of taxes, the suit asked the court to instruct the Internal Revenue Bureau to give Emmitt credit on his 1951 taxes.[10]

 က

By 1954, George Cochran Doub had replaced Bernard Flynn as US Attorney in Baltimore. Doub was eager to bring Emmitt Warring to court. He had already successfully secured a conviction against DC gambler Sam Beard, and had seen the "Pickle King" off to serve another stretch in the Atlanta Penitentiary.

The government opened its case against Emmitt by making sure the jury understood how the numbers business operated. Doub traced the flow of bets through number writers, pickup men, and runners all the way to the "backer."[11] Perhaps because it was the Yuletide season, Doub drew a Christmas tree image on a board to outline the typical numbers network. At the bottom of the pyramid-like diagram were the numbers writers who initially took the daily bets. Above them were the pickup men and runners. Daub depicted and characterized all of the employees in the network as "ornaments" on the tree. He described how "each worker in the vineyard" received his commission. Emmitt, the "backer" or "banker" and ultimate beneficiary of the network, was perched at the top of the tree.

The prosecution described Emmitt as a man who disdained "any normal business methods in handling his affairs," who used cash for purchasing everything, including real estate, and who would never think of using a checking account. Of course, the prosecution kept coming back to all that cash in the safety deposit box.

Emmitt's lawyers countered that the government was making no attempt to establish that all of the money in the box was Emmitt's. How much belonged to the other legal box holder, Charles Warring? Charlie's name was only on the box in the event that Emmitt would suddenly die. It was a tricky act for Emmitt's lawyers to deflect part of Emmitt's income tax liability towards his brother. Charlie was married with two young boys, and Emmitt certainly did not want to shift the weight of the Internal Revenue Bureau and the Justice Department onto his brother. Of course, Charlie stayed away from the court proceedings just as he had avoided the televised US Senate hearings.

But on the third day of the trial, the prosecution presented a witness who put all of the weight of the ownership of the safety deposit box squarely back on Emmitt's shoulders: William R. Grady, a cashier at the Hamilton National Bank on the corner of 20th and Pennsylvania Avenue NW. Grady testified that he had known Emmitt for the last twenty-five to thirty years through his visits to the bank. In fact, they called each another by their first names. The cashier told the court that prior to 1947 Emmitt Warring had come to the bank an average of three times a week with a bag of coins and checks to be exchanged for $100 bills. He said the bag was about a foot wide and two feet deep. However, Grady said, starting in 1947 Emmitt began exchanging coins, checks, and now smaller bills for $1,000 bills. Once, early in 1948, Emmitt bought a $10,000 bill from the cashier.[12]

The next damning witness was also someone very familiar to Emmitt—his former lawyer, F. Jiggs Donohue, whom he had used in his last tax trial in 1939. The attorney testified that in 1939, while Emmitt sat in jail, he had instructed Donohue to go with Charlie and Leo to the home of their sister, Mrs. Esther Cady, to get $10,000 to pay the government as a "settlement" for Emmitt's tax liability. Evidently, Emmitt had transferred the money in his own safe to one in his sister's home before going to jail. Donohue said that he went to Esther's house with Charlie and Leo, who opened a wall safe and removed $10,000. After the safe was opened, he testified that either Charlie or Leo took $10,000 from the safe. He recalled that he was given ten $1,000 bills to settle Emmitt's tax liability. Donohue added that after the bills were withdrawn from the safe, there was still more money "than I have ever seen."[13]

Emmitt clearly did not appreciate that personal observation. During a recess, he sarcastically asked Donohue, "Did you get your witness fee yet?"

The government was clearly building its case around the theory that the evidence of cash in the box and cash expenditures proved that Emmitt's income for 1947 had to be more than he had stated on his income tax return. Prosecutor Doub asserted that some of the Emmitt's cash payments were to buy off the police. Doub pointed out to the jury of eight men and four women that Emmitt's numbers business flourished without interference by law enforcement.

"They corrupted the police, obviously," Doub declared. "It could not be done in any other way."[14]

But Judge W. Calvin Chesnut interrupted the prosecutor's comments regarding police corruption to observe, "I don't know that there is any evidence on that, Mr. Doub." At that point the US District Attorney offered to withdraw his statements. But of course, the jury had already heard his remarks.

Doub continued with his "soap box" oration, adding that "when you have a flagrant, deliberate, calculated tax evasion, it is not only an offense against the Government of the United States; it is an affront to those millions of conscientious taxpayers [who make complete returns]."

Doub then confidently concluded his argument. "We say the Government has presented to you a copper-riveted, cast-iron case that shouldn't take you 30 minutes to decide."

One of Emmitt's lawyers, G.C.A. Anderson from Baltimore, told the jurors to remember that the case before them involved a tax-evasion charge, not a gambling offense. Anderson argued that the prosecution had sought to prejudice the jury with Emmitt Warring's numbers game background. He concluded his portion of the defense's closing arguments by declaring, "If ever there was a case where you were asked to find anybody guilty predicated on an assumption, this is the case."[15]

Emmitt's Washington lawyer, Charles E. Ford, then reminded the jury that the safe deposit box was rented jointly in the names of Emmitt Warring and Charles Warring. Ford noted the government had not called Charles Warring as a witness, and that the prosecution had made no effort to determine what amount of the cash belonged to Emmitt, to Charles, or to anyone else.

Ford went on to declare:

"I, in closing on this eve of Christmas [December 20] would like to put to you this: Please don't hold him responsible for the human mistakes of the [Internal Revenue] agents."[16]

The man who some called the Cicero of Washington lawyers wrapped up the defense with some typically flamboyant oratory: "When the day comes for me to lay down my head, I hope that I have the comfort of a dying man that I never asked anyone to acquit or convict on a prejudice."[17]

But despite the pleas from Emmitt's attorneys, the jury came back with a guilty verdict after only three hours of deliberation. Emmitt was his usual impassive self as the foreman read the verdict. Before sentence was passed, the U.S. District Attorney recounted the facts of both Emmitt's 1939 income tax trial and his jury tampering trial. The prosecutor added that while serving time in Lorton, Emmitt had been a bookkeeper in the prison bakery—so he knew how to keep proper books.[18]

Judge Chesnut sentenced Emmitt to three years and a $10,000 fine—the same amount leveled against him in 1939. Of course, Emmitt had already paid the Bureau of Internal Revenue approximately $160,000 in taxes, penalties and interest related to his 1947 income tax return.[19]

ᔕ

Much of Foggy Bottom and Georgetown took the news of Emmitt's pending departure fatalistically. "There's Sadness in Foggy Bottom—Emmitt's Gone," was the byline in the *Washington Daily News*.[20] The article quoted a Georgetown priest as saying, "I thought when I saw the headlines, it's going to bring a lot of sadness to Foggy Bottom. Christmas isn't the same with Emmitt in the clink."

A friend of Emmitt's said, "He did more for charity for people of Georgetown than those prosecutors and judges ever did. He always gave to the Police Boys Club. They wouldn't take it if they knew where it came from, so he put it in the mails. He paid a $1,000 hospital bill for the wife of a guy in Georgetown that he didn't even know that didn't work for him or anything."

Another clergyman added, "I wouldn't condone [the illegal things attributed to the Warring gang] that are bad, but I wouldn't mind saying they're my friends. They aren't the damn frauds that don't drink, don't smoke, don't gamble, but wouldn't give you yesterday's headlines [newspapers]."

But the Georgetown priest put it another way. He spoke of the people who make "no errors, but no hits and no runs, either." He added, "I think it's the guys who get the big hits and big runs that the Big Umpire up there says will win the game."

Charlie Ford might have won that battle, but the odds were stacked against him in the one he waged to overturn Emmitt's conviction for the 1947 return. In front of the United States Court of Appeals, Ford challenged the way the government had computed Emmitt's tax liability based almost solely on the cash found in a safe deposit box."[21]

However, the judges decided that "Warring received an eminently fair trial under the guidance of a capable, experienced and dispassionate judge."[22]

Emmitt's last hope was the Supreme Court. But the justices declined to review the case.[23] All legal maneuvers had been exhausted. Emmitt was given ten days to get his affairs in order.

On October 28, 1955, shortly after his fiftieth birthday, Emmitt Warring presented himself to the federal authorities in Baltimore to begin his three-year sentence. Charlie drove him to the prison, accompanied by their sister Esther and her daughter, Tibby. The *Washington Post* later described Emmitt that morning as "calm and neat, clad in a blue suit and a light gray tie." Esther and Tibby cried as Emmitt tried to console them.[24] He would later be transferred to the federal prison in Lewisburg, Pennsylvania.

If Emmitt was listening to the radio in his cell during the 1956 Republican National Convention in San Francisco, he would have heard the attorney general of the United States cite the accomplishments of the Eisenhower Justice Department:

Well-known racketeers convicted of tax evasion included Frank Costello [New York], Benny Binion of Texas and Nevada, Sam Beard and Emmitt Warring, who operated in the Nation's Capital, and Umberto [aka Albert] Anastasia of New Jersey.[25]

ꟹ

Even in jail Emmitt Warring could not keep his name out of the courts and the newspapers. The genesis of this latest development started back in January of 1954, less than three weeks before the federal grand jury in Baltimore would return an indictment against Emmitt for evasion of taxes.

In January 1954, federal agents raided a huge moonshine still in Fairfax County, Virginia near Jefferson Village between the towns of Falls Church and Annandale (just miles from Washington, DC). According to the Treasury agents, the thirty-six-foot-high still was capable of producing 1,200 gallons of whiskey a day.[26] The distilled product was intended to be shipped to East Coast cities for sale at $10 a gallon.

Four men were arrested during the raid, but the arresting agents described them as "small fry." The Treasury suspected that there was big money behind the operation, described as the "largest of its kind found since Prohibition."[27] All the materials and machinery in the still were described as "top notch," and chlorophyll compound had been spread around the still site to kill the resulting odor.[28]

The agents also seized a blue 1949 Chevrolet panel truck found parked in the 2500 block of G Street in Foggy Bottom. The agents said they had observed the truck making several trips to the site of the still while it was under construction. The truck was registered to Bill Cady, Emmitt's brother-in-law, described in the newspapers as "Emmitt Warring's bodyguard."[29] Bill was almost twice the size of the diminutive Emmitt, but in 1954, he was over sixty years old. The description of him as "Emmitt's bodyguard" seems nothing more than newspaper sensationalism.

Three days following the raid, agents called Bill Cady in for questioning. They were surprised when Cady arrived at the Treasury office accompanied by Emmitt Warring. The *Washington Post* seized upon Emmitt's appearance and proclaimed in its lead headline the next morning, "Warring Quizzed in Still Raid."[30] Cady told the Treasury agents that the truck was registered in his name, but it actually belonged to Emmitt Warring. Emmitt claimed the truck had been registered in Cady's name because he didn't want friends asking him to use it. Both men told the agents that they had not used the truck in years. The agents bought their story, given the lack of evidence to the contrary. Eleven months later, the four men arrested at the still pled guilty. That should have been the end of the story as far as Emmitt was concerned—but it wasn't.

Two of the men who pled guilty were Walter W. "Bill" Pickett and Michael Lee. A resident of Virginia, Bill Pickett claimed to be a descendant of the Confederate general who led the fateful "Pickett's charge" at Gettysburg.[31] Michael Lee made no claim to General Robert E. Lee, but one afternoon approximately a month after they had pled guilty but before they were sentenced, Pickett and Lee had their own civil war in a car going down M Street in southeast Washington. Pickett called Lee up and asked him to come for a ride to carry out some errands. Apparently, the relationship between the two men had soured somewhat since the trial. Lee would later testify that Pickett was singing something about "heavenly portals" when Lee entered Pickett's automobile. Pickett seemed to be singing a phrase from the popular song "With a Song in My Heart." Lee later said that he feared for his life and felt that Pickett's reference to heaven was his sick way of hinting what was to come of him. It is unclear who actually pulled out a gun as they were driving, but the weapon discharged three times as they struggled, still driving down M Street. Pickett was struck twice, once in the arm and once in his leg. Lee was hit once in his arm.[32] As the car slowed almost to a stop, a truck driver fueling his truck nearby ran to Pickett's car and broke up the fight by grabbing the gun from the two men still struggling for it.

When the police arrived, they heard Pickett ask Lee, "Oh, why, oh, why did you shoot me?"

"Oh, shut up. You're not dead yet, but you might as well be. I'm going to finish you sooner or later," exclaimed Lee.[33]

Despite not wanting to press charges against Lee, Pickett eventually did. He said that Lee was a "dirty dog to shoot someone who didn't do anything to him."

At Lee's trial, his defense lawyer called John A. Kendrick to the stand. Kendrick was serving time in Alcatraz for shooting a smalltime racketeer. Kendrick testified that Pickett had offered him money to shoot Lee in 1954, before the fracas in the car. Kendrick said he turned down the offer of $2,500 because "when I get done paying taxes out on that, what would I have left?"[34]

Kendrick said he called Pickett's offer "pretty cheap."

"We'll get more money afterward ... but in a check or a note," Pickett allegedly told him, but Kendrick insisted that he would not take a check or note.

When the prosecutor accused Kendrick of coming to Washington to testify in order to get away from Alcatraz for a few days, the convict retorted that "Alcatraz is 100 percent better than the District Jail anytime."

Kendrick then stunned the court by testifying that Pickett told him the offer to kill Lee came at the request of Emmitt Warring. This was not something that Emmitt, preparing for a parole hearing to facilitate his release from the Lewisburg penitentiary, wanted to have declared in a court of law. During the height of Emmitt's power around Washington, it was common for a lot of smalltime racketeers to invoke Emmitt's name to garner credibility and influence.

I got to know Bill Pickett pretty well while growing up. He was a frequent customer at Pete Dailey's. He had a likeable side to him, and he certainly was nice to me as a youngster. But he also had a reputation as a schemer—not someone who you would trust in a high-risk deal. And of course I knew Emmitt. I can state with absolute certainty that there was no way in hell Emmitt Warring would have sent Bill Pickett to negotiate an arrangement to have somebody killed. Anyone who knew both men would find the idea laughable.

Fortunately for Emmitt, the authorities did not believe the accusation either. He would be released six months early from serving his full three-year sentence.

CHAPTER TWENTY-TWO

Enter the FBI

At an early age, I realized that my dad was not like the dads of TV sitcoms like *Father Knows Best* or even the average dad in our neighborhood. But I loved his uniqueness.

He did not leave first thing in the morning to go to work. He slept in. He did not wear a suit, except for church, funerals, and weddings. He did not lounge about the house after dinner in his coat and tie like TV dads. He did not drive a late-model car, preferring instead his beloved black and well-worn 1948 Plymouth Coupe, which he affectionately referred to as the "junk box" or "shit box," depending on the audience. But he loved that car. At times he seemed to express his affection by leaning forward in the driver's seat and hugging the top half of the steering wheel with his hands and forearms.

When my dad did wake up, he would just slip on his pants and come down shoeless and still wearing his pajama top. It was just black coffee for breakfast plus a cigarette that would cause him to eventually go into a coughing fit, turning his face red. He was addicted to Camels. Many times, he sent me to the store to get "his last pack" before he quit. I can still see him lighting up one of those unfiltered Camels with his yellow-stained fingers and then making two or three slow, deliberate shakes with his right hand to put out the match flame. Often the newly lit unfiltered cigarette would leave a small piece of tobacco in his mouth that he discharged by sticking his tongue out between slightly clenched teeth and blowing a small puff of air.

My dad had a folksy way of talking. He spoke with the slight southern accent common to most Washingtonians of his generation. He slurred his "ing" words by dropping the "g" sound, so his last name sounded like "Warrin." The name of the nation's capital became "Washintin." And of course, there was the double negative was common to both my dad and Emmitt. "Don't tell them nothin'," would be their advice for handling most questions from outsiders. Other times he would revert to the Pig Latin phrase "ixnay" to tell me to stop talking when strangers were around.

Although my dad freely used certain curse words around the house, I never heard him use the "F word" in the company women and youngsters. "Goddamn" was usually the first word out of his mouth when something really upset him. And he had a way of stretching the enunciation of the word out for almost 5 seconds.

Our neighborhood was a newly-developed area about a mile west of Georgetown Hospital, between Foxhall Road and MacArthur Boulevard. It was a combination of two-story homes and ramblers. Our street, Q Place, had a cul-de-sac at one end and was intersected by 45th Street and Indian Rock Terrace. The homes were mostly bought by young, professional families with children. It had the benefits of suburban living, plus it was only a ten-minute drive to DC's memorials and downtown. It was a great place to grow up.

One of the first friends I remember was Steven, who lived in a rambler around the cul-de-sac. When I was about five years old, we were playing with a metal Ferris wheel toy about two feet high. Steven attempted to spin the wheel around while the little finger of my left hand was in the wheel. When my finger stopped the wheel from turning, Steven kept forcing the wheel to turn with more determination, not knowing my finger was the problem until I started to scream in pain. The result was a long and deep cut that came close to severing my small finger. Off I went to the emergency room at Georgetown Hospital with my worried mother. I kept the finger but still sport a scar of over two inches long today. Steven's family put their house up for sale a week after the incident.[1] Apparently, they had heard of the Warring name and my father's reputation. Of course, their fear was completely unfounded. If they had really known my father, they would have realized that he would never have taken retribution against their family for any true accident to me. He wouldn't shy away from a fight, but he would never purposely harm any innocent person. He had a general love of people, especially kids. And kids loved him.

Perhaps because he remained a kid at heart, he loved to be around young people, and they loved to be in his presence. Some of the most ordinary delights could bring a smile to his face. My close childhood friends have told me that some of their best memories as kids were times spent around my dad.

My oldest and most enduring friend from the neighborhood, Ron Levin, frequently tells me how important a figure my dad was in his childhood. He points to the warmth and respect that my dad always showed him as a kid. My dad's ability to see the world in an almost childlike innocence allowed him to relate so well to kids and to rarely "speak down" to them.

My dad always had some amazing stories for us. And, boy, did he have some tall tales. One of them was the one about a rabbit who ran so fast that he went right through the spokes of a bicycle. Another had a cat jumping or being thrown from the Washington Monument and surviving the fall, only to be killed shortly thereafter by a dog. Years later I learned that he actually was repeating a story from Washington folklore. As kids, we were mesmerized by his stories.

One of his most delightful stories came from playing for the local St. Stephen's Church football team. As he told it, St. Stephen's once played a team whose players were so big they wore horse collars instead of shoulder pads. Adding to the incredulity of the story, he claimed that after a few plays trying to tackle and stop their offense, the St. Stephen's players realized their jerseys were torn to shreds. A close examination of their opponents' football cleats revealed that they were using razor blades for cleats. There were individual skirmishes throughout the game, but the real melee ensued when a blimp pilot flying overhead did not watch where he was going and ran into electrical wires, setting off an explosion. Order was restored only when the band at the game began playing the national anthem and the players halted their fighting to come to attention.

One Easter when I was young, my dad impulsively bought a number of baby chickens whose feathers had been painted with bright Easter colors. Concerned that our basement would be too cold for the newborn chicks, he made a cardboard box in our living room as their home. Years later, a neighbor would remind me how she'd had to watch her step while visiting in our living room as the baby chicks temporarily exercised their freedom from the box and scampered across the floor. It was a scene that could have fit right into the *Beverly Hillbillies* TV show.

Part of my dad's allure to kids was his "junk box" automobile that he used for most occasions, often a ride to a toy store, ice cream shop, amusement park, or other fun place. The coupe did not have any back seats, but there was enough space behind the front seats for two or three kids to stand and rest their arms on the top of the front seats while maintaining the same eye level of any adult sitting in the front. It had an exhaust system more suited to a hotrod and a unique horn that my dad frequently discharged for our amusement.

My two best friends from grade school, John Viehmann and Barry Byrne, were with my dad and me the night we "christened" the new K Street tunnel that runs under Washington Circle in Foggy Bottom. Although the tunnel was not officially open and the road was still unpaved, my dad felt like checking it out. So he just maneuvered the "junk box" around the temporary barricades and entered the tunnel. We decided to see how loud a "cherry bomb" firecracker would sound in the tunnel. When it went off, anyone nearby must have thought that half of Foggy Bottom had just exploded. Leaving a cloud of smoke and a smell of sulfur behind, we quickly exited the tunnel joining the normal K Street traffic and a few startled pedestrians.

The Fourth of July was a special holiday for him. Back in the '50s and '60s, illegal fireworks were accessible in DC for those who knew where to buy them. Unless you were willing to travel some distance from Washington, you had to know someone. My father did not seem to have a problem acquiring loud explosives and various pyrotechnics. One Fourth of July night, a "friendly" policeman slowly pulled his cruiser through a thick wall of smoke approaching our house and declared he had not seen anything like it since he had fought in Korea.

Ever one to celebrate holidays with flare, my dad made sure Halloween saw our dining room table covered with bowls of various candies and treats. The kids would fill up their bags as they circled the dining room table, some of them two or three times.

"Dutch" Becker, who grew up in our neighborhood, included the following in a Christmas card to me decades later: "The best thing about Halloween and the Fourth of July was going to Charlie Warring's house."

And of course, Christmas was a big deal in our house. My mother took great effort to decorate our home with many Christmas ornaments. She even took to the ladder to put up our outdoor Christmas lights rather than wait for my father to get around to it. We always had a large tree in our living room adorned with lights and expensive Christmas balls. On Christmas Eve, most of the guys who worked for my dad dropped by to have a drink and pick up their Christmas bonus. The party went late into the night, making it even more difficult for my anxious brother and me to sleep. And "Santy Claus," as my dad referred to him, never missed our house. My brother and I always seemed to get what we asked for, plus plenty more. Years later, my best friend Ron Levin admitted that besides celebrating Hanukkah at his home, he was always excited to come over to our house to check out the array of Christmas gifts that I received. Yes, my brother and I were spoiled at a young age.

If my dad provided most of the fun in the family, my mom guaranteed that all the basic needs of the family were met. She held it all together day after day. Like my dad, she enjoyed having a family. The truth is that my dad provided the income but did little else around the house. My mom did all the cooking of the meals, cleaning of the house, washing of clothes, running of the errands, disciplining of the kids, etc. She seemed to always be giving her time for the family and asking for little in return.

Once our family dog did not return home until the middle of the night and began banging his paw against our front door. As my dad and my brother and I stayed in bed, it was my mom who took the initiative to let the dog in to stop his banging. While descending the stairs, she tripped over some shoes left on one of the bottom stairs and fell down the remaining stairs. Her screams got my dad out of bed and from the top of the stairs he called down to see if my mom was hurt. When my mom reported that she had broken her leg, my dad dejectedly responded, "Goddamn it. Everything happens to me." Not only was his wife laying at the bottom of the stairs, but his "chief cook and bottle washer."

When it came to everyday living expenses, my mom did all the shopping. She was not an extravagant spender. But she always bought quality. She would say, "Buy cheap, get cheap." Whenever my dad would complain that she must be spending too much, my mom's retort would be that familiar refrain of many housewives, "If you think that you can do better, you're welcome to try."

But the money made during the heydays of the family numbers business was drying up by the middle of 1950s.

ꕤ

Only Emmitt and Charlie knew the exact arrangement for splitting the profits from their operations. Even my mom did not know. My mom was sociable to Emmitt but she was certainly not fond of him. She had a general feeling that my dad was not given his fair share but never pressed my dad to create waves with Emmitt. She knew and respected my dad's relationship with his older brother.

Whatever the income sharing arrangement was, I am confident that Emmitt unilaterally decided what it would be. Apparently, Emmitt maintained a balance for my dad, crediting as profits came in and debiting as my father drew from the balance. There had been heavy expenses from paying teams of lawyers over the years. There had been four income tax cases, one jury tampering case, and two appearances before congressional investigative committees.

What became evident was that after Emmitt retired, my father could no longer support our family solely from the remaining balance. Therefore, my dad had to back his own numbers business. For that he hired James "Prim" Kyle.

Kyle had managed the "office" for the Warring's in the 1940s, after Leo's death. He wore half-framed glasses and usually dressed like a legitimate businessman. His name had surfaced in connection with the Warring number business during Emmitt's latest income tax trial in 1954. According to the records Emmitt had presented to support his income tax payments, Kyle was a twenty-five percent partner. Perhaps because the Internal Revenue Bureau had dismissed those records as inconsequential during Emmitt's trial, they did not pursue any income tax indictment against Kyle, so he was available to run a numbers game backed by my father in the mid-50s.

The "office" for that operation was located on a farm in Fairfax County, Virginia, not far from the Arlington County line, only about a twenty-minute drive from our home in northwest Washington. Always one for company, my dad would take me to the "office" many days. I guess he was ahead of his time with the "Take your Child to Work Day" phenomenon.

Crossing the Chain Bridge into Virginia and proceeding north on

Chain Bridge Road, we would turn left onto Kirby Road, just south of the CIA Headquarters. Then we turned right onto a dirt and stone road that led to a farmer's house. The farmer's property was quite wooded, and the only thing that he seemed to raise was chickens. To fight boredom, I once went into the chickens' fenced-in area to examine them. That in itself was not a problem, but when I failed to close the door behind me and many of the chickens escaped—that was a problem. I still remember my dad giving me hell as he and the farmer chased down and rustled up the escaped chickens.

The numbers operation was headquartered in a large room on the second floor of the farmer's home. Of course, my father paid the farmer for use of the room and to keep his mouth shut. A number of card tables were set up with phones, writing pads, and adding machine. Besides Prim Kyle, Don Wallace, who was lifelong friend of my dad, was also regularly there.

I think after a few trips to the "office," I started to decline my dad's invitations at times out of boredom with the farm, and my dad started to bring my younger brother, Richard. Only my dad would be crazy enough to bring minor children to a gambling establishment that might be raided by the authorities.

But usually my brother and I loved to go anywhere with our dad. And in this case, we had a job to do for him—as he put it. And that job? It was to help him detect anybody following us as we drove to the farm. There was a need to determine whether anyone (especially undercover law enforcement) was on our trail to find the headquarters for the numbers operation. That is why we seldom went to the farm in the direct route.

My dad was always suspicious of being followed. He explained to me the many ways that the cops can "tail" a car. For example, they may use more than one car so different cars can drop out of sight at times to confuse anyone trying to detect them. One of the cars can actually be positioned in front, watching in the rear-view mirror. So my dad always took a circuitous route with stops on the way. As my brother is fond of saying, "If you were going to follow Charlie Warring, you better bring a lunch."

By the 1950s, a bookmaker had to worry about more than violating local gambling laws. In 1951, Congress passed and the president signed a national law that required anyone who accepted bets to purchase a $50 federal gambling stamp in order to operate. The Supreme Court finally struck down the law in 1968 because of its self-incriminating aspect, but it was a federal law until then. Its primary effect was to authorize the Federal Bureau of Investigation (FBI) to pursue anyone who did not come out of the shadows to buy the required stamp but still maintained gambling operations. Congress recognized that local governments were overmatched in the battle against organized crime and theorized that local law enforcement could be bought – but the federal government could not.

Of course, the FBI assigned the responsibility to curb local gambling to its Washington, DC offices. One of the agents responsible for that job was James (Jimmy) Collins.[1] Ironically, he was a local boy who was a star baseball pitcher for a local high school and went on to pitch for a local university. As an FBI agent, he pitched for the local FBI sandlot team that played its games on the Ellipse, just south of the White House. At that time, the Ellipse was equipped with regulation baseball infields and pitching mounds. The games were played after work and the league schedule and results were listed in the local papers. My dad used this public display of local FBI agents to learn the faces of the players and other agents in the FBI office who came to watch them compete with other local talent. And being my dad, and to borrow a line from Frank Sinatra, he did not do it "in a shy way." He plumped himself down in the grass just a few feet behind the FBI bench. Jimmy Collins and a few of the other agents recognized him and spoke to him as he became a regular at most of their games. He even arranged for me to be an unofficial bat boy for the team.

Once, a player for the FBI went to his car for something when his team was at bat and then made a dash for the field when the FBI made a quick third out to end the inning. On his way to the field, the agent accidently stepped on my father's hand as sat in the grass. The player's spikes cut my father's hand badly. It was strange to see Jimmy Collins, who earlier that day may have followed my dad in order to find his gambling headquarters, now administering to my dad's bleeding hand with bandages.

With a catalog of the agents' facial features in his head, my dad

---

1 The author has changed his name in order to protect his family from any innuendo that he did not perform his job to the fullest. I am sure that his family knows the integrity that he brought to his job, but those not familiar with him may naively question it.

could easily spot agents in a trailing car. Once after noticing Jimmy Collins in a trailing car, my dad pulled over and turned off the engine. The car holding Collins and another agent quickly pulled over. They parked it between other cars, hoping not to be noticed. But my dad, always willing to pull someone's leg, emerged from his car and walked back to where the agents were parked. "Why don't you guys just get out of your car and come with me. We could save gas and keep each other company." Of course, Collins declined, fighting back a smile.[2]

My dad seemed to have a sixth sense of knowing when he was being watched and followed. At least Collins thought so. A few years after my father's death, Collins, now working in California, contacted Washington Redskins assistant coach Ralph Warring Hawkins. Collins knew Ralph, also a fine DC athlete in his own right, and phoned him when the Redskins played a game in Los Angeles. During their conversation, Collins relayed a story about the time the FBI had set up nondescript trailer near a phone booth in a shopping center parking lot that my dad seemed to use daily to make "work-related" calls. They had installed a secret telescope and cameras in the trailer to observe the number being dialed or watch for any meetings with other numbers operators. On the first day at the location, they were surprised to see my dad walking over to the trailer. He kicked the door of the trailer and nonchalantly said, "Jimmy Collins, I know that you are in there."[3]

Once, my dad invited Jimmy Collins to come to our house to watch the All-Star baseball game on TV. He parked a few blocks from our house and walked to our front door. Later my dad found out that one of our next-door neighbors had been assigned the job of writing down the tag numbers of all visitors to our house. I took the seat closest to the TV while my dad laid on the couch with his head close to Jimmy Collins' chair. I do not remember the specifics of their conversation during the game but I do remember my dad was not talking baseball. He clearly seemed to be doing most of the talking. Because I found it somewhat distracting to me as I tried to watch and listen to the broadcast and felt that Jimmy Collins was also being distracted from the game, I foolishly spoke up and suggested to my dad that he let the FBI agent watch the game without the distraction. My dad said nothing as Jimmy Collins jumped in to save me by assuring me that he was fine. But afterwards my dad told me to never interrupt when he was talking business. Years later when I saw Sonny Corleone of "The Godfather" movie fame be scolded by his father for speaking out of turn, I certainly could relate.

Despite having some affinity for my dad, Collins pursued him in order to find evidence that he was engaged in "accepting wagers," as defined by the federal law requiring the gambling stamp. Fortunately, he was never able to accomplish that mission. But my dad never believed he had been given a pass by Jimmy Collins and the FBI. He constantly took precautions to avoid arrest despite his effort to court Collins' friendship.

During the Kennedy years in the White House, my brother became good friends with his classmate, Joe Kennedy—Attorney General Robert Kennedy's eldest son. Joe often visited our house and made the rounds with my father in the "junkbox." I remember distinctly when Joe announced that he had to leave a toy gun my dad had bought for him at our house because he could not have it at his house. This was before the assassinations of his father and uncle.

I saw the surprised expressions of the faces of the regulars at Pete Dailey's when my dad introduced them to the attorney general's son and the president's nephew. I would have loved to have seen the reaction of any FBI agent who might have trailed my dad while Joe was in the "junkbox" when they realized that the son of the Attorney General was in the car they were following.

By the mid-1960s, my dad decided it was too risky to continue to go into the "office" in person. Now in his fifties, serving jail time was unthinkable. Therefore, he had to totally rely on others to totally run the office.

CHAPTER TWENTY-THREE

Old Habits Die Hard

In the fall of 1967, my father began to distribute and back "football cards." These were not the football cards that came wrapped with bubble gum. These cards listed some of the top college games to be played on the coming Saturday and all of the pro games for that coming weekend for gambling purposes. All wagers made using one of these football cards was by a parlay bet. The bettor had to pick at least three games and had to win all three to collect any winnings. A one dollar bet on three winning games generally would return six dollars. Betting on more games and winning all of them would yield a higher payback. The cards were illegally and discretely created by a local printer and distributed at bars, diners, and barber shops early in the week. Later in the week, before any games were played, bettors completed them and turned them in to designated pickup men.

All of the cards showed the "point spread" for each game, giving the underdog team a certain number of points to be added to their actual score to determine the betting winner. Thus, the underdog team could lose the actual game but win for those who bet on them if they had the higher score after the betting points (spread points) were added. In contrast, the favored team had to "cover" the point spread in order for a bettor to win on the favored team.

It was about this time that I became acquainted with Nick Valltos. His older brother, Steve, had worked for my dad in the "office," and my dad had Nick distribute and pick up the football cards that he backed weekly. Nick looked like the 1940s screen idol John Garfield, and he enjoyed the comparison. He usually dressed in black-and-white clothing, accentuating his Greek looks.

During my Christmas break of 1968, I came home from college in the middle of a snafu with the football cards that nearly cost my dad thousands of dollars. In making up the cards for the week, the printer mistakenly gave the Green Bay Packers seven points instead of giving the points to the underdog San Francisco 49ers. Unfortunately, my dad and Nick did not discover the error until the cards had been distributed to the betting public. The bettors noticed the printer's error and jumped all over the Packers-49ers' game, betting on the Packers and getting seven points instead of giving seven points to the 49ers, like most of the country was. An overwhelming number of the bettors picked the Packers as part of their parlay and put a significant amount of money on their picks.

Since the game was in San Francisco, it was the last one played on the weekend. Many people had successfully picked two or more winners and now were only waiting for a Packers win that they thought of as a "mortal lock." The Packers were playing the first year without now-retired coach Vince Lombardi, but they still had many of their great players including quarterback Bart Starr. Facing the possible loss of thousands of dollars if the Packers won, my dad got out his rosary and the prayer card to St. Jude, the patron saint of hopeless cases. Somehow the 49ers pulled off the upset and won by seven points—twenty-seven to twenty. This created a tie game when adding the seven points to the Packers. The rules dictated that the bettor loses all tie games. Therefore, anyone who bet on either team in that game lost. It was a grand Sunday dinner in the Rags Warring home that night.

ᔕ

Since Emmitt had returned home from prison, he turned further inward and distrustful and became even more isolated from the outside world.

Emmitt now very carefully chose whom he allowed in his circle. Everyone seemed to be a potential G-man, or just someone looking for a handout. He knew that he could no longer turn to illegal rackets such as numbers to support himself. Now he had to manage on what he had in his coffers for the rest of his life. Emmitt had not invested in legitimate businesses like some other bookmakers, probably due to lack of trust in other people. The simple pleasures that he had indulged in before now became fewer and simpler.

Welcoming would be the last word to describe his home. All of the doors were always locked. Dogs would bark at any hint of a stranger. He continued to use his one-way mirror on the front door to examine potential visitors before opening the door to just a few trusted individuals. The window blinds were closed and the curtains were drawn. Besides an iron fence, the backyard was bordered by a wall of tall, thick Leland cypress evergreens.

Emmitt did not answer his phone unless someone called who knew the code (call three times hanging up the first two times after only one ring) or the time was prearranged. He rarely went out to eat at Billy Martin's or Britt's cafeteria in Georgetown as he had in years past. He no longer took his dog for walks in the neighborhood, partly because his current dog, Mark, was much more aggressive than his Great Dane, Duke.

Any yard work was carried out by Carolyn Rainear, Emmitt's near-constant companion for the rest of his life. I qualify the use of the term "constant" because Emmitt insisted that she move out for a while before every seven years elapsed so she would not gain the rights of a "common-in-law" wife. He would even anonymously mail letters to her at his Macomb Street address so he could then formally advise the U.S. Post Office that she no longer lived there. But the redhead who was almost twenty years younger than Emmitt would remain with Emmitt the rest of his life.

If Emmitt was now living an almost Howard Hughes-like existence of withdrawal from society, his brother, Charlie, did the opposite. The front door of our house was unlocked a good amount of the time to accommodate kids coming in and out of the house. My dad did not live in fear and remained his usual outgoing self. Every once in a while, he received a threatening phone call, but he dismissed them in the belief that "if somebody was really going to try something, they wouldn't warn you in advance."

By this point, I had graduated from grade school and was attending St. John's College High School in Washington. Many of my cousins had attended the school, which had a good academic record and a great sports history. My dad drove me and my friend, John Viehmann, to school each day during our freshman and sophomore years in his beloved "junk box." The school was about five miles from our house in upper northwest Washington but it took about twenty minutes to get there in the morning. My dad would then come back in the afternoon to pick us up. Sometimes we would find ourselves sitting at a red light next to a junior or senior in one of the hot rods of the day. As the hot rod sat there revving its engine, it became too much for my dad not to show up this guy and his car when the light turned green. The opposing teenager had no idea that the guy in the old, beat up car next to him was a former bootlegger who'd run moonshine from southern Maryland to DC. Usually the duel would start somewhere on Nebraska Avenue and continue through the busy Tenley Circle with its curves and turns.

I'm partly embarrassed to admit to the speeds that we (and the opposing car) usually reached as we sped down Nebraska Avenue past Wilson High School and through busy streets. Looking back, I can see it was totally irresponsible for my dad to reduce himself to the antics of a teenager. But that was just another example of the irrepressible kid in my dad.

I shared a love of sports with my dad. Despite his reluctance to mingle in crowds, he brought me out to some Washington Senators baseball games. Those times with my dad at Griffith Stadium and later at DC Stadium (which became Robert F. Kennedy Stadium) stand out in my childhood memories. We usually sat behind the visiting team's dugout where he knew an usher who I only knew by the nickname of "Shirts." Ironically, my dad's sister Lillian sat with her husband, Dr. James Lyons, next to the Senators dugout in seats usually reserved for VIPs. Though they had season tickets to the Senators' games for many years, we never used their seats or even walked over to their seats to visit with them. At the time I thought it was strange. But looking back now, I realize that my dad did not want to do anything to cast any aspersion on the respectable life that his sister and her physician husband enjoyed. Most of the respectable people who knew my aunt probably only knew her by her married name. My dad did not want to publicize the fact that she was a Warring by associating with her in a public place. It was something that did not particularly bother my dad. He was happy that his sister was living a good life.

I did not have the athletic ability required to play on the varsity teams at St. John's. I knew that had to disappoint my dad. Therefore, I tried to excel in my studies and enjoyed some success at it. When it came time to go to college, I chose to go to the University of Kentucky where my second cousin, Ralph Warring Hawkins, was an assistant football coach. He arranged a job for me as an equipment manager for the football team that came with a partial scholarship covering my room, board, and books. I worked for the team during my four years at Kentucky and learned an immense amount about college football. And for the first time in a while, another Warring was actually "away at college" and not in some penal institution. I continued to get good grades earning the Dean's List at least twice. I still treasure the memory of my dad's proud and joyful response when he read the notices regarding the Dean's List.

By the mid-1960s, Pete Dailey's second location was demolished to make room for the Kennedy Center of Performing Arts. But my dad found new places to spend some evenings with his pals. One of the places was the Cold Duck Restaurant on Connecticut Avenue, two blocks down from the Washington Hilton. Many former patrons of Pete Dailey's, including police, hung out at the Cold Duck. It was a place where everybody knew your name before there was a *Cheers* and its theme song. Unlike Pete Dailey's, the Cold Duck had good food backing up an American and Greek menu.

And Rags Warring wasn't the only bookmaker who frequented the Cold Duck. Pete Gianaris was probably the most well-connected bookmaker in Washington and was fond of the Cold Duck's owners, Jimmy and Angie Geralis. Gianaris dressed and carried himself like a leading executive or lobbyist. Allegedly Gianaris "fixed" a game in 1943 between the Redskins and the Steagles,[1] a temporary merger of the Pittsburgh Steelers and Philadelphia Eagles during the war. Known for running the highest-class sports booking operation in the city, his cultured manner endeared Gianaris to doctors, lawyers, sports figures, and politicians.[2] They went to Pete because they trusted him and his ability to keep everything confidential. When Gianaris was arrested and placed on trial for running a gambling operation in 1977, as many as 60 prominent figures in Washington wrote letters to the presiding judge on his behalf, citing his generosity to religious and cultural organizations. Their names were kept out of the public record. But at least one of the letters was publicized. That came from a local orphanage where the children knew Gianaris as "Peter Rabbit" and were praying for him.[3] Despite a long record of arrests for gambling, Gianaris got off with a six-month sentence.

Besides the Cold Duck, my dad also found the Good Guys on Wisconsin Avenue in upper Georgetown to replace Pete Dailey's as a nighttime stop. Certainly more of a bar than a restaurant, the Good Guys was run by Ernie Byrd, a transplant from Tennessee who was a wannabe gangster. He had a picture of himself holding a gun while standing with one leg resting on the floorboard of an old gangster-style roadster a la Bonnie and Clyde. Such characters seemed to be drawn to my dad.

For a guy who ran a bar, Ernie was always well-dressed in a dark suit and white shirt, usually with small bowtie. He had the face of a retired boxer, with a nose that had once been re-arranged by somebody or something, rather than a restaurateur. Riding around town in nothing less than a new Cadillac convertible, he played the role of a big shot with a wet cigar usually protruding from his mouth. After challenging DC's decency laws in the late sixties by converting the Good Guys and a couple other establishments to topless go-go bars, he earned the title of "Go-Go Impresario" from the *Washington Daily News*.

One spring night in 1969, my dad and Ernie Byrd closed the Good Guys at 2:00 a.m. and cruised down to Chinatown to a hole in the wall of a place called Ho Wah's on H Street. It was open late to attract the crowd who had been drinking all night and could stand a serving of greasy Chinese food. I am probably not doing justice to the food, but the cramped, dingy restaurant that you walked down to from street level did not suggest gourmet dining. I had accompanied my dad and Ernie to Ho Wah's on a previous visit during my Christmas break from college, but I was not with them this particular evening.

Sometime during the night, a drunken vagrant came into the restaurant and created a disturbance with the manager. My dad and Ernie observed the argument and had an uneasy feeling that the drunk would be back after being kicked out by the manager.

The drunk returned, but this time he was brandishing a knife and threatening the manager.

My dad's shouts of "leave that man alone" were to no avail and the manager seemed frozen in fright. When it became obvious that Ernie, who was carrying a small pocket pistol, was not going to do anything to help the frightened and cornered manager, my dad asked Ernie to give him the gun.

At least two shots rang out. The drunk now lay motionless on the floor.

My dad disregarded a burning pain in one of his calves as he stared at the apparently lifeless body on the floor. Blood started to run down the man's expressionless face.

"Is he dead, Ernie?"

Ernie kicked the victim and replied, "I'm afraid he is."

"Goddamn, and I promised my wife that I wouldn't shot nobody no more," my father said as only he could say it.

Suddenly, low, guttural sounds came from the presumed corpse. The bullet had only grazed his forehead enough to open a wound.

The restaurant manager grabbed the phone on the wall behind him and called the police. In no time, the cops and an ambulance arrived.

But there were two victims of the shooting. Apparently, one of the bullets had entered my dad's calf. The vagrant drunk was carried on a stretcher to the back of the ambulance while my dad limped with assistance before being lifted into the vehicle and placed on a side bench.

Before they reached the hospital, the drunk regained consciousness and observed the medics treating my dad's leg.

Addressing my dad, the wounded and delirious drunk said, "I guess the same guy that shot me must have shot you."[4]

When I returned from college during spring break, there was my father in his favorite chair in the living room with the foot of his injured leg in a pan of water, washing his calf wound with a sponge. Luckily the bullet had not struck any bone and passed clear through the fatty part of his calf.

Surprisingly, there were no charges stemming from the Chinatown incident, but word leaked back to Emmitt, and he was livid. Emmitt could not understand why a man my father's age was running around on the streets at 3:00 in the morning. Again, my dad was the recipient of a lecture from his older brother, something that really rankled him.

ꟹ

At some point in most people's lives, the subconscious idea that one's parents will be around forever starts conflicting with what they see.

People seemed to age faster in those days than they do now, perhaps because they smoked so much. My father was no exception. He continued to smoke unfiltered Camel cigarettes. But he was showing signs of serious health problems during the late 1960s, such as difficulty with climbing stairs.

During breaks from college I spent more time and did things with him one-on-one. I even convinced him to go see a new gangster movie that I had seen in Kentucky, *Bonnie and Clyde*. We had not been to the movies since we went as a family to the drive-in. I had been excited with the realism of the movie's gunfight scenes. How naïve I was not to realize that my dad had already experienced the reality of a shooting in his own life that could not be matched by anything in a film. He was generally unimpressed and pointed out afterwards that in reality Bonnie and Clyde had actually been a couple of young punks slaying cops and unarmed bankers—not the folk heroes portrayed by Warren Beatty and Faye Dunaway. I guess that I, like most of the public, had mistakenly lumped famous bank robbers during the "gangster era" with those racketeers in the big cities who made their money without holding people up with a gun.

Along with my father's waning health, there was the matter of the family's waning finances. If there was any money set aside for my father in Emmitt's safe, it appeared to be almost gone. For sure, large bank accounts, bonds, stocks, were nonexistent. My mom had to take a saleslady job at a Lord and Taylor department store on upper Wisconsin Avenue. The earnings from that job primarily went towards running the house. The job also allowed her to buy clothes for herself and other family members at a discount. But most important for her, it alleviated the need to ask my dad for money. It was hard for him to accept that he was barely making enough money to provide for his family, and any requests from my mother for money only accentuated that fact. My mom accepted the job willingly and liked being around fine clothes and apparel. She accepted my father's continued involvement in illegal gambling and his fraternizing with his questionable friends as nothing more than an extension of the man she married. But I do not think she envisioned a time when money for household necessities would be an issue. When my parents were dating and during the early years of marriage, money was plentiful and the steady flow into their pockets seemed like it would have no end. Now times had changed. Sure we still lived a middle class existence but we were one of the last, if not the last house on our block to get central air conditioning and a color television in the late sixties.

Most of the bookmakers and number backers in DC were now African American. The city's demographics had changed with the desegregation of public schools and subsequent "white flight." By the spring of 1969, my dad was down to three small numbers books manned by small-time numbers writers.

After having his coffee and reading the *Washington Post*, my dad now usually started his day by going to Mass at St. Dominic's Church in southwest Washington. He had been attending St. Dominic's for years since it was near his favorite hangout, Pete Dailey's, and could conveniently drop by on his way home from Mass. Now, was he praying for a good number to come out that day? You better believe it. Since he started backing his own number business after Emmitt retired from it, my dad started to attend mass daily.

My dad's "office manager" in the late 1960s was Eddie Lawler. He had married the daughter of Toots Juliano, who had been with my dad at the U Street shooting in 1933. Since my dad was no longer willing to risk going to the "office," Eddie would call my dad at home and advise him on what numbers were attracting the most bets and then notify him of the financial consequences as the three digits came out during the day after the race results.

After the three-digit number was finalized, Eddie would compute whether each individual book ended the day in the black or the red. My father took over at that point, delivering cash to those who ended the day in the red in order to cover the day's bets or pick up money from those who ended the day in the black (less their commission). My dad sometimes would talk my brother into accompanying him on the rounds. When I was home from college, I would almost always go (and drive). My dad kept his 38-caliber revolver by his side on all nightly trips to pick up or deliver. Perhaps my brother and I had become accustomed to accompanying my dad on his business meetings despite the inherent risk. Since we had been old enough to know the danger of a gun, my dad had kept his .38 revolver in a table next to his favorite living room chair so he could quickly respond to any intruder coming through the front door. So we were not intimidated by the gun.

We would leave the house after supper and first meet with Al Harvey, an African American guitarist with over forty years of experience. In addition to having a numbers book with my dad, Harvey had a nightly gig at Mr. Smith's, a nightspot on M Street in Georgetown.[5] It was important for us to be across the street from Mr. Smith's when Al Harvey arrived for work and had not yet entered the nightspot. The routine was that I would drop my dad off on the northwest corner of

31st and M, and he would wait there until the veteran musician, carrying his guitar and its case, pulled up and got out of a cab on the same corner. I would drive around the block until Al Harvey arrived and the exchange was made. Because no numbers slips were involved, only the exchange of money, we were probably safe from any arrest. The mere exchange of money was not sufficient evidence of gambling.

Next we headed up Georgetown, turning east onto Q Street. We would proceed on Q Street crossing the Buffalo Bridge (known for its buffalo statues that stand guard on either side of the bridge) and continue east, passing north of Dupont Circle. Shortly before reaching 17th Street NW, we stopped at a house on the south side of Q Street. Years have caused me to forget the name of the bookmaker who lived on that block. Before the area was "gentrified," street crime was common in that neighborhood.

After I parked the car, my dad would get out, carrying his .38-revolver covered by a small paper bag. He looked like an old man with a newly purchased pint of whiskey in a paper bag swaying by his side. He would stroll down the street, and people would pass him on the sidewalk—unaware that the man who just walked by them had his finger on the trigger of a loaded gun. Some young men hung around the bookmaker's house, and my dad suspected they were aspiring "stick up" men looking for an easy score. He made a point of letting them see his revolver and made sure they knew that a man need not be shot in the chest with a bullet from this gun to die. Anyone shot in the artery of a leg with a .38 caliber probably would bleed to death before an ambulance arrived. Fortunately, he never had to put the gun to use.

Leaving the location on Q Street, we proceeded east until we turned left onto 16th Street. Driving past the historic Woodner Apartments, we continued a few more blocks before turning onto Arkansas Avenue and working our way to 14th Street until we reached Shepherd Street, which dead-ended at a park. "Fat Betty" lived almost at the bottom of the hill on Shepherd Street. I don't think that I ever knew her real name. She was an African American whose figure supported her moniker. It wasn't that she was grossly heavy, but her lack of height accentuated her girth. She lived with her adolescent children in two-story home that sat up from the street and required a walk up a number of cement steps.

My dad had a love-hate relationship with Fat Betty. Betty knew how get to my dad's soft side, and he hated it. Betty was notorious for always being a bit short on the nights when she had to pay my dad. Blocks away from arriving at her house, he would start swearing he was not going to let her come up with any excuses that night for not paying all that she owed. I usually asked to stay in the car to listen to the radio and avoid hearing the endless wrangling between Fat Betty and my dad. He would eventually come out to the car claiming some minor victory and promising to "clip" (short) her the first time he would have to pay her on a winning day by her bettors. My father's nature did not allow him to stay mad at anyone for long, including Fat Betty.

ᔓ

Sometime in the early summer of 1969, my dad started to complain of a burning sensation when he urinated. He was never one to see a doctor, but he finally agreed after the discomfort did not go away. I don't remember the details, but I know that the "C-word" (cancer) was not mentioned in his initial treatment. By mid-summer the problem had not gone away.

In August, I headed back for my final year of college. Of course, I was concerned about my dad's health, but I still had not recognized his problems as life threatening. Around September 9, my father entered Georgetown University Hospital for exploratory tests. Nick Valltos drove him to the hospital, which was less than a mile from our house.

Upon checking in, my dad felt well enough to flirt with the young woman who was doing the paperwork. She could not get over the fact that he had no Social Security number. She kept repeating that she had never met anyone who did not have one. Between working for his father as a youth and then operating only in illegal activities, my dad had never gotten around to applying for a Social Security card.

One evening soon after my father was admitted to the hospital, I got a phone call from my mom telling me that my dad had a procedure on his bladder. A small cancerous tumor had been removed. She worried about how my dad would react when told he had cancer. Back in the 1960s, a cancer diagnosis was more often a death sentence than it is now. I was worried about my dad's physical and emotional state of mind but tried to concentrate on my studies and my job with the football team.

Then on the evening of September 18, I received a call from my mom saying that I should come home: my father was asking for me. The next afternoon, I took a flight from Lexington to Washington's National Airport.

Nick Valltos picked me up at the airport around 4:30, and we were at Georgetown Hospital within a half an hour. During the ride to the hospital, Nick was vague about my father's condition. However, when I went into the intensive care unit and saw my dad, it was much worse than I had imagined. Even with an oxygen mask, he was struggling to breathe. His chest rose and fell rapidly, and his hands were moving constantly as if they were reaching for something to grab hold onto. I moved closer to him and leaned over him and, for the first time, I saw something that I had never seen in my father's eyes before—fear. I had seen joy, anger, even tears on very rare occasions—but never fear. The man who had never feared for his life, despite being threatened by dangerous men, had finally found something to be fearful of. Without having thought in advance of what I would say to my dad, I mumbled something about knowing he had been in tough spots before and he could beat this.

I went into the waiting room where my mother, Nick, and my Uncle Emmitt were waiting. Emmitt had not only had an interest in the welfare of his brother; he had a special interest and a layman's knowledge of medicine that he thought could be helpful.

I was still stunned by what I had just seen at my father's bedside. I am sure there must have been some small talk in the waiting room at that time. For one thing, Nick was always willing to fill the silence with a story of some local character. But I cannot remember anything that was said.

It seems that we were only sitting there for less than ten minutes when a doctor emerged from the intensive care unit and walked slowly up to my mother.

"Mrs. Warring, I'm afraid that we've had a setback," he began. The physician advised us that my father's heart had suddenly stopped. He then went on and gave a protracted description of all of the vain attempts the doctors had made to revive him. He then broke the news to us that my dad was gone.

At the time, "setback" seemed a poor choice of words. But I soon appreciated his method of breaking the news to my mom in stages. I am not sure whether it was the doctor's approach in gently informing my mom of my father's death or if she had prepared herself for this moment, but she took the news with sad resignation rather than uncontrollable grief.

As thoughtful and considerate as he had been in breaking the bad news to the family, the doctor immediately and coldly requested permission to do an exploratory autopsy on my dad as a learning experience for young doctors studying at Georgetown. My mom was still processing the sudden news of my father's passing and looked to me to respond to the doctor.

I knew that I instinctively did not like the idea of anyone cutting up my father. Immediately, I looked to Emmitt who was standing about five feet behind the physician. Would this man who was known for unemotional decisions and who had an extraordinary respect for those who practiced medicine think we should give our permission and allow my dad to be cut open for the sake of science? I wanted to turn down the doctor's request, but I also wanted the respect of my uncle, who now was going to have a more important role in my life with my dad gone.

I did not have to wait for an answer. Somewhat to my surprise, Emmitt immediately gave me a slow but distinct negative gesture of his head without changing the expression on his face. So on behalf of my mother, I turned down the physician's request.

The cause of death was listed as "pulmonary embolism," a blockage of an artery in the lungs. My brother Richard swears that he heard that Emmitt had my father's body taken out of Georgetown Hospital and had an autopsy performed by another physician at another hospital. Who knows?

I guess that all sons go through the same emotion that I dealt with that night, trying to accept that the unbelievable had just happened—that the man I thought could conquer anything had just lost to death.

You can't help being around someone as close as a father without taking something away from the experience. He certainly did not want me to follow the example of an uneducated convicted felon who had to derive his family's income by illegal means. But he taught me plenty of important principles: it's essential for family members to stick together, you should share what you have been given, people deserve courtesy and respect regardless of their status in life. I have met some very important individuals in government and private industry during my life, and often found that their graciousness and fairness to people paled in comparison to the uneducated, convicted felon who raised me.

The *Washington Post* noted my dad's passing in an article, which began:

> "They buried Charles R. (Rags) Warring yesterday in Mt. Olivet Cemetery – all the way across the city from his beloved Foggy Bottom and the scenes of this headline-making heyday as the youngest of a triumvirate of brothers who ruled Washington's gambling world some three decades ago." [6]

The headline of his obituary was "'Rags' Warring, Gang Chief." Perhaps it was nothing more than an attempt to sensationalize the story, but my dad would have appreciated the promotion to "Chief," a title more befitting to Emmitt. But the exalted title was in the headline only. In the text of the article, he was reduced to "triggerman," the *Post's* favorite moniker for him.

I would now enter a period of my life where I became closer to my Uncle Emmitt, a man whose presence I had never been in before without my father.

CHAPTER TWENTY-FOUR

Facing the End

A few days after my father's funeral, I flew back to Lexington, Kentucky. I had missed working the sidelines during the first game of the season (a loss to Indiana), but I was back to see Kentucky pull an upset over Archie Manning (father of Peyton and Eli) and the University of Mississippi to give Kentucky's new coach, John Ray, his first win.

However, except for a one-point win over Virginia Tech, only losses followed the win over Mississippi. Nick Valltos came down to Lexington to see me one weekend when the team played the Louisiana State Tigers at home on a Saturday night. I got Nick a sideline pass and tried to stand by him for most of the game while still doing my job.

I had shown some guys on the team my dad's obituaries from the Washington newspapers. I also made it a point to introduce Nick to my roommate, Jerry Bentley, and a couple of other players. The guys on the team who'd read about my dad saw me with Nick on the sidelines and immediately concluded that Nick was in the rackets. And Nick looked the part. His dark glasses and tailored clothes along with his olive skin and slick, black hair combed straight back gave him the look of a gangster straight out of the movies. But Nick's presence did not bring Kentucky any luck. We lost by the lopsided score of thirty-seven to ten.

A few weeks later, after more football losses, head coach John Ray's secretary called me and asked me to come to his office. I couldn't imagine what business that the head football coach had to speak to me about that was so important and urgent that required a private meeting. Ray, who had played and previously coached at Notre Dame, could be blustery in his manner, but I had no previous problems with him. He had come to Kentucky with outstanding credentials as the defensive coordinator of Notre Dame's 1966 championship team, but Kentucky's repeated losses were leaving him very frustrated.

Upon entering his office, he asked me to take a seat next to his desk. He might have engaged in some small talk at first, but I don't remember. My mind was searching for some reason why he had called me into his office in the middle of the day. He then got to the point, saying it had come to his attention that I knew some gamblers. I suddenly began to wish that I had kept my mouth shut about my family's business. I confessed that my father was a bookmaker but said he was dead, and my connection to that business was completely over.

Ray then leaned over and pointedly asked me, "So tell me the goddamn truth. Have you ever bet against our team or told anybody to bet against our team and then given out information like our game plan?"

I never imagined a question like that was coming. To be accused of a serious crime that I was totally innocent of, and never for a second thought of perpetrating, almost left me speechless. With all the surety that I could muster, I emphatically answered, "No sir. I never would ever think of doing something like that." And that was the God's truth.

He then warned me that if he ever found out that I did something like that, he would ruin me. After that warning, he leaned back and took on a relaxed composure and thanked me for coming in to see him and clearing up that little matter.

☙

With my dad gone, it seemed natural that I should begin to regularly visit my Uncle Emmitt. Since my dad called him by his family nickname, "Pudge," he was always "Uncle Pudge" to me. Growing up as a kid, I did realize the liberty that I was taking by calling him by this nickname. His home at 3900 Macomb Street was conveniently less than a ten-minute drive from our house on Q Place. I began stopping by his home starting with the Thanksgiving break of my senior year of college. That I was one of the few people he would allow in his house was reassuring, but it did little to make me feel comfortable.

By now the German shepherd, Mark, who Emmitt had since the early '50s, had passed away. Emmitt replaced him with two fairly large dogs that were only part German shepherd. Emmitt's live-in girlfriend, Carolyn, had two grey, miniature Schnauzers. Ringing the doorbell would spark a cacophony of barking from all four dogs.

My visits to his house usually were no more than twenty or thirty minutes. They were always a bit awkward and were confined to the kitchen. At times, silence would reign in the air, only disturbed by the gurgling of the large fish tank in the kitchen. I found myself usually having to bring up some subject to try to pass the time. He was not one to ask you a lot of questions about your personal life. Even on rare occasions when he had phoned our home when my dad was alive, there was no small talk when I answered the phone. He only said, "This is Emmitt. Is your father home?" It wasn't that he was not interested in my welfare; he was not into idle chit-chat.

Emmitt's girlfriend Carolyn would often join us in the kitchen and join in the conversation which helped limit the moments of silence. Although possessing a strong mind of her own, she was careful not to say anything in front of visitors that would displease Emmitt.
In the evenings, he would usually offer me a beer. He bought Iron City Beer, one of the cheapest beers you could buy at that time. I am not sure whether he was actually pinching pennies or continuing his portrayal of a man without riches that he had pushed during the first IRS trial.

Sometimes current events would capture his interest. When J. Edgar Hoover died in 1972, Emmitt was intrigued as to the disposition of Hoover's "secret files," which allegedly contained the dirt on politicians, entertainers and whomever else Hoover might have had an interest in manipulating.

Occasionally, Emmitt had other visitors when I dropped by to see him. One was my cousin, Johnny Warring, the son of Emmitt's brother, Jonesy. I had heard that Emmitt helped him purchase a small elevator company in DC which he grew into a very successful enterprise. John had started as an employee of the company and impressed Emmitt with his willingness to work hard and provide for a growing family. He became probably the closest family member to Emmitt in his last years.

Another occasional overlapping visitor was Joe Nesline. He usually brought his girlfriend (soon to be wife), Becky, or another friend or two. Joe spoke slowly and tended to draw out his enunciation of some words. After spending a year in jail for carrying a concealed weapon in the Harding shooting, Nesline parlayed some of the contacts he had made while working at Jimmy La Fontaine's in Bladensburg, Maryland, "the biggest gambling house between Palm Beach, Florida, and Saratoga, New York."[1] "Fontaine's" was where he met Dino Cellini, who had cut his teeth by working gambling joints in Steubenville, Ohio, with singer Dean Martin. More importantly, Cellini would go on to become the right-hand man for National Crime Syndicate figure Meyer Lansky. Through that connection, Joe got a job working the craps tables in Las Vegas and then at the Tropicana in Havana, Cuba. He went on to establish himself as a technical expert in setting up and running casinos.[2] But Joe's stay in Cuba was interrupted by the Castro-led revolution which ended the mob's hold on Havana. However, his work with international gambling figures did not end in the Caribbean. Nesline went on to set up and operate casinos in Yugoslavia and London. FBI agents once testified that Nesline boasted that he was "one of the best crapshooters and dealers in the world." According to the agents, Nesline went on to claim that he had been gambling since he was fifteen years old and assured the agents that "I only walk on one side of the street, so don't think I'll ever rat on any of my buddies."[3]

It was also in Cuba where Nesline met Charles "The Blade" Tourine, alias Charlie White, who ran the Capri in Havana. Reputedly, his nickname "came from his proficient use of the knife when dealing with recalcitrant debtors and rival gangsters."[4] Tourine was allegedly a top member of New York's Genovese crime family and earned a reputation as an enforcer besides running a number of gambling joints for the mob. Tourine often stayed with Nesline when he was in Washington and accompanied Joe a number of times to visit Emmitt. When my Italian grandfather died in 1964, Emmitt showed up at the wake with Tourine and Nesline. When my grandparents' Italian family and friends who came down from New York saw Charlie the Blade in attendance, their jaws dropped.

Emmitt especially enjoyed Tourine's "old country" ways. Specifically, he was tickled that Tourine navigated through life managing to speak only broken English and without learning to read at all. While struggling to tell me the story without laughing, Emmitt told me of the time that Tourine, Nesline and Gladys, Nesline's wife at the time, had taken an airplane flight together. Joe Nesline bought tickets for each of the three travelers and, thanks to the lax security of the times, randomly distributed the tickets to the travelling party. Upon landing in Miami, the federal authorities spotted Charlie Tourine and took him into custody for questioning. Of course, Tourine played dumb to most of the questions. When asked by the federal agents who he was travelling with, Tourine answered that he was travelling alone. When asked if he was sure, Tourine became indignant and snapped back with a question, "Ya tink I'm a child and need somebody to go with me?"

Showing Tourine the writing on his plane ticket, the agent then asked, "Well, if you are travelling alone, how long have you been travelling under the name of Gladys Nesline?" Tourine was flying under Gladys Nesline's ticket and was completely unaware of the mistake because he could not read the name on the ticket.

The guy, who visited Emmitt's at least once, and I really would have liked to have met was Charlie Tourine's paid "greeter" at casinos and sometimes part owner of multiple gambling joints worldwide, movie gangster George Raft. In real life, Raft grew up in New York's Hell's Kitchen and became associated with one of the city's more notable gangsters during Prohibition, Owney Madden.[5] That history lent credibility to his gangster character in those Warner Brothers' movies. At the height of his movie career, many actual gangsters modeled themselves after Raft's dress and grooming. Perhaps uniquely, when it came to George Raft, art first imitated life, and then life imitated art.

ᔕ

Despite giving up cigarettes years before, Emmitt had suffered from emphysema for some time, and his breathing now became more difficult. He was not the kind of person who voluntarily shared much personal information, and I felt too intimidated to ask him any direct questions about his health. Later, I only learned he was in Sibley Hospital by dropping by his house one day and being advised by Carolyn. She said something about his doctor wanted to run tests on his lungs at the hospital.

Emmitt was not your typical hospital patient. First, they were never going to get him in one of those hospital gowns that open in the back. He dressed as though he was sitting at his kitchen table in the familiar dark trousers, shoes, socks, and a white T-shirt. Ironically, the same man who practically hid from the world in his home on Macomb Street now transformed himself into an outgoing personality at the hospital.

He brought a large coffee maker from his home and set it up in his hospital room. First thing in the morning, Emmitt would make coffee for the nurses in his unit so they would not have to go down to the cafeteria for their morning jolt.

After the doctors made their rounds visiting patients, Emmitt would make his rounds visiting the same patients, most of whom he had built relationships with during his short stay in the hospital. In those days, the patient's charts were kept on a clipboard hanging on the end of the patient's bed. Always fascinated with medicine, Emmitt would examine the patient's chart and explain to the patient what their doctor had written that day. He brought a weighty *Merck Manual* from home and lugged the voluminous medical reference guide around from room to room in order to look up unfamiliar conditions or drugs prescribed by the patient's doctor.

Later, a priest assigned to the hospital spoke of how he witnessed Emmitt "pushing a cart to another patient's room even while he himself had to be equipped with a tube down his throat because of his condition."[6]

He also took many of his meals in the ground-floor cafeteria instead of in his room. One evening I found him downstairs having dinner with his nephew Johnny. He was sitting at a table near the cash register at the end of the cafeteria line. He seemed to purposely have chosen that location to stop any doctor, or more so, any nurse that caught his attention. Before we left the table, he took a $5 dollar bill and placed it on our table. When an older African American lady who was cleaning tables came by, he asked her to take the bill because "it was in our way." He gave her a sly smile, and you could see he was pleased with himself and his wry sense of humor.

I came to visit Emmitt at Sibley Hospital one evening and found Joe Nesline and his entourage in Emmitt's room—but no Emmitt. When I asked where the patient was, I was told that he had gone to the grocery store to buy some snacks for his guests. Emmitt returned in a short while with two grocery bags of party snacks.

I was also present one day when Emmitt's sister, my Aunt Lillian, came to visit. Married to a doctor, she tried to engage him in a conversation about his medical condition but was only able to elicit minimal information. For me, the visit was memorable because of what she asked Emmitt upon leaving his room. Playing her longtime role as an older sister, she asked her brother, "Boy, do you need any money to buy anything while you're here?"

The question itself was not remarkable. But to hear a man whose power and demeanor made most men fear him addressed as "boy" was not anything I was expecting. But it was a nickname from decades earlier. Lillian was merely continuing the family practice of addressing some of the young boys in the family with the simple title of "boy."

By 1973, the C-word became part of the discussions about Emmitt's health. My cousin, Johnny Warring, who was very close to Emmitt, was the first one to inform me that Emmitt had been diagnosed with cancer. By the spring of 1973, I noticed that Emmitt was losing weight on an already frail body. My visits to his house became even more difficult as I found myself carrying most of the conversation. I did not ask many questions regarding the specifics of his illness or treatment, and he did not offer much information in return. By June, Emmitt was back in Sibley Hospital.

❧

My brother Richard ("Bo") did not take my father's death well. Even while my dad struggled for his life in Georgetown Hospital, my brother could not bring himself to visit my dad and witness his last days. He was far from apathetic—he just couldn't deal with it.

Our father's absence allowed my brother to break out on an unfettered way of his own. He had dropped out of St. John's High and its military school environment and enrolled in George Marshall High in Fairfax County. During that time, he became friends with many in the motorcycle crowd in Northern Virginia.

One guy in the motorcycle crowd that he became good friends with was somewhat older guy named Frankie. From my limited exposure to Frankie I was convinced that he was a loud, headstrong individual who had opinions on most any subject. He also seemed to match or exceed my brother's 6' 3", 225-pound frame. He was the natural leader for a small group of young men and women whose preoccupation in life was to have a good time.

It was in pursuit of a good time that my brother suggested that the gang take a short respite from Fairfax County and head south along the Potomac River to Westmoreland County, Virginia.

Apparently, my brother had scouted out Emmitt's cottage at Colonial Beach and found that no one had used it in years. Emmitt had stopped visiting the beach in the late 1940s and my Aunt Esther and her grandson, Ralph Warring Hawkins, had been the only ones using the cottage since then. Ralph had used the cottage to entertain his fellow University of Maryland football players during breaks from school. Good times had been had in the small beach town, with a speedboat that Emmitt had bought Ralph and a decent nightlife while the slot machine-filled casinos were still active off of the Colonial Beach piers. But by the '60s, Ralph was off coaching and living in Texas and then Kentucky. Esther was getting older and had no desire to make the trip to the beach alone. The cottage had deteriorated through neglect. Two hurricanes in the 1950s had also washed away the private pier and a good portion of the backyard. When my brother saw the condition of the place, he had an idea. Specifically, he and his friends would paint the cottage, make some other minor repairs, and just enjoy their stay at the beach while they worked. It sounded like a reasonable trade-off. But there was one problem—no one ever asked Emmitt, the owner.

Besides having multiple eyes and ears around Washington, Emmitt also had informers in Colonial Beach. It did not take long for them to advise Emmitt that a gang of about four to five motorcycle riders and their girlfriends had moved into his cottage. Whoever was acting as Emmitt's eyes and ears in Colonial Beach was brave enough to inquire at the cottage and was told there was no problem because Emmitt's nephew, Bo, was among the squatters.

Word got back to Emmitt. Needless to say, he was not happy. Too sick with cancer to drive down to the beach, Emmitt dispatched Ralph Warring Hawkins down to Colonial Beach to tell the squatters to get out immediately. Ralph was now living in the Washington area and working as an assistant coach to George Allen and the Washington Redskins.

When Ralph got to the cottage, the scene conjured up images of a Charles Manson-like group in the mind of the strait-laced football coach. The Manson murder story was still fresh in the minds of most Americans, so the scene of long hair and scantily-clad girls quickened the comparison in Ralph's mind. They seemed to have a blatant disregard for authority and convention. In blustery Frankie, Ralph saw a Manson-like leader who the others followed. Looking back, it was a significant stretch to make that comparison, but that is what Ralph reported to Emmitt. Worse, he told Emmitt that the group said they were not planning on leaving until they finished the paint job on the cottage. It was a paint job that Emmitt did not want.

The man who had stood up to criminal thugs and the Department of Justice was now being challenged by a small band of long-haired hippies. Times had certainly changed for the man who was once one of the most powerful men in the city.

Although few knew it at the time, the doctors had given Emmitt a very pessimistic prognosis. His cancer had spread and his probable lifespan was reduced to months. For someone who strove to be in control of things around him, this challenge to his authority could not be taken standing still. If Emmitt wouldn't be threatened or pushed around when he was well, he was now in no mood to be challenged by some "young punks" and was unconcerned about the consequences of any violent action on his part. To put it simply, when facing a death sentence, some men are prone to irrational responses and actions. This was certainly true in Emmitt's case. Fortunately, Bo and the rest of the gang decided to suddenly leave without finishing the paint job.

On a visit to his house sometime after he received the report from Ralph Hawkins, after I settled down in my usual place in the kitchen table booth, Emmitt surprisingly started the conversation.

"Your brother and his friends are lucky that they got out of Colonial Beach when they did," Emmitt stated as a matter of fact. I said nothing in return. "I arranged for some guys to go down there and spray the place," he added.

For a second, I assumed that he was talking about painters. I was momentarily confused because I was aware that Emmitt did not want the cottage painted.

"But lucky for them, they all left with their lives," he said to my amazement as I realized that he was talking about the cottage being sprayed with bullets, not paint. I knew that he could make some cold and calculating decisions if he had to, but now, overwhelmed by the physical and emotional pain of dying, he was irrationally striking out at this perceived threat.

"Do you know how they carry out a job like that?" he asked me knowing that I didn't have a clue.

"The men go in one car and the hardware goes in another," he calmly said. I did not ask any follow-up questions but assumed that the men and the guns were combined only for the short duration in case the gunmen were ever stopped by the police.

This all seemed surreal and a gross overreaction. Combining the unbearable pain of the cancer, the influence of the drugs, and his impending loss of his life, Emmitt had lost touch of reality. Fortunately, my brother had no more interaction with our uncle.

ဢ

As 1973 came to an end, it was obvious that Emmitt was lucky to have finished the year alive. The cancer had reportedly spread to his stomach. He was nothing but preverbal skin and bones. My visits were becoming more difficult.

My last visit was on the evening of January 13, 1974. I am not sure why, but I had started a pattern of dropping by his home on alternating Sunday nights. On that night, I was surprised to have his girlfriend Carolyn open the door for me. She explained to me that Emmitt was in his bedroom and I had to go upstairs for the first time to see him.

Emmitt was sitting on the edge of the bed, dressed more in street clothes than in bed clothes. His eyes were sunken well into his head and he had a feeding tube in his nose. In the same bedroom where robbery thugs had once threatened him with immediate death, he was now slowly dying.

If I had found our conversation strained before, it was now extremely difficult as he offered nothing to the conversation other than very short comments or responses to anything that I said. I frantically searched for something relevant to say but was always fearful that the logical response of this dying man to a mundane remark by me would be, "Who gives a shit?"

I did share one bit of news. I had taken a government job with the Treasury Department. It was not the Internal Revenue Bureau—renamed the Internal Revenue Service in 1953—that had hounded him for so many years, but another bureau in the same organization. He did not comment.

My stay was brief and absent of any syrupy goodbyes. When I pulled away from his home that wintery night, I did not realize that I had seen my uncle for the last time.

Two weeks rolled by, and it was another Sunday evening. According to my recent schedule, I should have visited my uncle once more, but I didn't. I do not recall why I did not go the Sunday night of January 27, 1974. However, I am sure that I was reluctant to stare again at a dying man and try to make small talk.

The news the next morning made me regret my decision. I received a phone call from my cousin Johnny Warring. His words, "Emmitt is dead. He shot himself," stunned me. At first it seemed totally out of character that Emmitt would kill himself. How could the man who had stood up multiple times against hoodlums and the prosecutorial powers of the United States government cash in his chips by his own hand?

Later it all made sense to me. He no longer wanted to demand the care of his constant companion, Carolyn, or any more medical personnel. Enough was enough. The physical pain and hopelessness became too much to bear. With a concern for others in his last seconds on this earth, he laid out newspaper on his bathroom floor to make it easier for them to clean up. He went back to his bedside to get a revolver out of the nearby stand, returned to the bathroom, sat on the toilet, placed the pistol to his temple with his right hand, and pulled the trigger. The bullet exited the left side of this head and penetrated the nearby bathroom window.

Emmitt was buried in Mount Olivet Cemetery with most of his family members, including his mother and father. He was laid next to his brother, my father, Charlie.

Not surprisingly, Alfred E. Lewis, who had chronicled Emmitt's public life with personal details for the *Washington Post*, co-wrote Emmitt's obituary for the paper. While describing Emmitt as the onetime "kingpin" of the numbers game in Washington, Lewis highlighted Emmitt's criminal career and his almost never-ending problems with the Bureau of Internal Revenue and the Department of Justice. But like most of the articles that Lewis had written about Emmitt over the years, he balanced it with descriptions of Emmitt as a "quiet man who enjoyed raising dogs, doing small favors for his neighbors, helping various charities and looking out for neighborhood children."[7]

Bill Gold, who wrote a column on District matters for the *Washington Post* for thirty-four years, told a nice story regarding Emmitt in a column a few days after his death. According to Gold, he received a phone call from Emmitt one night about a lost cat.

"The cat is nothing to me," Emmitt explained. "It's just an alley cat that has been hanging around my house because I feed it. But the kids in the neighborhood have become very attached to that cat, and they asked me to find it for them."

"And you want me to run something in the column about the cat?" Gold asked.

"That's right," Emmitt said. "And I'll send you a couple bucks for Children's Hospital."

"Emmitt," Gold replied. "I would swim the river in January for Children's Hospital, but I can't run any lost-and-found items. There are two dozen lost cats in Washington every day. If I ran one, I'd have to run them all."

"You don't understand," Emmitt countered. "This is a special cat the kids are attached to. I'll send you $20 if you run it."

"I do understand," Gold said, "but what you don't understand is that kids are attached to pets that get lost every day.

"Sorry, but I just can't do it," Gold insisted.

"You're impossible," Emmitt said and he slammed down the phone.

But about two days later, a letter arrived from Emmitt with just a brief note that said:"You are a stubborn mule, but this is for the hospital anyhow."

There was a $100 bill in the envelope. Gold closed his column with the following about Emmitt:

"A tough guy in some respects, perhaps. But a pretty good man to have on your side."[8]

Epilogue

The names of the Warring brothers and other associates who were engaged in the business of supplying alcohol and gambling to the public when it was outlawed by the government have occasionally surfaced in print or on the internet in the last few years.

Perhaps it is because their activities were centered in the nation's capital—right under the nose of the United States government. Their exploits seem mild compared to the heartless brutality of the drug wars of today. Though long gone, the Warring brothers are still remembered.

In the late '80s when there was a concern that big-time organized crime was moving into the District, the *Washington Post*'s Sunday edition published remembrance of the bygone days titled "Our Gang—With the Mafia Muscling In, We Soon May Long for the Good Old Bad Days."[1] The story came complete with photos of the Warring brothers, Joe Nesline, and Roger "Whitetop" Simkins. In the article, Emmitt captured most of the print as usual. The nostalgic piece detailed the Warring brothers' rise in Prohibition, their entry into the numbers business, and their headline-making trials. Of course, the infamous opening of the safe deposit box was once again was detailed for the reading public. Joe Nesline's shooting of George "Mad Dog" Harding also was retold. And not surprisingly, the appearance of Emmitt and Whitetop Simkins as witnesses before the Senate District Subcommittee was covered. The article specifically mentioned how Emmitt and Whitetop took the "constitutional duck," invoking the Fifth Amendment of the Constitution.

I was working for the Treasury Department in 1993 when I dropped by a coworker's cubicle as she was having lunch. As I spoke to her on some matter, my eyes were drawn to an extraordinarily large photo in a newspaper on her desk of Emmitt raising his hand, being sworn in at the 1950 Senate hearing. Because Mayor Sharon Pratt Kelly had proposed bringing casino gambling to Washington, the *Washington Post* had run an article on how Washington had once once "had its own small-scale, illegal version of Las Vegas." In "Gamblers Once Thrived in the City," the paper told how "three men cornered the market on notoriety in the gin joints and numbers games," i.e., Emmitt "Little Man" Warring, Roger "Whitetop" Simkins and "Jimmy" La Fontaine.[2]

When searching for the name of "Emmitt Warring" online, you find Emmitt's name in the strangest places. In the 2005 edition of the *New Partridge Dictionary of Slang and Unconventional English*,[3] the authors used the following example of the verb "pinch" from the book *Washington Confidential*: "Since Emmitt seems immune, it makes Georgetown a lovely place to live—nobody gets pinched here."[4]

I am indebted to the skillful reporters and writers who worked for the Washington newspapers during the years of this story. Without the details culled from their stories, the book would not have been the same. I am also grateful to a number of people who lived in Washington during the time covered herein and knew one or more of the Warring family members. I feel especially lucky to have spoken to those who have passed on in the last few years.

But most importantly, I hope that this book has provided a full and accurate telling of the saga of Emmitt, Charlie, and Leo Warring. If my relationship to these men has caused me to portray them more sympathetically than they deserve, I assure the reader that I tried to avoid doing so. Even though I relied heavily on the newspaper archives, my ultimate goal was to provide a more rounded picture of these men and their activities than was first told by the Washington papers.

The Warrings' story certainly can be seen in a different light, in view of the changes in the law and in society that have transpired over the decades. The lengths at which the federal government went to "get" Emmitt Warring and his brothers seem somewhat surreal in the context of today's legalized gambling environment. When one considers that their business catered to people who voluntarily spent a few coins in return for a bit of daily diversion, one could argue that the government overreached and overreacted.

As for my son, the law student who once researched his name on a legal database and thus created the reason for writing this book? Well, he graduated from law school and his first job was working as a contractor that provided paralegal services to government agencies. And where was he assigned to begin his working career? The Tax Division of the Department of Justice. That's right—the same office that prosecuted Emmitt twice for evasion of taxes. As they say, you can't make this stuff up.

If the words of George Eliot are true and "Our dead are never dead to us until we have forgotten them," I hope this book will keep their memory alive.

Notes

Chapter 1

[1] Lewis, Alfred E. and Richard Morris, "Charmed Life of Emmitt Warring," "Barrel Boy of Foggy Bottom Rose to Riches in Numbers," *Washington Post*, Sept. 16, 1951; Pg. 1

[2] Gabbett, Harry, "Rags Warring, Gang Chief," *Washington Post*, Sept. 24, 1969; Pg. C6

[3] "Jail Warring, Get a Promotion, Says Barrett," *Washington Post*, Feb. 3, 1951; Pg. B1
[4] "A National Disgrace," *Washington Post,* Feb. 17, 1939; Pg. 8

[5] "There's Sadness in Foggy Bottom," *Washington Daily News*, Dec. 27, 1954

[6] Buchanan, Pat. "Hail to the Redskins!," *Townhall,* Oct. 22, 2013

[7] Kilian, Michael; "250 Years of Georgetown History," *Chicago Tribune*, June 3, 2001

[8] "Foggy Bottom Historic District," National Park Service; https://www.nps.gov/nr/travel/wash/dc20.htm

[9] Sherwood, Suzanne Berry (1978); *Foggy Bottom 1800-1975*; Center for Washington Area Studies; The George Washington University, No. 7

[10] Both of the stories in this chapter were told to the author by his father (Charles)

Chapter 2

[1] Peck, G. (2011). *Prohibition in Washington, D.C. How Dry We Weren't,* Charleston, S.C.: History Press

[2] Ibid.

[3] As told to the author by World War I veteran, Joseph William Cannella, and confirmed by Frank Cady Jr.

[4] "Police Raiders Find Underground Stores of Alleged Bootleggers," *Washington Post,* Nov. 3, 1921; Pg. 1

[5] "Police Shoot One, Arrest Three; Get Back Some of Leiter Liquors," *Washington Post,* Nov. 2, 1921; Pg. 1

[6] "Virginia Drops Leiter Wine Robbery Charge," *Washington Post,* May 20, 1923; Pg. 3

[7] As told to the author by his father and Emmitt's brother, Charles

[8] Lewis, Alfred E. and Richard Morris; "Gunfire Punctuated Early Career of Georgetown Mob," *Washington Post,* Sept. 19, 1951; Pg. 1

Chapter 3

---

[1] Lewis, Alfred E. and Richard Morris, "Cloak of Anonymity Hides Numbers Racket Mystery Man," *Washington Post,* Sept. 17, 1951; Pg. 1

[2] Lewis, Alfred E. and Richard Morris, "Barrel Boy of Foggy Bottom Rose to Riches in the Numbers," *Washington Post,* Sept. 16, 1951; Pg. 1

[3] Lewis, Alfred E. and Richard Morris, "Cloak of Anonymity Hides Numbers Racket Mystery Man," *Washington Post,* Sept. 17, 1951; Pg. 1

[4] As told to the author by Ralph Warring Hawkins

Chapter 4

---

[1] As told to the author by Arthur Cranston, second cousin to the three Warring brothers

[2] As told to the author by Mary Brown, member of Oldest Inhabitants of Washington D.C.

[3] Okrent, Daniel (2010), *Last Call, The Rise and Fall of Prohibition*, New York, N.Y.; Scribner

[4] "Capt. Little: Scourge of Bootleggers." *Washington Post,* June 3, 1954; Pg. 20

[5] As told to the author by Joe Osterman in 2009

[6] Peck, Garret (2011), *Prohibition in Washington D.C. – How Dry We Weren't,* Charleston, S.C.: History Press

[7] Borchert, James (1982), *Alley Life in Washington,* Urbana and Chicago: University of Illinois Press

[8] Sherwood, Suzanne Berry (1978), "Foggy Bottom 1800-1975, A Study in the Uses of an Urban Neighborhood," *Center for Washington Area Studies, The George Washington University, No. 7*

[9] The author draws this information from stories heard from a number of people who lived in Washington during Prohibition and from observation of newspapers during that time

[10] This information on "Chick" Edmonds was told to the author in 2012 by Joseph Goffney, a 91 year old African-American who lived in Foggy Bottom during his younger years.

Chapter 5

---

[1] "Gambler Killeen Slain," *Washington Post,* Nov. 24, 1935; Pg. 1

[2] "Jury Clears Killeen," *Washington Post,* April 1, 1921; Pg. 1

[3] "Rum Thief with Bitten Finger Sought as Envoy's Assailant," *Washington Post,* May 14, 1931
[4] "Arrest May Clear Legation Rum Case," *Washington Post*, Oct. 21, 1931; Pg. 1

[5] "Rum Thief with Bitten Finger Sought as Envoy's Assailant," *Washington Post,* May 14, 1931

[6] "Jury Clears Killeen," *Washington Post,* April 1, 1921; Pg. 1

[7] "Police Arrest Man in Killing of Cunningham," *Washington Post,* May 25, 1931; Pg. 1

[8] "Gun Links Slaying Of Police Tipster To Envoy Assault," *Evening Star,* June 3, 1931

[9] "Day's Slayers Known, Police in Hunt Claim," *Washington Post,* May 19, 1931; Pg. 1

[10] "Talley Day's Death Fight Told at Trial," *Washington Post,* Dec. 8, 1931; Pg. 20

[11] Day Funeral Rites Enlivened by Fight" *Washington Post,* May 21, 1931; Pg. 1

[12] "Convict Sends Note to Court In Fight for Custody of Son," *Washington Post,* Jan. 5, 1936

[13] "Bryant McMahon's Wounding Mystery," *Washington Post,* Mar. 2, 1932; Pg. 18

[14] "Quartet Grilled In Hotel Killing; Police Baffled," *Washington Post,* Sep. 16, 1934; Pg. 2

[15] "T.F. Tobin Gets Writ for a Test of Detention," *Washington Post,* Jan. 3, 1935; Pg. 5

[16] "Nalley Killing Blamed on War Over Gambling," *Washington Herald,* Nov. 8, 1933

[17] "Arrest Two In Assault," *Washington Post,* Aug. 6, 1921; Pg. 7

[18] "Three in La Plata Jail Beat Guard and Escape," *Evening Star*, Feb. 22, 1923; Pg. 3

[19] Near-beer was beer that contained less than 0.5 percent alcoholic content and was deemed legal during Prohibition

[20] "Held For Murder in Second Degree," *Evening Star,* Mar. 30, 1925; Pg. 2

[21] "Gunman Is Slain; Three Questioned," *Evening Star,* Nov. 7, 1933; Pg. 16

Chapter 6

---

[1] "Nalley Killing Blamed on War over Gambling," *Washington Herald,* Nov. 8, 1933

[2] "Warring Slew Nalley, Charge of Witnesses," *Washington Post,* Nov. 8, 1933; Pg. 1

[3] Lewis, Alfred E. and Richard Morris, "Gunfire Punctuated Early Career of Georgetown Mob," *Washington Post,* Sept. 19, 1951; Pg. 1

[4] "'Numbers' Writer Dies of Shot Fired by Rival After Argument," *Washington Post*, Dec. 17, 1936; Pg. 21

[5] As told to the author by a second cousin, Arthur Cranston, who knew Don Wallace

[6] "Black Broadway–A vintage look at U Street," NBC Washington https://www.nbcwashington.com/news/local/black-broadway-a-vintage-look-at-u-street/8403/

[7] "Gunman Is Slain," Three Questioned," *Evening Star*, Nov. 7, 1933; Pg. 16

[8] "Warring Held After Nalley Killing Query," *Washington Post,* Nov. 9, 1933; Pg. 19

[9] "Myron Ehrlich, Famed Lawyer, Dies," *Washington Post*, Dec. 23,1960; B3

[10] "Warring Slew Nalley, Charge of Witnesses," *Washington Post,* Nov. 8, 1933; Pg. 1

[11] "Nalley Killing Blamed on War Over Gambling," *Washington Herald,* Nov. 8, 1933

[12] "Warring Slew Nalley, Charge of Witnesses," *Washington Post,* Nov. 8, 1933; Pg. 1

[13] "Club Hostess Fails to Name Death Suspect," *Washington Herald,* Nov. 14, 1933

[14] Ibid.

Chapter 7

[1] "Capital Gambler Under Suspicion in Wilson Murder," *Evening Star,* Oct. 17, 1935; Pg. 1

[2] "Planned to Quit Her, Confession Declares," *Evening Star,* Nov. 24, 1935; Pg. 1

[3] "Wilson Murder Net Is Tightened," *Evening Star,* Apr. 2, 1936; Pg. 3

[4] Johnson, Nelson (2002). *Boardwalk Empire,* Medford, N.J.: Medford Press; Plexus Publishing

[5] Richardson, Selden (2012); "*The Tri-State Gang in Richmond,*" Charleston, S.C. History Press

[6] "Gunmen's Slugs Kill Silver Spring Resident In Error," *Evening Star,* Oct. 23, 1934; Pg. 1

[7] "Cugino Is Named As Wilson Killer; Shotgun Studied," *Evening Star,* Oct. 23, 1935; Pg. 1

[8] "Gang's Ambush Kills Innocent Man in Takoma," *Washington Post,* Oct. 24, 1934; Pg. 1

[9] "Pistol Is Seized, Police Question Two in Murder," *Washington Post,* Oct. 25,1934; Pg. 1

[10] "Building Owners Renting To Gangs Face Prosecution," *Evening Star,* Oct. 26, 1934; Pg. 1

[11] "Police Crash Into H St. Resort," *Washington Post,* Oct. 31, 1934; Pg. 1

[12] "Publicity Is Urged By La Roe As Check On Parole Action," *Evening Star,* Nov. 23, 1934

[13] "Wilson Case Row Perils Crime War," *Evening Star,* Sept. 25, 1936; Pg. 21

[14] "Philadelphia's No. 1 Gunman Nabbed in N.Y.," *Washington Post,* Sep. 5, 1935; Pg. 3

[15] "'The Stinger's Widow Rushed Here for Wilson Murder Quiz," *Washington Post,* Nov. 21, 1934; Pg. 1

[16] "Mrs. Maddock Freed In Killing of Gaming King," *Washington Post,* Apr. 9, 1936; Pg. 1

[17] "Gambler Killeen Slain; Girl Admits Shooting, Says He Tortured Her," *Washington Post,* Nov. 24, 1935; Pg. 1

[18] "Gambler Killeen Shot to Death By Scorned Woman After Drink Orgy," *Evening Star,* Nov. 24, 1935; Pg. 1

[19] "Killeen Given Simple Burial As Killer Prepares Defense," *Evening Star,* Nov. 26, 1935; Pg. 4

[20] "Eddie Killeen's Rites Attract Curious Crowd: Floral Tributes From the Boys Mark Passing of Gambler," *Washington Post,* Nov. 27, 1935; Pg. 6

[21] "Wife of Cugino, Dead Gangster, Kills Herself," *Washington Post,* Oct. 18, 1936; Pg. M 18

[22] "Captain of Police Linked to Crime As Inquiry Begins," *Evening Star,* Jan. 28, 1935; Pg. 1

[23] Lewis, Alfred E. and Richard Morris, "Gunfire Punctuated Early Career of Georgetown Mob," *Washington Post,* Sept. 19, 1951; Pg. 1

Chapter 8

[1] "Who gets What Share of the Gambling Profits?," *Washington Post,* Jan. 1958; Pg. A1

[2] "Police Smash Numbers Ring In U.S. Bureau," *Washington Post*, Oct. 20, 1962; Pg. A3

[3] "Captain of Police Linked To Crime," *Evening Star,* Jan. 28, 1935; Pg. 1

[4] "Dimes and Pennies Finance City's Crime," *Washington Post*, Oct. 27, 1934; Pg. 1

[5] "Prince Georges Tax Rate Fixed at $1.38," *Washington Post,* Mar. 21, 1929; Pg. 5

[6] As told to the author by Jack Sweeney's daughter, Jackie

[7] "U.S. Indicts 34 in War to Rout Illicit Liquor," *Washington Post,* Mar. 28, 1935; Pg. 5

Chapter 9

[1] "Atlantic Seaboard Suffers Under Sun," *Washington Post,* July 10, 1936; Pg. 1

[2] "Record Throng of 37,500 Crowds Stadium," *Washington Post,* July 5, 1936; Pg. 1

[3] "Gang Warfare Holds Five," *Washington Herald,* July 22, 1936; Pg. 1

[4] "Jury Convicts Warring Mob Of Shooting," *Washington Post,* Dec. 9, 1936; Pg. 1

[5] "Police Arrest 'Rags' Warring In O'Brien Case," *Washington Post,* Aug. 2, 1936; Pg. 6

[6] "Six Warring Mobsters Get Prison Terms," The *Washington Herald,* Feb. 3, 1937

[7] "Gang Warfare Holds Five," *Washington Herald,* July 22, 1936

[8] "Gunfire Punctuated Early Career of Georgetown Mob," *Washington Post,* Sep. 19, 1951; Pg. 1

[9] "3 Bootleggers Raise $60,000 Bond Quickly," *Washington Post,* July 25, 1936; Pg. 1

[10] "Arrest of Warring Ordered," *Washington Herald,*; July 31, 1936; Pg. 1

[11] From transcript of interviews with Collas G. Harris, Executive Officer, the National Archives by Joseph C. Welch, Assistant to the Chief, Investigation Division, Civil Service Commission of May 12, 1939 and June 14, 1939

[12] "Police Arrest 'Rags' Warring in O'Brien Case," *Washington Post,* Aug. 2, 1936; Pg. 6

[13] "O'Brien Names 'Rags' Warring As Assailant," *Washington Herald,* Aug. 2, 1936

[14] "Hunt at Beach Fails to Locate Warring Mob," *Washington Post,* Aug. 10, 1936; Pg. 13

[15] "Suspect Admits Turning Over Proceeds to Collector for Gang; Thompson Calls for Gaming Laws 'With Sharper Teeth,'" *Washington Post,* Aug. 16, 1936; Pg. M12

[16] "Gaming Raid On L St. Nets 13 Prisoners," *Washington Post,* Aug. 22,1936; Pg. 13

[17] "Inquiry Forces 2 To Surrender In O'Brien Case," *Washington Post,* Sept. 2, 1936; Pg. 1

[18] "Gunfire Punctuated Early Career of Georgetown Mob," *Washington Post,* Sept. 19, 1951; Pg. 1

[19] "Court Refuses To Remove Guard From Witnesses," *Evening Star,* Nov. 24, 1936; Pg. 23

[20] "Six Are Indicted In O'Brien Case," *Evening Star,* Nov. 19, 1936; Pg. 1

[21] "Smoke Screen Charge Costs Tear 18 Months," *Washington Post,* Oct. 25, 1936; Pg. M15

[22] "Shots Halt Wild Pursuit," *Evening Star,* April 2, 1936, Pg. 23

[23] As told to the author by second cousin, Arthur Cranston Jr. circa 2010.

Chapter 10

[1] "Memory of O'Brien, Gang's Victim, Lapses On Stand Under Eyes of 6 Indicted Mobsters," *Washington Post,* Dec. 8, 1936; Pg. 1

[2] "O'Brien Refuses To Identify Gang," *Washington Times,* Dec. 8, 1936

[3] "Jury Convicts Warring Mob Of Shooting," *Washington Post,* Dec. 9, 1936; Pg. 1

[4] Ibid.

[5] "'Rags' Warring and Four of Gang Sentenced, Sixth Gets Longer Term in Hijack-Shooting," *Washington Post,* Feb. 3, 1937; Pg. 1

[6] "Bond Confesses O'Brien Shooting To Aid Friends," *Evening Star,* Feb. 3, 1937

[7] "Six Warring Mobsters Get Prison Terms," *Washington Herald,* Feb. 3, 1937

[8] "O'Brien Guilty of Perjury in Gang Shooting," *Washington Post,* Feb. 9, 1938; Pg. 1

[9] Ibid.

[10] "Numbers Raid Nets 3 Captives, $1,971 in Coins," *Washington Post,* Feb. 17, 1937; Pg. 1

[11] "Numbers King to Surrender For Arrest Today After Raid," *Washington Post,* Feb. 18, 1937; Pg. 1

[12] "'Numbers Writer' Is Arrested As Police Seek Link Between Raid and Taxi Pushed in River," *Evening Star,* Feb. 17, 1937; Pg. 1

[13] "Numbers King to Surrender For Arrest Today After Raid," *Washington Post,* Feb. 18, 1937; Pg. 1

[14] "Man Is Indicted For 'Revenge' Wreck of Taxi," *Washington Post,* July 3, 1937; Pg. 6

[15] "Numbers King to Surrender For Arrest Today After Raid," The *Washington Post,* Feb. 18, 1937; Pg. 1

[16] "Woman Indicted in Traffic Death," *Evening Star,* Aug. 20, 1937; Pg. 2

[17] "Area's Gambling Czar Sam Beard Dies at 76," *Washington Post,* May 26, 1965; Pg. B 13

[18] "Raid Gave Little Hoped-for Chance Of Meeting Beard," *Evening Star,* Oct. 6, 1934; Pg. 21

[19] "Headquarters Raided, Gambling King Seized," *Washington Post,* Oct. 6, 1934; Pg. 1

[20] "Raid Gave Little Hoped-for Chance Of Meeting Beard," *Evening Star,* Oct. 6, 1934; Pg. 21

[21] "Witnesses Tell of Phone Bets In Beard Trial," *Washington Post,* May 3, 1935; Pg. 6

[22] "Coercion Laid to Beard Jury Foreman In New Trail Plea," *Evening Star,* May 10, 1935; Pg. 1

[23] "Jailer Aids Beard, Off to Cell, In Obtaining Liquor License," *Evening Star,* April 10, 1936; Pg. 1

[24] "Sam Beard May Reach Through Lorton Bars To Take Over Nuckols' Gambling Throne," *Washington Post,* Jan. 11, 1938; Pg. 1

[25] "U.S. Orders Sam Beard Returned to Atlanta," *Washington Post,* Jan. 15, 1938; Pg. 1

[26] "Lorton Trades 13 For D.C. Gaming Czar, 12 Others," *Washington Post,* Jan. 8, 1938; Pg. 13

[27] "Transfer Of Beard To Lorton Is Hit," *Evening Star,* Jan. 12, 1938; Pg. 21

[28] "'Nubby' Nuckols, Czar of Gamblers, Suicide" *Washington Post,* Jan. 9, 1938; Pg. M1

[29] As told to the author by James Geralis whose brother attempted to deliver the take out order

[30] "Nolan Demands Beard Removal From Lorton," *Washington Post,* Jan. 12, 1938; Pg. 17

[31] Ibid.

[32] Ibid.

[33] "Warring Is Given Two Years And His Attorneys Acquitted In Jury-Tampering Scandal," *Evening Star*; Feb. 24, 1939: Pg. 1

[34] Eig, Jonathan, *"Get Capone,"* Simon and Schuster, Inc. (2010); Pg. 374

Chapter 11

---

[1] Lewis, Alfred E. and Richard Morris, "Barrel Boy of Foggy Bottom Rose to Riches in the Numbers," *Washington Post,* Sept. 16, 1951; Pg. 1

[2] Ibid.

[3] "The Museum at Colonial Beach," www.museumatcolonialbeach.com

[4] "U.S. Closing In On Overlords Of Crime Here," *Washington Post,* Dec. 10, 1936; Pg. 1

[5] "Grand Jury To Get Evidence Against Three Warrings," *Evening Star*, Mar. 20, 1938; Pg. 1

[6] "Jury Indicts Warrings As Evaders of Taxes; 'Protection' Is Hinted," *Evening Star,* April 4, 1938; Pg. 1

[7] "Warring Kept Busy by Woes, Jury Is Told," *Evening Star,* Nov. 22, 1938; Pg. 1

[8] Told to the author by the owner of the Macomb Street home circa 2008

[9] "Warring Kept Busy by Woes, Jury Is Told," *Evening Star,* Nov. 22, 1938; Pg. 1

[10] "Numbers' Ring Heads Face Tax Fraud Charge," *Evening Star,* Mar. 20, 1938; Pg. 1

[11] "$4,000,000 Bets Taken by Warrings," *Washington Post,* Nov. 18, 1938; Pg. 1

[12] "D.C. Heads Map Secret Attacks On Racketeers," *Washington Post,* April 9, 1938; Pg. 3

[13] "Not Guilty Plea Made in Tax Case by Rags Warring," *Evening Star,* June 3, 1938; Pg. 21

[14] "Warring Brothers Will Be Tried November 15," *Washington Post,* Oct. 13, 1938; Pg. 1

[15] "Laws Will Serve As Toastmaster," *Washington Post*, Feb. 26, 1939; Pg. 16

[16] "Bolitha Laws Sworn In as D.C. Jurist," *Washington Post,* Sept. 11, 1938; Pg. 13

[17] "Judge David Pine, D.C. Native, Got His Start by 'Being Brash'," *Washington Post,* April 27, 1952; Pg. M10

[18] "Warring Trio To Trial Today in Fraud Case," *Washington Herald*; Nov. 15, 1938; Pg. 3

[19] "Watergate Attorney John J. Wilson Dies," *Washington Post,* May 20, 1986; Pg. C4

[20] "Courts Honor H. T. Whelan," *Washington Post,* Feb. 15, 1947; Pg. B8

[21] "William B. O'Connell, 72, Attorney; Crash Victim," *Evening Star,* Aug. 22, 1960; Pg. 24

[22] "Judge Leo A. Rover Dies of Heart Attack," *Washington Post,* Nov. 12, 1966; C3

Chapter 12

[1] "CCC Begins Removing Historic Trees at Basin," *Washington Times,* Nov. 16, 1938; Pg. 1

[2] "Army of Citizens to Defy Tree Movers at Basin Today," *Washington Herald,* Nov. 18, Pg. 1

[3] "Prospective Jurors Who Read Story of Warring Trial Excused," *Evening Star,* Nov. 15, 1938; Pg. 1

[4] "3 Warrings Face Trial On Tax Evasion," *Washington Post,* Nov. 14, 1938; Pg. 1

[5] "$4,000,000 Bets Taken By Warrings," *Washington Post,* Nov. 18, 1938; Pg. 1

[6] "Warring Agents Revealed At Trial," *Washington Herald,* Nov. 17, 1938; Pg. 3

[7] "Warring 'Protection' Payment Claims Recounted at Trial," *Evening Star,* Nov. 16, 1938; Pg. 1

[8] Ibid.

[9] "Warrings' Income Tax Return Lists 75 Persons As Employees; Gives Names, Dates and Places," *Washington Post,* Nov. 17, 1938; Pg. 6

[10] "Hazen Probes Warring Charge of Police Bribes," *Evening Star,* Nov. 17, 1938; Pg. 1

[11] "$4,000,000 Bets Taken By Warrings," *Washington Post,* Nov. 18, 1938; Pg. 1

[12] "Bribe-Takers' Names Shielded By Warring," *Washington Post,* Nov. 22, 1938; Pg. 1

[13] Eig, Jonathan; "Get Capone." *Simon & Shuster Paperbacks*; 2010; Pg. 277

[14] "Hazen Probes Warring Charge of Police Bribes," *Evening Star,* Nov. 17, 1938; Pg. 1

[15] "Warring 'Protection' Payment Claims Recounted at Trial," *Evening Star,* Nov. 16, 1938; Pg. 1

[16] "Prison Hint Delays Trial of Warrings," *Washington Post,* Nov. 19, 1938; Pg. 1

[17] "Warring Trio's 'Pickup' Men Once Quizzed," *Evening Star,* Nov. 21, 1938; Pg. 1

[18] "Judge Seeks Data on Warring Charge of Bribing Police," *Evening Star,* Nov. 18, 1938; Pg. 1

[19] "Warring Kept Busy by Woes, Jury is Told," *Evening Star,* Nov. 22, 1938; Pg. 1

[20] Lewis, Alfred E. and Richard Morris, "Cloak of Anonymity Hides Numbers Racket Mystery Man," *Washington Post,* Sept. 17, 1951; Pg. 1

[21] "Warrings' Income Put At $238,000 For 3 Years," *Washington Post,* Nov. 23, 1938; Pg. 1

[22] "Mistrial Denied for Warrings; Scherr Freed," *Washington Post,* Nov. 24, 1938; Pg. 1

[23] "Warrings Charge U.S. Broke Faith," *Washington Post,* Nov.30, 1938; Pg. 1

[24] Ibid.

[25] "Warrings Paid Police $60,000 in Year, Is Intimation at Trail," *Washington Post,* Nov. 30,1938; Pg. 1

[26] Ibid.

[27] "Warring Case Due to Reach Jurors Today," *Washington Post,* Dec. 2, 1938; Pg. 1

[28] "Mistrial Is Denied In Warring Case On 'Mob' Reference," *Evening Star,* Dec. 1, 1938; Pg. 1

[29] Ibid.

[30] Ibid.

[31] "Bribes Held Key to Warring Case," *Washington Herald,* Dec. 2, 1938; Pg. 3

[32] "Warring Case On Tax Charges Goes to the Jury," *Evening Star,* Dec. 2, 1938; Pg. 1

[33] "Warring Jury Rests after 11 Hour's Study," *Washington Post,* Dec. 3, 1938; Pg. 1

[34] "Warring Jury Nears Record Deliberation," *Washington Post,* Dec. 5, 1938; Pg. 1

[35] "Allen v. United States," 164 U.S. 492 (1896) https://supreme.justia.com/cases/federal/us/164/492/; Sept. 18, 2019

[36] "Warring Case Is Mistrial," *Washington Herald,* Dec. 6, 1938; Pg. 1

[37] "Warring Case Mistrial; Jury Out 4 Days," *Washington Post,* Dec. 6, 1938; Pg. 1

[38] "Warring Case Retrial Set for January 23," *Evening Star*, Dec. 6, 1938; Pg. 17

Chapter 13

[1] "Jury Chosen For Retrial of Warrings," *Washington Times Herald,* Feb. 2, 1939; Pg. 1

[2] "Lawyer Challenges Theory of Warring Tax Conspiracy," *Evening Star,* Feb. 2, 1939; Pg. 2

[3] "U.S. Witness Stalls Trial of Warrings," *Washington Post,* Feb. 3, 1939; Pg. 1

[4] "Two More Marshalls Ousted in Warring Probe," *Washington Times Herald,* Feb. 18, 1939; Pg. 1

[5] "Warrings Released on $150,000 Bail in Jury Tampering Case," *Washington Post,* Feb. 7, 1939; Pg.1

[6] "Warrings Go Free Under $150,000 Bail," *Washington Times Herald,* Feb. 7, 1939; Pg. 1

[7] "Emmitt and Marshal To Answer Monday On Jury Tampering," *Washington Post,* Feb. 9, 1939; Pg. 1

[8] "Warrings' Tax Case Lawyers Cited in Jury-Tampering Trial As Emmitt, Deputy Admit Guilt,"

Evening Star, Feb. 13, 1938; Pg. 1

[9] "Trial of A Racket," *Washington Post,* Feb. 14, 1939; Pg. 8

[10] "A Smell of Corruption," *Washington Post,* Feb. 9, 1939; Pg. 10

[11] "Further Inquiry Due In Warring Jury Tampering," *Evening Star*, Feb. 25, 1939

[12] "F. Joseph Donohue Dies; Lawyer Headed D.C. Board," *Washington Post,* April 5, 1978; Pg. C4

[13] "4 More Cited in Growing Warring Jury Scandal," *Washington Post,* Feb. 14, 1939; Pg. 1

[14] Ibid.

[15] "Warrings' Tax Case Lawyers Cited in Jury-Tampering Trial As Emmitt, Deputy Admit Guilt," *Evening Star,* Feb. 13, 1938; Pg. 1

[16] Ibid.

[17] "Three More Ordered Held for Contempt in Warring Inquiry," *Evening Star,* Feb. 14, 1939; Pg. 1

[18] "Marshal Outs Two Aides in Suppression of Warring Evidence," *Washington Post,* Feb. 18, 1939; Pg. 1

[19] "2 More Deputies Out," *Washington Post,* Feb.15, 1939; Pg. 1

[20] As told to the author by his dad, Charles (Rags) Warring

[21] "Three More Ordered Held for Contempt in Warring Inquiry," *Evening Star,* Feb. 14, 1939; Pg. 1

[22] Ibid.

[23] Ibid.

[24] Ibid.

[25] "2 More Deputies Out," *Washington Post,* Feb.15, 1939; Pg. 1

[26] "U.S. Marshal Drops Two More Aides," *Times Herald,* Feb. 15, 1939; Pg. 1

[27] "Warring Jury Case Spurs Reform in All U.S. Courts," *Washington Post*, Feb. 17, 1939; Pg. 1

[28] "Policy Game Abandoned, Warrings Say," *Washington Post,* Feb. 22, 1939; Pg. 1

[29] Ibid.

[30] "Warring Is Given Two Years And His Attorneys Acquitted In Jury-Tampering Scandal," *Evening Star,* Feb. 24, 1939; Pg. 1

[31] Ibid.

[32] "Emmitt Warring Goes to Jail Church Service; Date of Third Trial to Be Set Wednesday," *Washington Post,* Feb. 27, 1939; Pg. 13

[33] "Warring Jury Hears Tax Agents Quizzed," *Evening Star,* Apr. 26, 1939; Pg. 1

[34] "Warring Gang Chief Enters Plea of Guilty," *Washington Post,* Apr. 29, 1939; Pg. 1

[35] "2 Warrings Pay Fines, Go Free; Emmitt Gets 3 to 9 Months," *Washington Post,* May 3, 1939; Pg. 1

[36] "Emmitt Warring Sent to Jail; Brothers Fined in Tax Case," *Evening Star*; May 2, 1939; Pg. 1

[37] Ibid.

[38] "Watergate Attorney John J. Wilson Dies," *Washington Post,* May 20, 1986; Pg. C 4

Chapter 14

[1] Lewis, Alfred E. and Richard Morris, "Cloak of Anonymity Hides Numbers Racket Mystery Man," *Washington Post,* Sept. 17, 1951; Pg. 1

[2] Lewis, Alfred E. and Richard Morris, "Uncle Sam Dealt Gambler Only Serious Blow in Career," *Washington Post,* Sept. 20, 1951; Pg. 1

[3] As told to the author by his mother, Vincenza (Vince) Mary Warring

[4] As told to the author by Ralph Warring Hawkins

[5] Lewis, Alfred E. and Richard Morris, "Uncle Sam Dealt Gambler Only Serious Blow in Career," *Washington Post,* Sept. 20, 1951; Pg. 1

Chapter 15

[1] National Archives; https://www.archives.gov/founding-docs/declaration; Sept. 21, 2019

[2] Letter from Harry B. Mitchell, President of the Civil Service Commission to Dr. R.D.W. Connor, The Archivist, National Archives dated Aug. 7, 1939

[3] "Collas G. Harris, Retired CIA Official," *Washington Post,* May 16, 1981; Pg. D6

[4] Letter from Harry B. Mitchell, President of the Civil Service Commission to Dr. R.D.W. Connor, The Archivist, National Archives dated Aug. 7, 1939

[5] Lansky, Sandra and William Stadiem; "*Daughter of the King,*" Weinstein Books, New York; Pg. 30

[6] As told to the author by his older cousin, Philip Warring

Chapter 16

[1] Casey, Phil; "Pete's (Goatless) Closes Forever," *Washington Post,* Sept. 16, 1957; Pg. B1
[2] Ibid.

[3] Ibid.

[4] As told to the author by his older cousin, Frank Cady Jr.

[5] Ibid.

[6] As told to the author by Ralph Warring Hawkins

Chapter 17

[1] Lewis, Alfred E.; "Out-of-Town Trio Hunted In Holdup," *Washington Post,* Jan. 13, 1950; Pg. 1

[2] As described to the author by Emmitt Warring circa 1972

[3] "Biggest Liquor Seizure Made Since Repeal," *Washington Post,* Oct. 30, 1937; Pg. 3

[4] "Harding Remanded By Coroner Verdict In Killing Of Davis," *Washington Post,* April 23, 1933; Pg.18

[5] "3-6 Year Term Given to Harding," *Washington Post,* June 17, 1933; Pg. 18

[6] From National Archives; Proclamation 2676 – Granting pardon to certain persons who have served in the Armed Forces of the United States; Dec. 24, 1945

[7] "Man Accused in Kidnapping of Woman," *Washington Post,* Oct. 2, 1947; Pg. B 2

[8] "'Caveman' Wooing Tactics Lead to Indictment Here," *Washington Post,* Oct. 21, 1947

[9] "Ex-Suiter Found Guilty On 3 Counts In Assault Case," *Washington Post,* Mar. 12, 1948; Pg. B1

[10] "Ex-Convict Held in $1100 As Assailant Of Gambler," *Washington Post,* Aug. 30, 1949; Pg. B1

[11] "Club Where Gambler Was Shot to Death Defies Order to Close," *Evening Star,* Jan. 11, 1951; Pg. 1

[12] "Arthur Pelkisson, 40, Accused of Series of Bronx Holdups; $50,000 Bond Set," *Washington Post,* May 2, 1950; Pg. B1

[13] Lewis, Alfred E. and Charles E. Davis, Jr.; "Two suspects Identified As Warring Holdup Men," *Washington Post,* April 4, 1950; Pg. 1

[14] "Subpoena Issued for Warring As Probers Arrange Showdown Of Richett and Barrett Today," *Evening Star,* Mar. 3, 1950; Pg. 1

[15] Lewis, Alfred E. and George T. Draper; "He Could See Only Big Feet Of Robber, Court Told," *Washington Post,* Sept. 12, 1951; Pg. 1

[16] Many critical details of this story were relayed to the author by his father, Charles Warring, and

Cady family members throughout the years.

[17] Lewis, Alfred E. and Charles E. Davis, Jr.; "2 Suspects Identified As Warring Holdup Men," *Washington Post,* April 4, 1950; Pg. 1

[18] "Warring Holdup Probe Pressed Despite Denials," *Evening Star,* Jan. 12, 1950; Pg. 1

[19] Ibid.

[20] "Warring Holdup Search Centers on Ex-Friends," *Evening Star,* Jan. 13, 1950; Pg. 32

[21] "Police Check Phone Tip in Warring Case," *Washington Post,* Jan. 14, 1950; Pg. B 1

[22] "Stromberg Identified By Warring Maid In $24,000 Robbery," *Evening Star,* April 4, 1950; Pg. 25

[23] Paull, Joseph; "Crime Wave Here Deplored by Warring," *Washington Post,* April 14, 1950; Pg. 1

[24] "Knew Harding, Stromberg Says, But Denies Warring Holdup," *Evening Star,* Sept. 12, 1951

[25] Lewis, Alfred E. and Richard Morris; "Numbers Business Thrived During Grand Jury Probe," *Washington Post,* Sept. 22, 1951; Pg. 1

[26] "Club Where Gambler Was Shot to Death Defies Order to Close," *Evening Star,* Jan. 11, 1951; Pg. 1

[27] "Swears He Fell Out With Pal a Year Ago, Lived in Fear of Life for 4 or 5 Months," *Washington Post,* April 18, 1951; Pg. B1

[28] Ryan, Edward F. and Thomas Winship; "Bottle-Club Crackdown Under Way," *Washington Post,* Feb. 19, 1950; Pg. 1

[29] "Club Where Gambler Was Shot to Death Defies Order to Close," *Evening Star,* Jan. 11, 1951; Pg. 1

[30] "Gambler Slain In Gun Attack at After-Hours Club," *Evening Star,* Jan. 10, 1951; Pg. 1

[31] "'I had to do it,' Nesline Says; Threat Made by Harding Told by Waitress," *Washington Post,* Jan. 11, 1951; Pg. 1

[32] Ibid.

[33] "Charles E. Ford Is Dead From Coronary Attack," *Washington Post,* Oct. 27, 1957; Pg. B2

[34] "Bernstein, Carl; "Judge Alexander Holtzoff Dies; Controversial U.S. Court Figure," *Washington Post*, Sep. 7, 1969; Pg. 1

[35] "Jury Chosen To Try Nesline For Murder," *Washington Post,* Apr. 11, 1951; Pg. C12

[36] "Jury Told Shot Killed Harding At Point Blank," *Washington Post,* Apr. 12, 1951; Pg. 22

[37] "Murder Scene At Club 'Quiet' Police Testify," *Washington Post,* Apr. 14, 1951; Pg. 27

[38] "Nesline Murder Trial Expected to Continue Through Next Week," *Evening Star,* Apr. 14, 1951; Pg. 20

[39] "2 Witnesses Hit Nesline Defense Case," *Washington Post,* Apr. 17, 1951; Pg. 17

[40] "Swears He Fell Out With Pal a Year Ago, Lived in Fear of Life For 4 or 5 Months," *Washington Post,* Apr. 18, 1951; Pg. B1

[41] Ibid.

[42] Yarbrough, Charles J.; "Holtzoff Indicates Nesline Murder Case Will Go to Jury Today," *Evening Star,* Apr. 18, 1951; Pg. 2

[43] "Nesline Has Oil Company Presidency," *Washington Post,* Apr. 18, 1951; Pg. B1

[44] Yarbrough, Charles J.; "Nesline Freed In Slaying, Gets Year for Gun," *Evening Star,* April 19, 1951; Pg. B1

[45] Ibid.

[46] Yarbrough, Charles J.; "Holtzoff Indicates Nesline Murder Case Will Go to Jury Today," *Evening Star,* Apr. 18, 1951; Pg. 2

[47] Bradlee, Benjamin; "Jury Frees Nesline of Harding Shooting," *Washington Post,* Apr. 19, 1951; Pg. B 1

[48] Lewis, Alfred E. and George T. Draper; "He Could See Only Big Feet of Robber, Court Told," *Washington Post,* Sept. 12, 1951; Pg. 1

[49] Ibid.

[50] Ibid.

[51] Paull, Joseph; "Prison Term Up to 30 Yrs. Ordered for Stromberg," *Washington Post,* Oct. 6, 1951; Pg. B1

Chapter 18

---

[1] Doherty, Thomas; "Frank Costello's Hands: Film, Television and the Kefauver Crime Hearings," *Indiana University Press*

[2] Aucoin, Brent J.; "The Southern Manifesto and Southern Opposition to Desegregation," *Indiana University Press*

[3] "Subpoena Issued for Warring As Probers Arrange Showdown of Richitt and Barrett Today," *Evening Star,* March 3, 1950; Pg. 1

[4] "Area Police Officials at Rites For Ex-Chief Robert Barrett," *Washington Post,* Nov. 3, 1966; Pg. B 6

[5] "Barrett Career Filled With Commendations and Pyrotechnics," *Evening Star,* Nov. 20, 1951; Pg. 1

[6] Moseley, William P.; "Posies and Brickbats Splatter Police Chief Barrett's Record," *Times Herald*, Jan. 12, 1950; Pg. 1

[7] "Robert J. Barrett Dies; Ex-Chief of D.C. Police," *Evening Star*, Oct. 30, 1966; Pg. 34

[8] "Is Barrett "The Boss"? *Washington Post,* Mar. 4, 1950; Pg. 10

[9] Dutkin, Howard L.; "Blick Brushed Off Suggested Raid In Third Precinct, Richitt Charges," *Washington Post,* Mar. 4, 1950; Pg. 1

[10] Ryan, Edward F. and Benjamin C. Bradlee; "Talked with Richitt, Wallrodt, Witness Testifies at House Committee Hearing," *Washington Post,* Mar. 4, 1950; Pg. 1

[11] Bradlee, Benjamin; "All's Quiet on Police Front – For Awhile," *Washington Post,* Mar. 7, 1950; Pg. B1

[12] Bradlee, Benjamin; "Conspiracy Charged at Crime Inquiry," *Washington Post,* Sep.13, 1950; Pg.1

[13] Ibid.

[14] Ibid.

Chapter 19

---

[1] Ryan, Edward F.; "'Charmed' Life Led by Gamblers Here, Davis Unit Tells Congress," *Washington Post,* Jan. 3, 1951; Pg. 1

[2] Ibid.

[3] "Jail Warring, Get Promotion, Says Barrett," *Washington Post,* Feb. 3, 1951; Pg. B1

[4] Lewis, Alfred E. and Richard Morris; "Barrel Boy of Foggy Bottom Rose to Riches in the Numbers," *Washington Post,* Sept. 16, 1951; Pg. 1

[5] "Post's Stories on Warring Win Grand Award of Guild," *Washington Post,* Apr. 5, 1952; Pg. 1

[6] Lewis, Alfred E. and Richard Morris; "Cloak of Anonymity Hides Numbers Racket Mystery Man," *Washington Post,* Sept. 17, 1951; Pg. 1

[7] Ibid.

[8] Editorial Page; *Washington Post,* Sept. 20, 1951; Pg. 14

Chapter 20

---

[1] "Special Committee On Organized Crime in Interstate Commerce," United States Senate; https://www.senate.gov/artandhistory/history/common/investigations/Kefauver.htm; Sept. 25, 2019

[2] "Probe of D.C. Crime Urged on Kefauver," The *Washington Post* (1923-1954); Mar. 22, 1951; Pg. 7

[3] "Bring It Here," *Washington Post* (1877-1954); Mar. 23, 1951; Pg. 22

[4] "Rally Hears Welker Blast McCarthy Foes," *Washington Post,* Nov. 12, 1954; Pg. 16

[5] "In the 83rd Congress, A Senate In Constant Turmoil," *Washington Post,* Dec. 15, 2006; Pg. 33

[6] Ryan, Edward F.; "New Yorker Appointed To Run D.C. Crime Probe," *Washington Post,* Oct. 3, 1951; Pg. B1

[7] Ryan, Edward F.; "D.C. Crime Prober No 'Sherlock' Type," *Washington Post,* Oct. 28, 1951; M11

[8] "Commissioners Hear Barrett in Revolt on Quiz," *Evening Star,* Nov. 2, 1951; Pg. 1

[9] "Welker Critical of D.C. Crime Probe Secrecy," *Evening Star,* Jan. 13, 1952; Pg. 1

[10] "Barrett Wins Fight to Bar TV While He Testifies At Hearings; Defends Record on Gambling," *Evening Star,* Jan. 14, 1952; Pg. 1

[11] Horner, John V.; "Crime Probers Question Barrett On Contracts With Gamblers; Neely Denounces 'Lax' Regime," *Evening Star,* Jan. 15, 1952; Pg. 1

[12] Draper, George T.; "Warring Has Few Answers But Knows Barrett," *Washington Post,* Jan. 18, 1952; Pg. 1

[13] "Text of Warring Questions (and Some Answers)," *Evening Star,* Jan. 17, 1952; Pg. 5

[14] Lewis, Alfred E. and Chalmers M. Roberts; "Gambler Mum Again; Caudle Failed to Act, Says Bauman," *Washington Post,* Jan. 19, 1952; Pg. 1

[15] "Warring Faces Baltimore Tax Trial Tomorrow, Old Subject in New Setting," *Sunday Star,* Dec. 12, 1954; Pg. 29

[16] Draper, George T.; "Warring Has Few Answers, But Knows Barrett," *Washington Post,* Jan. 18, 1952; Pg. 1

[17] "R.W. (Whitetop) Simkins Dies," *Washington Post,* July 17, 1973; Pg. C4

[18] "'Ex-Girl Friend' of Simkins Quotes Him as Declaring He Gave 'Ice' to Officers Who Called at Her Home," *Washington Post,* Jan. 17, 1952; Pg. 1

[19] Ibid.

[20] Draper, George T.; "Strange Story: How Simkins Rose to Riches," *Washington Post,* Jan. 22, 1952; Pg. 1

[21] Berryman, Jim; *Evening Star,* Jan. 18, 1952; Pg. 1

[22] Lautier, Louis; "Capital Spotlight"; *Afro-American,* Jan. 26, 1952; Pg. 4

[23] Brooks, Charles G.; "3 D.C. Gambling Bosses Reported Out of Business," *Evening Star*; Feb. 23, 1952; Pg. 1

[24] Winship, Thomas; “Senate Cites Warring, Simkins For Contempt of Subcommittee,” *Washington Post,* Feb. 26, 1952; Pg. 1

[25] “Innocent, Say Both Simkins and Warring,” *Washington Post,* July 12, 1952; Pg. 11

[26] “Warring Is Acquitted Of Contempt Charge In Directed Verdict,” *Evening Star*, Oct. 23, 1952; Pg. 1

Chapter 21

[1] Jonas, Jack; “Warring Jury Gets Fill-In on Numbers Game,” *Evening Star,* Dec. 14, 1954; Pg. 1

[2] Kent, Jr., Frank R.; “Warring depicted as Spot Cash Operator,” *Washington Post,* Dec. 14, 1954; Pg. 1

[3] “$160,000 Lien For Taxes Hits Emmitt Warring,” *Evening Star,* Mar. 13, 1951; Pg. 1

[4] Bradlee, Benjamin; “$159,917.89 Tax Lien Filed On Warring,” *Washington Post,* Mar. 14, 1951; Pg. 1

[5] “Miscellany,” *Washington Post,* Mar. 14, 1951; Pg. B14

[6] “U.S. Charges Warring Owes Tax On $122,245,” *Washington Post,* June 7, 1951; Pg. B1

[7] Pearson, Drew; “Warring Tax Prosecution Tabled,” *Washington Post,* Sept. 23, 1951; Pg. B5

[8] “Grand Jury At Baltimore Accuses D.C. Gaming Czar,” *Washington Post,* Feb. 17, 1951; Pg. 1

[9] “Move in Tax Case Is Lost,” *Baltimore Sun,* Mar. 6, 1954; Pg. 14

[10] “Warring Files Suit Asking Court Order in Tax Fight,” *Washington Post,* Aug. 28, 1954; Pg. 14

[11] Jonas, Jack; “Prosecutor Draws Yule Tree To Show Warring Bet Setup,” *Evening Star,* Dec. 13, 1954; Pg. 1

[12] Jonas, Jack; “Warring Liked $1,000 bills, D.C. Bank Cashier Testifies,” *Evening Star,* Dec. 15, 1954; Pg. 1

[13] Kent Jr., Frank R.; “Warring Tax Settlement Detailed,” *Washington Post,* Dec. 15, 1954; Pg. 1

[14] Kent Jr., Frank R.; “$100,000 Warring Case Goes to Jury,” *Washington Post,* Dec. 21, 1954; Pg. 1

[15] Ibid.

[16] Jonas, Jack; Warring Guilty, Gets 3 Years, Fined $10,000,” *Evening Star,* Dec. 21, 1954; Pg. 1

[17] Kent Jr., Frank R.; “$100,000 Warring Case Goes to Jury,” *Washington Post,* Dec. 21, 1954; Pg. 1

[18] Jonas, Jack; “Warring Guilty, Gets 3 Years, Fined $10,000,” *Evening Star,* Dec. 21, 1954; Pg. 1

[19] Kent, Jr., Frank R.; “3-yr. Term, $10,000 Fine For Warring,” *Washington Post,* Dec. 22, 1954; Pg. 1

[20] Clark, Evert; “There’s Sadness in Foggy Bottom – Emmitt’s Gone,” *Washington Daily News,* Dec. 27, 1954

[21] "Court Hears Warring Tax Count Appeal," *Washington Post*, April 23, 1955; Pg. 21

[22] Westlaw; 222 F.2d 906, 55-1 USTC P9473, 47 A.F.T.R. 965

[23] Olsen, Don; "Supreme Court Declines to Review Tax Evasion Conviction of Warring," *Washington Post,* Oct. 18, 1955; Pg. 1

[24] Lewis, Alfred E.; "Warring Begins 3-Year Term for Tax Evasion," *Washington Post,* Oct. 29, 1955; Pg. 1

[25] "Brownell Report Cites 2 'Racket' Figures Here," *Washington Post,* Aug, 21, 1956; Pg. 8

[26] Baker, Robert E.; "Truck Listed to Warring's Bodyguard Seized by U.S. Agents in Raid on Still," *Washington Post,* Jan. 27, 1954; Pg. 1

[27] "Truck Used to Supply Moonshine Unit in Va.," *Washington Post,* Jan. 30, 1954; Pg. 1

[28] Ibid.

[29] Baker, Robert E.; "Truck Listed to Warring's Bodyguard Seized by U.S. Agents in Raid on Still," *Washington Post,* Jan. 27, 1954; Pg. 1

[30] "Warring Quizzed In Still Raid," *Washington Post,* Jan. 30, 1954; Pg. 1

[31] As told to the author by his father, Charles Warring

[32] "Two Men Shot as They Battle For Gun in Moving Car," *Washington Post,* Jan. 23, 1955; Pg. 1

[33] "A 'Dirty Dog to Shoot," Victim Testifies of Lee," *Washington Post,* Dec. 11, 1956; Pg. 3

[34] Dunie, Morrey; "Convicts' Data Spices Lee Trial," *Washington Post,* Dec. 12, 1956; Pg. B10

Chapter 22

[1] As told to the author decades later by his mother

[2] As told to the author by Arthur Cranston via "Jimmy Collins"

[3] As told to the author by Ralph Warring Hawkins

Chapter 23

[1] Loverro, Thom; "*Hail Victory: An Oral History of the Washington Redskins*," Turner Publishing Company (2008)

[2] House, Toni; "Gianaris Gets 6 Months for Bookmaking," *Evening Star,* Dec. 29, 1977; Pg. B1

[3] Kiernan, Laura A.; "Luck Fails Gambling King," *Washington Post,* Dec. 29, 1977; Pg. 1

[4] The details of the Chinatown story were told to the author by his father, Charles Warring, and Ernie Byrd

[5] Mr. Smith's moved to K Street in Georgetown around 2014.

[6] Gabbett, Harry; "'Rags' Warring, Gang Chief" *Washington Post*, ; Sept. 24, 1969; Pg. C6

Chapter 24

[1] Kuznick, Frank and Nigel Dickson; "Twilight of a Mobster," *Regardie's Magazine,* Spring 1987

[2] Browning, Frank; "Organized Crime in Washington,"; *Washingtonian Magazine,* (1976)

[3] Casey, Phil and David A. Jewell; "Ten Slick Guys and a Doll Glamorize Gambling Trial," *Washington Post*, July 19, 1967; Pg. B1

[4] Deitche, Scott M.; "The Blade," *American Mafia.com*; June, 2000

[5] "George Raft, Biography"; *International Movie Data Base*; https://www.imdb.com/name/nm0706368/bio

[6] Smith, J.Y. and Alfred E. Lewis; "Emmitt R. Warring Buried at Mount Olivet," *Washington Post,* Feb. 1, 1974

[7] Smith, J.Y. and Alfred E. Lewis; "Gaming Figure Emmitt Warring Dies," *Washington Post,* Jan. 29, 1974; Pg. C4

[8] Gold, Bill: The District Line; *Washington Post,* Jan. 30, 1974; Pg. C22

Epilogue

[1] Lewis, Nancy; "Our Gang – With the Mafia Muscling In, We Soon May Long for the Good Old Bad Days," *Washington Post,* Mar. 1, 1987; Pg. D1

[2] Hughes, Leonard; "Gamblers Once Thrived in the City,"; *Washington Post,* Sep. 30, 1993; Pg. DC1

[3] Dalzell, Tom and Terry Victor; "*New Partridge Dictionary of Slang and Unconventional English,*" John Wiley and Sons, (2005)

[4] Lait, Jack and Lee Mortimer; "*Washington Confidential,*" Crown Publishers, (1951)

Acknowledgments

Special thanks to my editor, Evelyn Duffy (Openboatediting.com) and my publishing agent, Dan Crissman (Parafinepress.com). I would have been lost without them. Also, many thanks to a few trusted friends who were willing to read my earliest drafts and provide advice and—more importantly—encouragement.

About the Author

Leo Warring, son of one of the members of the "Foggy Bottom Gang," has lived in the Washington, DC area his entire life. After retiring from a forty-year career at the US Department of the Treasury, he devoted his time in writing an account of the "Foggy Bottom Gang" drawing from newspaper archives and personal stories. He also has logged over 1,000 hours as a patient care volunteer at Children's National Hospital in Washington, DC. Leo and his wife Kathy have two adult children and three grandchildren.

You can contact him at Leo.Warring@gmail.com.

Author photograph by Wayne Bierbaum

CPSIA information can be obtained
at www.ICGtesting.com
Printed in the USA
LVHW050014090121
676101LV00013B/1609